A Card a Day

Paper Crafts MAGAZINE®   A Card a Day

Editorial

Editor-in-Chief Jennifer Schaerer
Managing Editor Brandy Jesperson
Creative Editor Cath Edvalson
Editors Susan R. Opel, P. Kelly Smith
Contributing Editors Andralynn Brown, Susan Hart, Kalyn Kepner, Melanie King, Shelisa Loertscher, Katie Pendleton, Erin Poulson, Nicole Thomas
Copy Editor Shelisa Loertscher
Editorial Assistant Brenda Peterson
Editorial Interns Brynn Lillywhite, Courtney Smith

Design

Art Director Stace Hasegawa
Designer Matt Anderson
Photography BPD Studios

Advertising and Events

Advertising Barb Tanner - 801/942-6080 barbara@tanneronline.net
Michelle Thorpe - 515/964-2410 mthorpe@ckmedia.com
Directory Sales Manager Alissa Norton, 303/215-5640
Online Sales Manager Kelly Workman- Flood, 303/215-5602
Online Advertising Operations Andrea Abrahamson, 303/215-5686
Senior Events Managers Danny Zoeller, Stacy Croninger
Events Coordinators Emily Haskell, Annette Hardy, Brooke Mathewson
Assistant Events Coordinators Lisa Sanders, Mandy Thacker, Micaela Zoeller

Operations

Circulation Director Nicole Martin
Human Resources Shoshanna Boothroyd
Production Director Tom Stuber

Offices

Editorial *Paper Crafts* magazine, 14850 Pony Express Rd., Bluffdale, UT 84065-4801
Phone 801/816-8300
Fax 801/816-8301
E-mail editor@PaperCraftsMag.com
Web site *www.PaperCraftsMag.com*

Published by Leisure Arts, Inc., 5701 Ranch Drive, Little Rock, Arkansas 72223-9633. 501-868-8800. *www.leisurearts.com*

Library of Congress Control Number: 2009931393
ISBN-13: 978-1-57486-031-3
ISBN-10: 1-57486-031-3

Leisure Arts Staff

Editor-in-Chief Susan White Sullivan
Special Projects Director Susan Frantz Wiles
Director of Designer Relations Debra Nettles
Senior Prepress Director Mark Hawkins
Publishing Systems Administrator Becky Riddle
Publishing Systems Assistants Clint Hanson, John Rose, and Keiji Yumoto

Vice President and Chief Operating Officer Tom Siebenmorgen
Director of Finance and Administration Laticia Mull Dittrich
Vice President, Sales and Marketing Pam Stebbins
Director of Sales and Services Margaret Reinold
Vice President, Operations Jim Dittrich
Comptroller, Operations Rob Thieme
Retail Customer Service Manager Stan Raynor
Print Production Manager Fred F. Pruss

CK Media, LLC

Chief Executive Officer Will Marks
Chief Financial Officer Rich Hybner
Controller Jill Collette
VP/Group Publisher Dave O'Neil
VP/Editorial Director Lin Sorenson
VP/Director of Events Paula Kraemer
Sr. Production Director Terry Boyer

PUBLICATION—*Paper Crafts*™ (ISSN 1548-5706) (USPS 506250) Vol. 32, is published 6 times per year in Jan/Feb, Mar/Apr, May/June, Jul/Aug, Sept/Oct and Nov/Dec, by CK Media LLC, 14850 Pony Express Rd., Bluffdale, UT 84065. Periodicals postage paid at Salt Lake City, UT and additional mailing offices.

REPRINT PERMISSION—For information on obtaining reprints and excerpts, please contact Wright's Reprints at 877/652-5295. (Customers outside the U.S. and Canada should call 281/419-5725.)

TRADEMARKED NAMES mentioned in this book may not always be followed with a trademark symbol. The names are used only in an editorial fashion and to the benefit of the trademark owner, with no intention of infringement of the trademark.

PROJECTS—*Paper Crafts* magazine believes these projects are reliable when made, but none are guaranteed. Due to different climatic conditions and variations in materials, *Paper Crafts* disclaims any liability for untoward results in doing the projects represented. Use of the magazine does not guarantee successful results. We provide this information WITHOUT WARRANTY OF ANY KIND, EXPRESSED, IMPLIED, OR STATUTORY; AND WE SPECIFICALLY DISCLAIM ANY IMPLIED WARRANTIES OF MERCHANTABILITY OR FITNESS FOR A PARTICULAR PURPOSE. Also, we urge parents to supervise young children carefully in their participation in any of these projects.

Printed in China

Posted under Canadian Publication Agreement Number 0551724

Contents

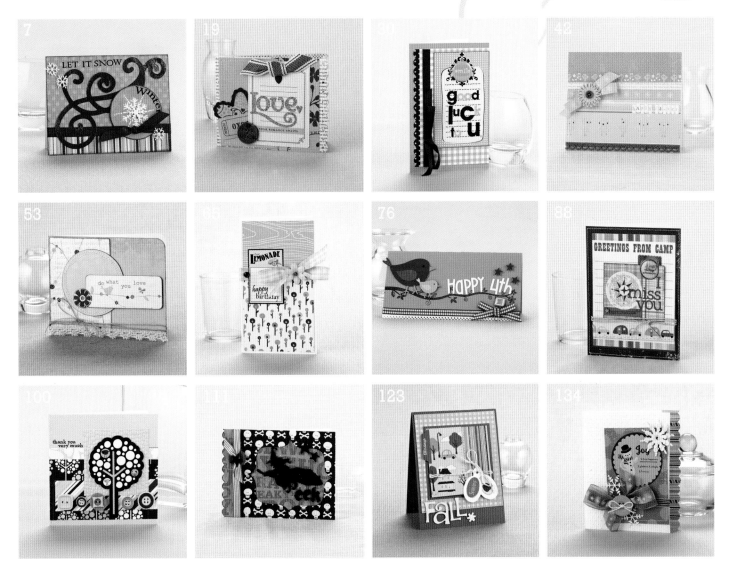

Editor's Note

One-stop Inspiration

Wendy Sue ANDERSON   **Jennifer** SCHAERER

Whether you're new to card making or a seasoned hobbyist, I think you'll agree that a handmade card is something unique and personal that you give of yourself. It's a wonderful way to let a friend, sister, neighbor, teacher, child, coach, or co-worker know that they are in your thoughts. No holiday or special occasion necessary.

With that in mind, we've gathered together the largest collection of card-making inspiration ever in this new book thanks to Wendy Sue Anderson, a talented designer and perennial favorite in the paper crafting community. When she suggested the card a day concept, we realized that in addition to holidays and special occasions, there is a special day set aside to recognize just about anything you can imagine. We asked her to create a special set of cards (featured on the opening page of each month) and, along with the designs from dozens of other designers, knew we had come up with a timeless and useful way to help you create a paper crafting connection.

This one-stop source for inspiration includes special sections on basic tools, color combinations, and even sketches you can use to build cards with whatever you have on hand. Complete instructions and supply lists for each card are right there for reference, and the designs that can be made in five steps or less are marked with this symbol: ⁙⁵⁙. We've also listed the cards by occasion in the back of the book for easy reference.

So here's to you on National Ice Cream Day! And Happy Talk Like a Pirate Day! Best wishes on National Grandparents Day! Celebrate the connection and creativity that is the heart of card making, and get inspired to make a card a day.

Jennifer

January

Let It Snow

Designer: Wendy Sue Anderson

1 Make card from cardstock. Adhere patterned paper piece and strip; ink edges. **2** Apply winter rub-on to snowflake circle, attach brad, and ink edges. **3** Tie on ribbon. Adhere swirl and adhere snowflake circle. **4** Apply let it snow rub-on. **5** Adhere snowflakes.

Designer Tip

If your rub-on sheets don't contain the words you want, combine letters from various words to create your own sentiment.

1 | ## Thanks a Bunch
Designer: Melanie Douthit

5 STEPS

Ink all paper edges.

1 Make card from cardstock. **2** Punch edge of cardstock strip and adhere to patterned paper piece. Stitch edges and adhere to card. **3** Tie on ribbon. Thread twine through flower and button; tie around ribbon. **4** Die-cut scalloped circle from cardstock. **5** Stamp thanks a bunch on cardstock and trim; mat with patterned paper. Adhere to scalloped circle; adhere using foam tape.

2 | ## Together Forever
Designer: Melissa Phillips

1 Make card from cardstock. **2** Stamp congratulations on cardstock strip; punch edge and adhere. **3** Ink patterned paper edges, adhere, and zigzag-stitch. **4** Attach brad to patterned tag, ink edges, and adhere. **5** Stamp large flower repeatedly on white tag; emboss. Lightly stamp tiny flower repeatedly on tag; ink edges. Tie ribbon, button, and twine to tag; adhere. **6** Affix label sticker. Ink edges of tag sticker and adhere using foam tape. **7** Adhere sentiment sticker using foam tape. Adhere pearls.

3 | ## Backwards in Heels
Designer: Melissa Phillips

5 STEPS

1 Make card from cardstock; paint edges. **2** Punch edge of patterned paper; adhere. **3** Cut patterned paper panel. Adhere trim and patterned paper strips. Tie on ribbon and adhere. Zigzag-stitch top and bottom seams. **4** Apply rub-ons and adhere rhinestones. Affix sticker. **5** Adhere glitter flowers together; tie to ribbon with twine. Thread floss through button; adhere.

National Bird Day

January 5th is National Bird Day. Take some time to appreciate the native birds in your neighborhood!

---

4 | To You from Me

Designer: Dawn McVey

5 STEPS

1 Make card from cardstock. **2** Punch edge of cardstock strip to create scallops; adhere. Adhere patterned paper strips. **3** Tie on ribbon. **4** Stamp sentiment on cardstock and punch into circle. Adhere to larger punched cardstock circle using foam tape. Adhere rhinestones. **5** Cut flower from cardstock. Adhere circle piece using foam tape. Adhere ribbon behind flower and adhere flower using foam tape.

5 | Happy Bird Day

Designer: Ashley Harris

1 Make card from cardstock; adhere cardstock piece. **2** Adhere chipboard house; cover with patterned paper. **3** Punch edge of patterned paper strips; adhere to house. **4** Stamp "Bird" on cardstock and apply rub-on. Trim into circle and mat with patterned paper; adhere to card. **5** Stamp birds on card and patterned paper. Trim patterned paper birds and adhere using foam tape. **6** Cut cloud from cardstock, ink, and adhere using foam tape.

6 | Hello Birdie

Designer: Kalyn Kepner

1 Make card from cardstock. **2** Trim patterned paper with decorative-edge scissors; adhere. **3** Trim patterned paper, round corners, ink edges, and adhere. **4** Trim patterned paper, round corners, and ink edges. Tie on ribbon and adhere using foam tape. **5** Spell "Hello" with stickers. **6** Affix bird sticker to cardstock, trim, and adhere using foam tape.

Doctor Thanks Day

Make sure you show your appreciation to the health care professionals in your life on January 7th, Doctor Thanks Day.

---

7 **Medical Thanks** ⟨5 steps⟩

Designer: Ashley C. Newell

1 Make card from cardstock. Adhere ribbon, leaving ends loose. Adhere vellum. **2** Stamp sentiment and adhere pearl. **3** Stamp stethoscope on cardstock, trim, and adhere using foam tape. Tie bow with ribbon. **4** Stamp hearts on cardstock, embossing one. Trim and adhere using foam tape.

---

8 **Wood Grain Thanks** ⟨5 steps⟩

Designer: Ashley C. Newell

1 Make card from cardstock; emboss. **2** Adhere cardstock strip; stitch. **3** Stamp sentiment. **4** Stamp leaves on cardstock, trim, and adhere. *Note: Adhere some leaves with foam tape.* **5** Tie on ribbon.

Designer Tip

Emboss the cardstock both vertically and horizontally to achieve a weave effect.

---

9 **Thinking of You Friend**

Designer: Wendy Sue Anderson

1 Make card from cardstock. **2** Trim patterned paper strip with decorative-edge scissors; adhere. **3** Stitch edges of patterned paper piece, tie on ribbon, and adhere. **4** Tie button to ribbon with twine. **5** Cut circle from patterned paper, stamp Tree, and adhere. **6** Apply rub-on. Spell "Friend" with stickers.

| **10** | **Bambino** | **11** | **Forever Begins Now** | **12** | **Husband & Wife** |

10 Bambino

Designer: Melissa Phillips

1 Make card from cardstock; ink edges.
2 Ink edges of patterned paper, adhere, and zigzag-stitch. **3** Trim label sticker, ink edges, and affix. **4** Stamp large motif, apply rub-on, and adhere rhinestones. **5** Tie on ribbon. Ink edges of bambino sticker and affix. Thread button with twine and adhere. **6** Paint chipboard house, coat with mica flakes, and adhere to card. **7** Trim separate chipboard roof piece, cover with sheet music, and ink edges. Cover with mica flakes. Adhere rickrack and adhere. Adhere keyhole.

11 Forever Begins Now

Designer: Julia Stainton

1 Make card from cardstock. **2** Score cardstock in diamond pattern and adhere. **3** Stamp image on cardstock, trim, and adhere. **4** Stamp sentiment. **5** Adhere flower. Tie ribbon and adhere. Insert stick pin.

Designer Tips

■ Layers of all white cardstock create a beautiful, elegant, and inexpensive card design.

■ Scoring is a great way to add texture to a design and is a very inexpensive embellishment.

12 Husband & Wife

Designer: Melissa Phillips

Ink patterned paper edges.

1 Make card from cardstock; paint edges.
2 Cut patterned paper block; mat with patterned paper. Punch edges of patterned paper piece; adhere. Stitch edges and adhere block. **3** Apply rub-on. Tie on ribbon and adhere flower and rhinestone. **4** Ink edges of sticker and adhere with foam tape. **5** Punch butterflies from patterned paper, apply glitter, adhere rhinestones, and adhere.

National Skeptic's Day

Do you know someone who is suspicious of reality, always questioning the facts, or doubting the truth? Then make a skeptical card every January 13th for the skeptic in your life.

National Strawberry Ice Cream Day

Celebrate this fun day every January 15th with a bowlful of your favorite strawberry ice cream.

---

13 | Skeptical?

Designer: Kim Kesti

5 STEPS

1 Make card from cardstock. **2** Mat patterned paper with cardstock; adhere. **3** Affix stickers. **4** Print sentiments on patterned paper; trim. Outline with pen and adhere using foam tape. **5** Attach brads.

14 | Happy 8th Son

Designer: Becky Olsen

5 STEPS

1 Make card from cardstock. **2** Adhere patterned paper pieces. **3** Punch circle from cardstock, spell "8th" with stickers, and adhere using foam tape. **4** Stitch around circle with floss. **5** Affix stickers to spell "Happy" and "Son".

15 | Strawberry Smile

Designer: Danni Reid

5 STEPS

1 Make card from cardstock. **2** Cut patterned paper panel. **3** Trim patterned paper, spell "Smile" with stickers, tie on ribbon, and adhere to panel using foam tape. **4** Tie strawberry and button to panel with twine. **5** Fasten flower with stickpin. Adhere rhinestones. Adhere panel to card.

National Thesaurus Day

January 18th is National Thesaurus Day so use a thesaurus to find synonyms of any word to create a unique card for any occasion.

16	Relax	5 STEPS
	Designer: Teri Anderson	

1 Make card from cardstock; cover with patterned paper. **2** Cut nested circles from cardstock; adhere. **3** Adhere chipboard chair; affix stickers to spell "Relax".

17	You Rock	5 STEPS
	Designer: Kim Moreno	

1 Make card from cardstock; tear right edge of card front. **2** Adhere strip of patterned paper inside card. **3** Adhere patterned paper and affix stickers to spell "You rock". Adhere rhinestones. **4** Adhere patterned paper strip. Trim guitars from patterned paper; adhere using foam tape.

Designer Tip

When using Black Magic paper, create a cool effect by tearing the paper to expose the colored core.

18	Get Well	5 STEPS
	Designer: Kim Kesti	

1 Make card from cardstock. **2** Print sentiments on cardstock; adhere. **3** Adhere patterned paper strip; zigzag-stitch seam. **4** Attach brads.

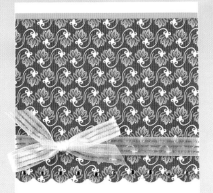

Celebrate!

"i have a dream"
-Dr. Martin Luther King, Jr.

Sending {{{Hugs}}}

Martin Luther King, Jr. Day
This holiday is always the third Monday in January, near King's January 15th birthday. It is one of only three holidays commemorating an individual.

National Hugging Day
Give all your loved ones a hug on January 21st, National Hugging Day.

---

19 I Have a Dream 5 STEPS
Designer: Kalyn Kepner

1 Make card from cardstock; cover with patterned paper. Round all corners.
2 Affix stickers to spell sentiment. **3** Die-cut quotation marks from cardstock; adhere.
4 Stitch around cloud shape with floss.
5 Write "-Dr. Martin Luther King, Jr." with pen.

---

20 Celebrate! 5 STEPS
Designer: Rae Barthel

1 Make card from cardstock; round bottom corners. **2** Adhere patterned paper strip. Trim patterned paper with border punch and adhere. **3** Adhere rhinestones. Tie on ribbon. **4** Apply rub-on.

Designer Tip

Let the patterned paper speak for itself on a card. To help the pattern stand out, keep the rest of the card design simple.

---

21 Sending You Hugs 5 STEPS
Designer: Julie Masse

1 Make card from cardstock; adhere patterned paper. **2** Attach brads to cardstock piece. Die-cut scalloped circle from patterned paper, trim to fit, and adhere. Adhere piece to card. **3** Stamp sentiment. Adhere flower.
4 Stamp image on patterned paper and cardstock. Trim patterned paper sections; adhere to cardstock image. **5** Color with markers. Mat with cardstock and adhere.

22	**You're a Knock-Out**	5 STEPS

Designer: Brandy Jesperson

1 Make card from cardstock. **2** Adhere patterned paper rectangle. **3** Trim knock-out from patterned paper and adhere using foam tape. **4** Affix stickers to spell sentiment.

23	**Wishes Do Come True**

Designer: Melanie Douthit

Ink all paper edges.

1 Make card from cardstock. **2** Adhere cardstock and patterned paper pieces. **3** Tie on ribbon; adhere rickrack. **4** Tie ribbon on ribbon. Attach button to flower with floss; adhere. **5** Adhere congratulations tickets. **6** Sew on buttons with floss.

24	**Miss You Flowers**

Designer: Jennifer Hansen

1 Make card from cardstock. **2** Adhere patterned paper. **3** Trim stems, leaves, and grass from patterned paper; adhere. **4** Punch flowers from patterned paper and adhere. *Note: Adhere the tallest flower using foam tape.* **5** Apply rub-ons to spell "Miss you". **6** Adhere rhinestones.

Designer Tip

The stems, leaves, and grass do not have to be green. Cut designs from patterned paper that match your card.

Spouses Day

On January 26th, celebrate your better half with Spouses Day. Let them know how much they are appreciated by spending some quality time together.

---

25 You Shouldn't Have

Designer: Melissa Phillips

Ink all paper edges.

1 Trim postcard from patterned paper. **2** Adhere patterned paper; zigzag-stitch. Adhere patterned paper strip. **3** Tie on ribbon. Tie twine to bow and adhere button. **4** Adhere die cut and affix sticker. **5** Punch butterflies from patterned paper, bend wings up slightly, and adhere. Adhere buttons.

---

26 Kiss Anytime

Designer: Alicia Thelin

1 Make card from cardstock. **2** Trim strip of cardstock with decorative-edge scissors; adhere. **3** Adhere patterned paper strip. **4** Stamp tickets on cardstock and trim. *Note: Use circle punch to trim corners and edges.* **5** Place tickets in cellophane bag, trim, and stitch to card. **6** Adhere flower and buttons.

Designer Tip

To help the cellophane bag stay in place when going through the sewing machine, adhere the bag to the card before stitching.

---

27 Thinking of You Today

Designer: Dawn McVey

1 Make card from cardstock. **2** Adhere cardstock using foam tape. **3** Stamp reeds, tops, and sentiment on cardstock. Tie on ribbon and adhere using foam tape. **4** Stitch buttons with linen thread; adhere.

28	**Take Care**	5 STEPS

Designer: Dawn McVey

1 Make card from cardstock; stamp finials. **2** Punch edge of cardstock, stamp finials, and adhere. **3** Adhere cardstock and patterned paper strips. **4** Stamp take care. **5** Adhere rhinestones; tie on ribbon.

29	**You're a Lifesaver**	5 STEPS

Designer: Jessica Witty

1 Make card from cardstock. **2** Stamp mini dots on cardstock. Mat with cardstock; distress edges and adhere. **3** Stamp sentiment on cardstock, trim, and adhere. **4** Punch life preserver from cardstock. Cut cardstock strips, fold over twine, and adhere. Adhere to card with foam tape.

30	**Cow Jumped Over the Moon**	5 STEPS

Designer: Maren Benedict

1 Make card from cardstock, adhere patterned paper, and adhere rickrack. **2** Cut cardstock rectangle, stamp images and sentiment, and mat with cardstock using foam tape. **3** Color stamped images, accent with glitter pen, and adhere using foam tape. **4** Tie on ribbon.

Designer Tip

By adding touches of contrasting colors to a stamp, you can really add variety and dimension to your card.

31 All Star Birthday

Designer: Betsy Veldman

1 Make card from cardstock. **2** Adhere patterned paper and cardstock. **3** Stamp "Happy birthday" on cardstock piece; trim with decorative-edge scissors and adhere. **4** Stamp sentiment circle, star, and numbers on cardstock strip; adhere. **5** Emboss cardstock, die-cut into star, and adhere. **6** Punch circles from cardstock. Adhere one using foam tape; adhere rhinestone. Attach brad to other circle; adhere. **7** Tie ribbon through brad loop.

February

True Romance Awaits

Designer: Wendy Sue Anderson

1 Make card from patterned paper. Punch right edge. **2** Adhere patterned paper piece. Stitch edges of patterned paper piece and adhere. **3** Die-cut heart and frame from patterned paper; layer and adhere to card. Adhere ticket. **4** Attach brad to tag and adhere. Spell "Love" with stickers and adhere knotted ribbon. **5** Attach brad to charm and adhere with foam tape.

Groundhog Day

On February 2nd all the eyes are on the official groundhog Punxsutawnay Phil as he officially pops out of his burrow. If he sees his shadow, legend has it that there will be six more weeks of winter. Send a quirky greeting to celebrate the hope of spring.

---

1 | XOXO Buttons

Designer: Rebecca Oehlers

1 Make card from cardstock; round corners. **2** Cut smaller square of cardstock; score edges and round corners. Mat with cardstock and adhere to card. **3** Punch circles from cardstock; adhere. **4** Stamp hearts and XOXO on cardstock; punch out. Thread small buttons with string; adhere to hearts. Adhere hearts to card with foam tape. Adhere XOXO. **5** Adhere large buttons.

2 | Groundhog Day

Designer: Teri Anderson

1 Make card from cardstock. **2** Print sentiment on cardstock; trim and adhere. **3** Cut branch, groundhog, and strips of patterned paper. Adhere. **4** Tie on twine.

3 | Kiss Me

Designer: Julia Stainton

1 Make card from cardstock. **2** Stamp image and sentiment; ink edges. **3** Attach brads to spell "XO".

American Heart Month

February is American Heart Month, a time to raise awareness of cardiovascular diseases and the research and education to combat them. Join in a walk-a-thon, make a financial donation, or bring it closer to home with a card for a loved one who is struggling with a cardiovascular disease.

4 Heart Possibilities

Designer: Melissa Phillips

Ink patterned paper edges.

1 Make card from cardstock; paint edges. **2** Cut patterned paper rectangle, mat with patterned paper, and zigzag-stitch seams. Adhere to card. **3** Cut strip of patterned paper and adhere. Apply glitter to sticker and affix. **4** Stamp flourish and sentiment. Paint chipboard frame; let dry. Stamp stars on frame and adhere. **5** Adhere ribbon bow. Thread buttons with twine; adhere. Adhere chipboard heart and rhinestones.

5 Thank You Butterfly

Designer: Betsy Veldman

1 Make card from cardstock. **2** Cut patterned paper smaller than card front. Trim cardstock strip with decorative-edge scissors; adhere to piece and adhere to card. **3** Cut cardstock piece; adhere. Cut and tear strip of patterned paper. Adhere and zigzag-stitch edge. **4** Stamp straight sentiment. Trim ribbon end, tie on twine, and adhere. **5** Punch circle from cardstock. Stamp decorative circle and circle sentiment. Adhere with foam tape. **6** Adhere butterfly with foam tape.

6 Love is All You Need

Designer: Anabelle O'Malley

1 Make card from cardstock. **2** Cut patterned paper to fit card. Adhere smaller patterned paper piece. Stitch edges and seams; adhere to card. **3** Affix scalloped heart sticker. Print sentiment on tag; adhere. **4** Spray chipboard swirl with shimmer spray; adhere. Adhere lined heart sticker with foam tape. Spray chipboard heart frame with shimmer spray; adhere. **5** Adhere flower die cut and rhinestones.

7   Hello Flower

Designer: Kim Moreno

1 Make card from cardstock. **2** Cut patterned paper rectangle; mat with cardstock and adhere. Adhere patterned paper strip. **3** Cut patterned paper, punch left edge, round right corners, and adhere. **4** Cut flowers, leaf, and stem from patterned paper. Ink edges of leaf and crease slightly. Turn up petals on flowers and adhere all pieces. **5** Attach brad to felt and paper flowers; adhere. **6** Spell "Hello" with stickers and outline with marker.

8   Live the Life

Designer: Jessica Witty

5 STEPS

1 Make card from cardstock. **2** Die-cut and emboss two labels from cardstock. **3** Stamp damask on one label and sentiment on other. **4** Cut sentiment label into strip and adhere to label. **5** Adhere rhinestones. Adhere label to card with foam tape.

9   Just For You

Designer: Melissa Phillips

1 Make card from cardstock. **2** Cut strip of patterned paper and adhere. Round right corners. **3** Cut cardstock and adhere. Emboss cardstock, cut into circle, and adhere. **4** Tie on ribbon. Stamp sentiment. **5** Cut cardstock circle. Lay circle over embossed circle and stamp reeds and tops. Adhere stamped circle with foam tape. **6** Punch butterflies from patterned paper, bend wings up slightly, and adhere. Adhere rhinestones.

10	**S.W.A.K.**	5 STEPS

Designer: Julie Masse

1 Make card from cardstock. Cut cardstock squares. **2** Die-cut hearts from cardstock and adhere to square, using foam tape for one. **3** Stamp sentiment and envelope on square. Stamp envelope on cardstock; color, trim, and adhere. **4** Cut smaller cardstock square; ink and emboss edges. Attach brad to button; adhere. Adhere embellished square to larger square with foam tape. **5** Stamp and emboss hearts on square. Adhere squares to card.

11	**Sweetie**	5 STEPS

Designer: Mary MacAskill

1 Make card from cardstock. **2** Cover card with patterned paper. **3** Cut square from patterned paper. Stamp and emboss flourish. Mat piece with cardstock; punch edges. Zigzag-stitch seams, tie on twine, and adhere. **4** Stamp Three Stitched Hearts on cardstock; apply chalk and trim. Stamp and emboss Sweetie; apply glitter glue. **5** Adhere heart with foam tape. Thread buttons with floss and adhere.

12	**Be Mine**	5 STEPS

Designer: Ashley C. Newell

1 Make card from cardstock. **2** Cut vellum square; mat with cardstock and punch edge. **3** Stamp and emboss hearts on cardstock; trim and adhere with foam tape. **4** Tie on ribbon and adhere block to card with foam tape. **5** Stamp sentiment.

Valentine's Day

Share the love with your special Valentine on February 14th with a beautiful handmade card.

---

13 | ## My Funny Valentine

5 STEPS

Designer: Maren Benedict

1 Make card from cardstock. **2** Cut patterned paper, lightly distress edges, and adhere. **3** Cut smaller rectangle from cardstock; adhere with foam tape. Cut funny valentine card from patterned paper and adhere with foam tape. **4** Tie on ribbon and adhere rhinestone heart.

---

14 | ## Be My Valentine

5 STEPS

Designer: Sherry Wright

1 Make card from cardstock. **2** Cover card with patterned paper. **3** Cut patterned paper slightly smaller, ink edges, and adhere. **4** Apply rub-ons. Cut flower and leaves from patterned paper and adhere. **5** Attach brad to flower; adhere flower and rhinestones.

---

15 | ## Pink & Green Thanks

5 STEPS

Designer: Anabelle O'Malley

1 Make card from cardstock. **2** Cover front with patterned paper; paint edges. Cut slightly smaller patterned paper rectangle. Paint edges, adhere, and zigzag-stitch seams. **3** Cut strip of patterned paper and trim with decorative-edge scissors. Adhere strip and trim. Stamp sentiment. **4** Affix stickers and adhere rhinestones. **5** Trim flowers from patterned paper and adhere.

Presidents' Day

The third Monday in February originally celebrated the birthday of George Washington. We added Abraham Lincoln's birthday and now call it "Presidents' Day," although it is still legally known as "Washington's Birthday."

---

16 | **Swirly Hi**

Designer: Daniela Dobson

1 Make card from patterned paper and emboss front. Lightly ink embossed dots. **2** Cut patterned paper and adhere. Adhere border. **3** Cut cardstock to fit behind tag and adhere. Adhere to card with foam tape. **4** Stamp branches and flowers on cardstock; color and trim. Stamp tree on buttons. Attach brads to flowers. Adhere buttons, flowers, branches, and rhinestones. **5** Spell "Hi" with stickers.

17 | **Celebrate**

Designer: Melanie Douthit

1 Make card from cardstock. **2** Cut patterned paper, mat with cardstock, and punch bottom edge; adhere. **3** Adhere patterned paper strip. Affix sticker and apply rub-on. **4** Tie on ribbon. Tie button to bow with twine. **5** Paint star; let dry. Paint star frames and apply glitter. Adhere.

18 | **Pink Birthday**

Designer: Daniela Dobson

1 Make card from cardstock. **2** Cut patterned paper; stitch edges and adhere. **3** Ink edges of patterned paper piece; adhere. Adhere border. **4** Apply rub-ons. **5** Adhere rhinestones and flowers.

Love Your Pet Day

Love Your Pet Day is February 20th. Shower your pet with attention by rubbing his belly a little longer or throwing the Frisbee a couple extra times. You can even make a delectable card with his favorite treat.

19 Best Friends	**20** Love Your Pet	**21** Grateful For You
Designer: Maren Benedict	Designer: Becky Olsen	Designer: Melissa Phillips

19 Best Friends · 5 STEPS

Designer: Maren Benedict

1 Make card from cardstock. **2** Cut rectangle from patterned paper. Cut shoes block from patterned paper and adhere. **3** Apply rub-on and adhere trim. Adhere piece with foam tape.

20 Love Your Pet · 5 STEPS

Designer: Becky Olsen

1 Make card from patterned paper by trimming 12" x 12" patterned paper at an angle. Accordion-fold piece in thirds. Adhere front two flaps together. **2** Cut strip of patterned paper, adhere, and zigzag-stitch sides. **3** Adhere ribbon and knot ends over dog biscuit. **4** Spell sentiment with stickers. **5** Stamp dog on patterned paper; trim, color, and adhere.

21 Grateful For You · 5 STEPS

Designer: Melissa Phillips

1 Make card from cardstock. Round bottom corners of card front. **2** Cut cardstock pieces, rounding one corner. Stamp flowers and sentiments; adhere. **3** Stamp flower center on cardstock; emboss. Trim and adhere. **4** Apply glitter glue and adhere rhinestone. Tie on ribbon.

22	You're So Sweet

Designer: Mary MacAskill

1 Make card from cardstock. Cover front with cardstock. **2** Cut cardstock panel; round top corners. Stitch edges of patterned paper piece; adhere. **3** Punch edge of cardstock strip; adhere. Adhere patterned paper strip and tie on string. Adhere panel to card. **4** Stamp and emboss "Soweet" on cardstock; trim and adhere. **5** In software, create text circle with sentiment "You are just so sweet!" Print on cardstock and cut into circle. Cut smaller cardstock circle; layer and adhere. **6** Adhere chipboard cherries. Thread button with string and adhere.

23	Black & Pink I Do

Designer: Susan R. Opel

1 Make card from cardstock. Cut patterned paper, fold around card, adhere, and trim. **2** Punch cardstock strip and adhere. **3** Adhere transparent damask to cardstock; adhere behind frame. Spell "I do" with stickers. **4** Adhere flower to card and adhere frame with foam tape.

24	Be Yourself Flower

Designer: Charity Hassel

1 Make card from cardstock. **2** Cut and affix strip of contact paper. **3** Cut flower and stem from patterned paper. Fold flower petals at base to add dimension and adhere. **4** Adhere felt flower and leaves. **5** Apply rub-on.

25 | Heartfelt Love

Designer: Melissa Phillips

1 Make card from cardstock and ink edges.
2 Cut square from cardstock. Trim patterned paper strip with decorative-edge scissors. Adhere to square and and zigzag-stitch to card. **3** Cut cardstock strip and ink edges; adhere. Punch square from patterned paper; adhere with foam tape. **4** Cut cardstock square, emboss, ink, and adhere. Stamp polka dot heart on cardstock and trim. Adhere with foam tape. **5** Tie ribbon in bow. Tie on button with twine; adhere. Adhere pearls.

26 | Always & Forever

Designer: Charlene Austin

1 Make card from cardstock. **2** Cut slightly smaller piece of cardstock. Tie knot in ribbon and adhere. **3** Adhere rhinestones and apply rub-on. **4** Adhere piece to card with foam tape.

27 | Little Prince

Designer: Heidi Van Laar

1 Adhere ribbon to card. Trim cardstock strip with decorative-edge scissors; adhere. Adhere ribbon. Tie ribbon bow; adhere. **2** Cut strip of ribbon and adhere. **3** Die-cut circle from patterned paper. Die-cut scalloped circle from cardstock; layer circles and adhere. **4** Make rosette from ribbon and adhere. **5** Make tag from cardstock and punch corners. Adhere label die cut; adhere to card. **6** Adhere crown die cut and rhinestones.

National Beaver Day

Occurring on the last Friday in February, this is a fairly new Canadian holiday, dating back only to the 1970s.

28 | Bucky the Beaver

Designer: Teri Anderson

5 STEPS

1 Make card from cardstock. **2** Cut paper pieces and adhere. Adhere ribbon over seam. **3** Staple ribbon loop. Tie on twine. **4** Punch circles from patterned paper; layer and adhere with foam tape. **5** Cut beaver from patterned paper; adhere. Cut heart from cardstock; adhere.

March

Good Luck to You

Designer: Wendy Sue Anderson

1 Make card from cardstock. **2** Cut patterned paper to fit card front; adhere. **3** Cut patterned paper strip; punch and adhere. Adhere patterned paper rectangle and ribbon. **4** Cut patterned paper; ink edges and adhere. **5** Affix journaling block and badge. Spell sentiment with stickers. **6** Tie ribbon bow; adhere.

Designer Tip

Don't be afraid to mix and match letter stickers in different sizes for a whimsical look.

1 | Bird on a Branch

Designer: Teri Anderson

5 STEPS

1 Make card from cardstock. **2** Cut patterned paper strips; adhere. **3** Cut patterned paper; adhere. **4** Cut out bird on branch; adhere. **5** Affix letter stickers to cardstock; trim and round end. Wrap thread and tie knot; adhere.

Designer Tip

If you're having a hard time matching patterned papers, use papers from the same collection.

2 | Read

Designer: Betsy Veldman

1 Make card from cardstock. **2** Cut patterned paper; adhere. **3** Trim journaling tag; adhere. **4** Die-cut reader icon from cardstock and sentiment from patterned paper; adhere. **5** Cover chipboard star with cardstock; adhere. **6** Knot ribbon on paper clip; attach.

3 | Button Tree Thanks

Designer: Melanie Douthit

Ink all paper edges.

1 Make card from cardstock. **2** Cut patterned paper; adhere. **3** Cut strip of patterned paper; adhere. **4** Stamp tree on cardstock; trim. Mat with cardstock trimmed with decorative-edge scissors; adhere. **5** Thread buttons with floss; adhere. **6** Apply rub-on to sticker; affix.

4 Love is Music

Designer: Beatriz Jennings

1 Die-cut card from cardstock; ink edges.
2 Die-cut card elements from patterned paper and sheet music; adhere and stitch. *Note: Ink sheet music.* **3** Apply rub-ons. **4** Die-cut flowers from patterned paper; bend petals up slightly and adhere. **5** Ink edges of sticker; adhere. **6** Tie twine through button; adhere. Tie bow, ink, and adhere.

5 Together

Designer: Melissa Phillips

1 Make card from cardstock; lightly distress edges. **2** Cut patterned paper; adhere. Cut cardstock; distress and ink edges. Stitch without thread; adhere. **3** Cut patterned paper strip; adhere and zigzag-stitch. Cut heart from patterned paper; lightly ink edges and adhere. **4** Cut cardstock; distress edges and stitch without thread. Tie on ribbon; adhere. **5** Stamp panel on cardstock; trim with decorative-edge scissors and ink edges. Adhere pearls; adhere with foam tape. **6** Apply glitter to flowers; adhere. Thread buttons with twine and adhere.

6 Loves You Still

Designer: Beatriz Jennings

1 Make card from cardstock. **2** Cut patterned paper; ink edges and adhere. **3** Cut felt; adhere and stitch edges. **4** Apply rub-on. **5** Cut lace trim; adhere. Adhere flowers. Thread buttons and adhere. **6** Tie on ribbon.

7 Flutterby	**8** Bunnies Missing You	**9** Get Well Oranges
Designer: Maren Benedict	Designer: Sherry Wright	Designer: Susan R. Opel

7 Flutterby

Designer: Maren Benedict

1 Make card from cardstock; die-cut circle. **2** Cut patterned paper; die-cut larger circle; adhere. **3** Apply rub-ons. **4** Adhere chipboard flower. **5** Tie on ribbon.

Designer Tip

Punch or die-cut windows so that you are using both the outside and the inside of your card.

8 Bunnies Missing You

Designer: Sherry Wright

1 Make card from cardstock; cover with patterned paper. **2** Cut patterned paper; ink edges and adhere. **3** Cut tree limb and bird from patterned paper and adhere. Punch circle from patterned paper, ink edges, and adhere. Cut rabbits from patterned paper and adhere. **4** Stamp tag and sentiment on patterned paper, trim, and adhere. **5** Adhere felt frame.

9 Get Well Oranges

Designer: Susan R. Opel

1 Make card from cardstock. **2** Cut cardstock; adhere. **3** Trim oranges from patterned paper; adhere. **4** Spell sentiment with stickers. **5** Tie ribbon bow; adhere.

10	Hockey Coach Thanks

Designer: Melyssa Connolly

1 Create skate, following pattern on p. 178; ink edges of dark gray cardstock pieces and assemble. **2** Attach eyelets. Draw stitching with gel pen, lace with twine, and adhere to card. **3** Pierce card near top and thread with twine; tie bow. **4** Stamp dotted oval; trim. Stamp sentiment; trim and adhere to oval. Adhere. **5** Punch holes in stars; thread cord and knot. **6** Cut cardstock, stamp "Coach", and adhere.

11	Enjoy Today

Designer: Danni Reid

1 Make card from cardstock. **2** Cut cardstock; dry emboss. Cut patterned paper; adhere. Tie on ribbon; adhere. **3** Form butterfly wings with twine; adhere. Twist wire; adhere. Adhere to ribbon. **4** Adhere felt cloud. Trim sentiment tag; adhere. **5** Apply rub-on, affix stickers, and adhere pearl.

12	Smile Crocodile

Designer: Angie Hagist

1 Make card from cardstock. **2** Cut patterned paper; mat with cardstock and adhere. **3** Cut cardstock; dry emboss. Mat with cardstock; adhere. **4** Stamp crocodile on cardstock; color, trim, and adhere with foam tape. **5** Create sentiment label; affix.

Pi Day

If you remember your math, you can recall that the mathematical symbol, pi, equals 3.14. Since "pi" sounds like "pie," get creative and celebrate "pi" day on March 14th—3/14.

---

13 | Where There is Great Love

Designer: Maren Benedict

1 Make card from cardstock. **2** Cut patterned papers; adhere. Tie on ribbon. **3** Stamp sentiment. **4** Die-cut scalloped rectangle from cardstock; adhere. **5** Stamp trees and scalloped edge on cardstock. Color with markers, die-cut and emboss into rectangle, and adhere with foam tape. **6** Adhere rhinestones.

14 | Sweetie Pi

Designer: Julie Campbell

Ink all paper edges.

1 Make card from cardstock; stitch edges. **2** Cut cardstock. Punch patterned paper strip; adhere. Cut patterned paper; adhere and stitch edges. Adhere piece to card. **3** Cut patterned paper; mat with cardstock and adhere. **4** Spell "Sweetie" with stickers; affix heart sticker. **5** Affix felt strip. **6** Stamp dashed circle on cardstock; die-cut and emboss into circle. Adhere with foam tape. **7** Ink chipboard pi sign; adhere.

15 | Lucky

Designer: Alli Miles

1 Make card from cardstock; sand. **2** Stamp lucky on cardstock. Trim, sand, and adhere. **3** Die-cut and emboss label from cardstock; adhere. Die-cut and emboss smaller label from cardstock; adhere with foam tape. **4** Stamp clover on patterned paper; trim and adhere with foam tape. **5** Adhere crown.

St. Patrick's Day
No matter what your heritage, celebrate the luck o' the Irish every year on March 17th.

16 Lucky Friend

Designer: Betsy Veldman

1 Make card from cardstock. **2** Cut patterned papers; adhere and stitch. **3** Stamp heart on cardstock four times, trim, and adhere with foam tape. **4** Freehand-cut stem from patterned paper; adhere. **5** Punch flower from patterned paper; attach brad and adhere. **6** Die-cut lucky from cardstock; adhere. **7** Print sentiment; trim and adhere.

17 Shamrock

Designer: Shanna Vineyard

1 Make card from cardstock; stitch edges. **2** Cut circle from cardstock; adhere and stitch. **3** Cut shamrock from cardboard; apply glitter and adhere. **4** Spell sentiment with stickers. **5** Tie button with floss; adhere.

Designer Tip

To create a shamrock pattern, find a clipart shamrock you like, resize it in your favorite software, print, and trim. Or, draw or stamp a heart and use it three times to create the leaves.

18 Happy Everything

Designer: Melissa Phillips

1 Make card from cardstock. Cut ½" from front flap and round right corners. **2** Cut cardstock; adhere. Cut patterned paper; round right corners and adhere. **3** Cut circle from cardstock; stamp polka dots. Cut circle from patterned paper; trim and adhere. **4** Tie on ribbon; adhere circle with foam tape. **5** Stamp sentiment and circle on cardstock; punch into circle and adhere with foam tape. **6** Stamp heart; trim, apply dimensional glaze, and adhere. Thread buttons with string and adhere. **7** Stamp hearts on cardstock; trim and adhere.

Spring Begins

In the United States, the first day of spring usually occurs on March 20th or 21st and is dependent on when the Vernal Equinox occurs—the moment when the hours of the day and night are equal and the northern hemisphere begins to tilt towards the sun.

---

19 Spring

Designer: Courtney Kelley

Distress all patterned paper edges.

1 Make card from cardstock. **2** Cut patterned paper piece and strip; adhere. **3** Cut patterned paper; trim with decorative-edge scissors, tear bottom edge, and adhere. **4** Spell "Spring" with stickers. **5** Cover chipboard flowers and butterfly with patterned paper; attach brads and adhere. **6** Stitch butterfly trail with floss.

20 Spring Time

Designer: Danni Reid

1 Make card from cardstock. **2** Cut cardstock; dry emboss. Round top corners and punch edge. Adhere ribbon and adhere to card with foam tape. **3** Apply rub-on. Adhere stick pins. Layer flowers and adhere with foam tape. Thread button and adhere. **4** Spell sentiment with stickers. *Note: Adhere orange stickers with foam tape.*

21 Beloved

Designer: Beatriz Jennings

1 Make card from cardstock. **2** Trim journaling card with decorative-edge scissors; ink edges, adhere, and stitch. **3** Tie on ribbon. **4** Stitch chipboard heart negative; adhere glitter. Adhere patterned paper behind heart; adhere. **5** Die-cut flowers from vellum; adhere. **6** Trim butterfly from patterned paper; adhere. Adhere pearls.

22   Smiles & Giggles

Designer: Danni Reid

1 Make card from cardstock. **2** Cut cardstock block; dry emboss. **3** Cut patterned papers; round corners and adhere to block. Apply rub-on. **4** Tie on ribbon and twine. Pull bows through chipboard flower frame; adhere. Adhere flower. Thread button with twine and adhere. **5** Adhere chipboard bee and rhinestones. Adhere block to card.

23   Many Thanks

Designer: Danni Reid

1 Make card from cardstock. **2** Cut cardstock; dry emboss and adhere. **3** Cut patterned paper; apply rub-ons and adhere pearl. **4** Punch patterned paper strip; adhere. **5** Loop ribbon; adhere. Adhere block. **6** Twist wire and adhere. Loop twine and adhere. Affix heart badge.

24   Get Well Soon

Designer: Sherry Wright

1 Make card from cardstock. **2** Cut patterned paper to fit card front; adhere. **3** Tie on ribbon. Adhere butterfly. **4** Stamp all images on cardstock; trim. Spray with shimmer spray. Adhere rhinestones. **5** Adhere berry branches. Adhere sentiment with foam tape.

---

25 | ## Tulip Hi

Designer: Teri Anderson

1 Make card from cardstock; round corners. Stitch edges. **2** Punch circle from patterned paper; adhere. **3** Spell "Hi" with stickers. **4** Tie ribbon around pins; adhere.

Designer Tip

Stitching around the borders of a card doesn't have to be perfect. A "wobbly" stitch adds character to your card.

26 | ## Celebrate Life

Designer: Melissa Phillips

Ink all patterned paper edges.

1 Make card from cardstock; round bottom corners of front flap. **2** Cut patterned papers; adhere. Zigzag-stitch left edge. **3** Cut patterned paper strip; emboss and punch; adhere. **4** Tie on ribbon; adhere die cut. **5** Adhere chipboard heart. Affix crown and adhere rhinestones and pearls. **6** Adhere flowers. Tie button with floss; adhere.

27 | ## Pink Floral Sympathy

Designer: Jennifer Hansen

1 Make card from cardstock; affix stickers. **2** Cut flowers from patterned paper; adhere. **3** Spell sentiment with rub-ons. **4** Attach brads.

28   Thoughts & Prayers

Designer: Sherry Wright

1 Make card from cardstock. **2** Cut tag from patterned paper; sand edges. Apply rub-on; punch hole in top. **3** Cut patterned paper to fit card front. Cut lace circle from patterned paper. Trim out flower; adhere. **4** Tie ribbon around patterned paper and through tag; adhere with foam tape. **5** Adhere lace circle; adhere block.

29   Quote of the Day

Designer: Shanna Vineyard

Ink all edges.

1 Make card from cardstock. **2** Cut patterned paper; adhere. **3** Tie on ribbon. **4** Apply rub-on to cardstock; trim with decorative-edge scissors and adhere with foam tape. **5** Spell sentiment with stickers.

30   Happily Ever After

Designer: Wendy Sue Anderson

1 Make card from patterned paper. **2** Cut patterned papers; adhere. Stitch around top block. **3** Adhere fibers; tie bow and adhere. Insert pin. **4** Apply rub-on.

31 | Husband Birthday

Designer: Betsy Veldman

1 Make card from cardstock. **2** Cut patterned paper; adhere. **3** Cut patterned paper; punch. Stitch; adhere with foam tape. **4** Stamp bracket repeatedly. **5** Stamp sentiments on cardstock; trim and layer together. Tie on ribbon; adhere. **6** Adhere chipboard sentiment circle.

April

🌼 Happy Easter

Designer: Wendy Sue Anderson

1 Make card from cardstock. **2** Adhere patterned paper strips. **3** Adhere felt trim and ribbon. **4** Tie ribbon bow; adhere. Adhere accent. **5** Affix stickers to spell "Happy Easter."

April Fool's Day

With April Fool's Day falling on April 1st it's a great opportunity to send a silly card to your friends or family.

---

1 | **Prank Me**

Designer: Teri Anderson

1 Make card from cardstock. **2** Print sentiment on cardstock and adhere. **3** Adhere patterned paper strips. Adhere ribbon. **4** Punch cardstock circle; adhere. Trim owl from patterned paper; adhere. **5** Affix stickers to spell "Prank me."

2 | **Right Now**

Designer: Jessica Witty

1 Make card from patterned paper; round bottom right corner. Adhere specialty paper. **2** Affix stickers and ink edges. **3** Ink edges of butterfly and adhere. **4** Adhere rhinestones.

3 | **Snail Hello**

Designer: Mary MacAskill

1 Make card from cardstock. **2** Cut patterned paper pieces, round corners, and adhere. **3** Punch cardstock and patterned paper circles; adhere. **4** Affix sticker and apply rub-on. Stitch below rub-on.

4   Elegant Anniversary   5 STEPS

Designer: Teri Anderson

1 Make card from cardstock; adhere patterned paper. **2** Tie ribbon bow around front flap. **3** Adhere patterned paper behind frame die cut; adhere. **4** Adhere flourish die cut and attach brad. **5** Apply rub-on.

5   Matthew 17:20   5 STEPS

Designer: Julie Masse

1 Make card from cardstock. **2** Trim patterned paper with decorative-edge scissors; adhere. Adhere patterned paper rectangles. **3** Cut triangles from patterned paper; adhere. **4** Open bracket frame in software. Print on photo paper, stamp sentiment, and color with ink and colored pencil. Trim and adhere. **5** Attach brads. Tie on trim and flower buckle.

6   Spread Your Wings   5 STEPS

Designer: Jessica Witty

1 Make card from cardstock. **2** Die-cut cardstock label; adhere. **3** Stamp butterflies and sentiment. **4** Adhere butterfly die cut.

7 Take a Load Off

Designer: Ashley Harris

1 Make card from cardstock. 2 Print sentiments on cardstock, mat with patterned paper, and adhere. 3 Punch cardstock circles and adhere to cardstock squares; adhere. 4 Trim laundry basket and clothes from patterned paper; adhere. 5 Adhere rhinestones.

8 Welcome Baby

Designer: Betsy Veldman

1 Make card from cardstock. Emboss, stitch, and paint edges. 2 Adhere patterned paper strip. Adhere starburst die cut with foam tape. 3 Die-cut owl and branch from cardstock and patterned paper. Adhere patterned paper owl to cardstock with foam tape. Adhere piece to card. 4 Die-cut sentiment from patterned paper; adhere. Adhere buttons.

9 Hey, Chickie

Designer: Julie Campbell

Ink all paper edges.

1 Make card from cardstock; score front flap. 2 Tie ribbon around patterned paper rectangle; adhere piece to card. *Note: Tie button to ribbon.* 3 Stamp sentiment and chick with egg on cardstock; color with markers and colored pencils. Apply dimensional glaze to egg. 4 Trim stamped piece and adhere with foam tape.

Easter

Easter is always on Sunday, but the specific Sunday changes depending on the stages of the moon and the spring equinox. Make sure you're prepared to celebrate this holiday by creating a religious or playful handmade greeting.

10   Worthy is the Lamb

Designer: Lea Lawson

1 Make card from cardstock. **2** Mat patterned paper with patterned paper. Zigzag-stitch edges and adhere. **3** Trim felt with decorative-edge scissors; adhere. **4** Print sentiment on cardstock, ink edges, affix cross, and adhere. **5** Die-cut brackets from patterned paper; adhere. Adhere rhinestones.

11   Hoppy Easter

Designer: Sherry Wright

1 Make card from cardstock; adhere patterned paper. **2** Adhere trim and tie on raffia. **3** Trim scalloped border from patterned paper, ink edges, and adhere. **4** Stamp scalloped border and hoppy Easter on cardstock, trim, and adhere with foam tape. **5** Fussy-cut bunny and flowers from patterned paper; adhere with foam tape. **6** Ink edges.

12   Easter Eggs

Designer: Maren Benedict

1 Make card from cardstock. **2** Adhere patterned paper; stitch edges. Tie on ribbon. **3** Cover chipboard eggs with patterned paper, ink edges, and adhere. **4** Stamp Hoppy Easter on chipboard egg. Color with markers and adhere flock.

Scrabble Day

Combine Scrabble Day (always on April 13th) with a note of congratulations by incorporating fun game tiles into the design of your card.

13 Scrabble Congrats	**14** Grow a Friend	**15** R-r-r-rev My Motor
Designer: Kim Kesti	Designer: Dawn McVey	Designer: Beth Opel

13 Scrabble Congrats

Designer: Kim Kesti

1 Make card from cardstock; adhere cardstock and sand edges. **2** Adhere patterned paper strips. *Note: Sand bottom edge of Good Fortune strip and curl torn top edge of Origami strip.* **3** Print "You did it!" on score sheet. Trim and tear edges; staple to card. **4** Adhere tiles to spell "Congrats."

14 Grow a Friend

Designer: Dawn McVey

1 Make card from cardstock. **2** Adhere patterned paper rectangles, tie on ribbon bow, and stitch edges. **3** Stamp snail and sentiment on cardstock. Affix rickrack and mat with cardstock. **4** Adhere piece to card with foam tape.

15 R-r-r-rev My Motor

Designer: Beth Opel

1 Adhere cardstock and patterned paper to card. **2** Select motorcycle image from web site and copy into software. Print on transparency sheet and adhere. **3** Affix stickers and apply rub-ons to spell sentiment.

Blah, Blah, Blah Day

April 17th marks Blah, Blah, Blah Day. This day was established to help people beat the blahs by quitting a habit, losing weight, or working on home projects.

National High 5 Day

National High 5 Day is always the third Thursday in April. Send someone a note of congratulations and commemorate this fun holiday by adding a high 5 to your project!

---

16 | Enjoy Life

Designer: Carla Peicheff

1 Make card from cardstock. Cover front with patterned paper **2** Adhere patterned paper pieces. Border-punch patterned paper strip; adhere. Stitch top and side edges. **3** Tie ribbon bow around front flap. Adhere flower and rhinestone. **4** Adhere journaling tag, chipboard life, and flower rhinestones. **5** Punch butterflies from patterned paper, adhere pearls, and adhere to card. **6** Affix stickers to spell "Enjoy."

17 | Blah. Blah. Blah.

Designer: Teri Anderson

1 Make card from cardstock; round top right corner. **2** Type "Blah." repeatedly in software. Print on cardstock, trim, round top right corner, and adhere. **3** Print "May your day be anything but..." on cardstock, attach brad, and adhere.

18 | High Five

Designer: Wendy Sue Anderson

1 Make card from cardstock. Adhere slightly smaller piece of patterned paper. **2** Adhere patterned paper strip to cardstock. **3** Stitch top and side edges and affix stickers to spell "High five!" **4** Punch circle from patterned paper, adhere hand, and adhere to piece. **5** Tie ribbon bow around piece and adhere to card. **6** Attach clip and fasten 5 to bow with safety pin.

19 Dreamer Butterfly
5 STEPS

Designer: Roree Rumph

1 Die-cut flower from patterned paper. Trace shape on cardstock card base, trim, and adhere. **2** Die-cut circle from patterned paper. Adhere, stitch edges with floss, and apply rub-on. **3** Fussy-cut butterfly from patterned paper; adhere. **4** Thread buttons with floss; adhere.

20 Style
5 STEPS

Designer: Dawne Ivey

1 Make card from cardstock; emboss Swiss Dots. **2** Punch scalloped square from cardstock, emboss Allegro, and adhere. **3** Adhere butterflies. *Note: Bend top butterfly wings to add dimension.* **4** Apply rub-on and adhere rhinestones.

21 Lavender Sympathies
5 STEPS

Designer: Rae Barthel

1 Make card from cardstock. **2** Cut patterned paper slightly smaller than card front; tie ribbon bow and adhere. **3** Apply rub-on and adhere pearls to tag; adhere. **4** Adhere flowers and button.

Earth Day

Celebrate Earth Day (April 22nd) by giving a handmade card and a bag of yummy organic fruit to someone special in your life.

Arbor Day

Founded in 1872, Arbor Day is celebrated on the last Friday in April. Send a simple card to a fellow nature lover and include a pack of seeds so they can plant a tree in honor of this special day.

22 Happy Earth Day

Designer: Nicole Maki

1 Make card from cardstock. **2** Double-mat patterned paper rectangle with patterned paper; adhere. *Note: Ink all patterned paper edges.* **3** Stamp Earth Topiary and Cathrine's Bow on cardstock. Color with colored pencils and water brush. **4** Trim stamped pieces and adhere together. Adhere piece to card with foam tape. **5** Stamp Happy Earth Day on cardstock, ink edges, mat with patterned paper, and adhere with foam tape.

23 Mushroom Hi

Designer: Sherry Wright

1 Make card from cardstock. Adhere slightly smaller piece of cardstock. **2** Stamp mushroom and frogs on cardstock, color with pen and markers, and trim. **3** Trim clouds, mushrooms, snails, and flowers from patterned paper. **4** Adhere patterned paper and stamped images. **5** Adhere chipboard pieces and spell "Hi" with stickers.

24 Happy Arbor Day

Designer: Susan R. Opel

1 Make card from cardstock; adhere patterned paper. **2** Die-cut tree from cardstock, adhere together, and attach brads. Adhere piece to card with foam tape. **3** Affix stickers to spell "Happy arbor day."

25 | Toadstool Thanks
Designer: Dawn McVey

1 Make card from cardstock. Adhere patterned paper strip and tie ribbon bow. **2** Stamp snail, mushrooms, and thanks on cardstock. Trim and mat with cardstock. Adhere with foam tape. **3** Adhere flower and pearls.

26 | Krafty Love
Designer: Wendy Price

1 Make card from cardstock. **2** Stamp flower repeatedly on cardstock. Color with colored pencils and water brush. **3** Mat piece with cardstock, adhere sticker with foam tape, and adhere to card.

27 | You're the Best Birds
Designer: Rae Barthel

1 Make card from cardstock; punch circles from patterned paper and adhere. **2** Tie ribbon bow around patterned paper square. Adhere piece and stitch sides with floss. **3** Trace template on patterned paper. Trim, sand, and stitch edges with floss. **4** Apply rub-ons to piece and adhere to card.

28 Vintage Kiss Me

Designer: Anabelle O'Malley

Ink all paper edges.

1 Make card from cardstock; adhere patterned paper and zigzag-stitch edges. **2** Adhere heart die cut. Accent with glitter glue. **3** Spell "Me" and apply heart on ticket with rub-ons; adhere. **4** Tie ribbon bow around front flap. Adhere trim, flowers, and button.

29 Butterfly Hello

Designer: Beatriz Jennings

Ink all paper edges.

1 Make card from cardstock. **2** Adhere patterned paper pieces and stitch edges. **3** Stamp flourishes and hello. **4** Adhere glitter to chipboard butterfly. Adhere tulle; adhere piece to card. **5** Attach flowers together with brad; adhere.

30 Simply Fabulous Friend

Designer: Kristen Swain

1 Make card from patterned paper. Adhere cardstock strip and ledger paper. **2** Stitch edges of cardstock rectangle; adhere. **3** Adhere ribbon around front flap. *Note: Tie bow with striped ribbon.* **4** Punch circle from patterned paper, affix bird, and adhere. **5** Affix alphabet stickers to spell "Simply fabulous". **6** Affix alphabet stickers to cardstock to spell "Friend". Trim and adhere.

May

Do What You Love

Designer: Wendy Sue Anderson

Ink all paper and die cut edges.

1 Make card from cardstock. **2** Cut patterned paper to fit card front; adhere. Round corner. **3** Cut rectangle of patterned paper; adhere. **4** Cut circle from patterned paper; stitch border and adhere. **5** Adhere die cuts with foam tape. **6** Adhere trim. Wrap twine around card front; tie bow.

Teacher Appreciation Week

The first full week of May, Teacher Appreciation Week was established by the National Education Association. Tuesday of that week is National Teacher Day. Show your appreciation to these courageous men and women by sending treats or a gift.

---

1 | Springy Hello

Designer: Jen del Muro

1 Make card from cardstock. **2** Cut square of patterned paper; mat with cardstock, stitch border, and adhere. **3** Cut square of cardstock; stamp images, color with markers. Double-mat with cardstock and adhere. **4** Stamp tree on patterned paper; cut out tree top and adhere. **5** Stamp Writing Paper Scrapblock on cardstock; punch flourish square. Stamp sentiment and attach with brad. **6** Emboss cardstock, using template. Punch flourish border; mat with cardstock and adhere. Adhere ribbon bow.

2 | Welcome Home

Designer: Heidi Van Laar

1 Make card from cardstock. **2** Cut rectangles of patterned paper; round two corners and adhere. **3** Cut strip of patterned paper; trim with decorative-edge scissors and adhere. **4** Adhere ribbon. Cut strip of cardstock; stamp sentiment and adhere. **5** Stitch alphabet stickers with floss. Adhere to spell "Home". **6** Die-cut and emboss circle from cardstock; die-cut scalloped circle from felt. Adhere. **7** Trim house, cloud, and tree from patterned paper; adhere. *Note: Adhere house with foam tape.*

3 | S is for School

Designer: Kim Moreno

5 STEPS

1 Make card from cardstock; trim right front edge with decorative-edge scissors. **2** Cut rectangle of patterned paper; distress edges and adhere. **3** Cut rectangle of patterned paper; adhere. **4** Affix stickers; attach brads. **5** Punch holes, thread string through, and tie bow.

Cinco de Mayo

Many Americans tend to think of Cinco de Mayo ("the fifth of May" in Spanish) as Mexico's Independence Day. This actually isn't true. On May 5, 1862, the Mexican army—outnumbered two to one—defeated powerful French forces at the Battle of Puebla.

---

4 | Take Care

Designer: Teri Anderson

1 Make card from cardstock. **2** Cut rectangles of patterned paper; adhere. **3** Adhere frame die cut. **4** Knot ribbon around card front. **5** Adhere sentiment die cut. *Note: Trim one edge.*

5 | Happy Cinco de Mayo

Designer: Kim Kesti

1 Make card from cardstock. **2** Cut rectangle of cardstock; apply ink and adhere. **3** Cut rectangle of cardstock; affix sticker border. *Note: Separate border into two pieces lengthwise before affixing.* **4** Die-cut "Cinco de Mayo" from cardstock; adhere. Mat piece with cardstock, adhere trim, and adhere to card with foam tape.

6 | Love You, Grandson

Designer: Betsy Veldman

1 Make card from cardstock. **2** Cut rectangles of patterned paper; adhere. **3** Adhere journaling card. Punch edge of cardstock strip; adhere. **4** Stamp sentiments and ship on cardstock; cut out and adhere. *Note: Adhere ship with foam tape.* **5** Stitch ribbon; wrap around card front and knot. Attach stick pin.

7 | Little Sprout

Designer: Kristen Swain

1 Make card from cardstock. **2** Cut rectangles of patterned paper and embossed cardstock; adhere. **3** Cut strip of cardstock; trim with decorative-edge scissors; adhere. Stitch border. **4** Cut rectangle of cardstock; apply rub-on and adhere. **5** Thread buttons with string; tie bows and adhere. **6** Affix sticker; adhere buttons and pearls.

8 | Greatest Teacher

Designer: Maren Benedict

1 Make card from cardstock; stitch. **2** Cut shape from patterned paper; stitch. **3** Cut heart from center of apple. Adhere patterned paper and acetate. *Note: Use foam tape between patterned paper and acetate layers.* **4** Cut stem and leaf from patterned paper; stitch leaf and adhere pieces. Tie ribbon bow; adhere. **5** Spell "Mom" with stickers on apple; adhere with foam tape. **6** Cut strip of patterned paper; trim with decorative-edge scissors and adhere. Adhere buttons. **7** Stamp "My greatest teacher" on patterned paper; trim and adhere.

9 | My Amazing Mother 5 STEPS

Designer: Alicia Thelin

1 Make card from cardstock. **2** Cut circles from cardstock; adhere. *Note: Create circle frame by cutting smaller circle from center of larger circle. Adhere cardstock strip; zigzag-stitch.* **3** Stamp first part of sentiment on cardstock rectangle; tear and curl part of one edge and adhere. **4** Stamp mother on cardstock; punch circle, attach brad, and adhere with foam tape. **5** Stamp images on cardstock; emboss, cut out, and adhere. *Note: Adhere large flower and bird with foam tape.*

Mother's Day

Celebrated on the second Sunday of May, Mother's Day is a fairly modern holiday. It was created by Anna Jarvis in 1914 and is now celebrated in the U.S. and countries as diverse as Romania, Kuwait, and Nepal.

---

10 | ## A Mother Understands

Designer: Wendy Sue Anderson

1 Make card from cardstock; ink edges. **2** Cut rectangle of patterned paper; stitch border and adhere. **3** Apply rub-on. **4** Thread ribbon through trim; adhere. **5** Thread button with twine; adhere to flower and adhere flower to card.

---

11 | ## Wonderfully Sweet

Designer: Melissa Phillips

Ink all paper edges.

1 Make card from cardstock. **2** Cut patterned paper slightly smaller than card front; adhere. **3** Stamp image on patterned paper; cut rectangle and round bottom corners. Wrap ribbon around and knot. **4** Cut border from patterned paper; zigzag-stitch to stamped piece. Adhere piece with foam tape. **5** Apply rub-on to chipboard rectangle; adhere. Apply rub-on to card. Affix sticker, adhere rhinestones. Draw cherry stem.

---

12 | ## Floral Love

Designer: Melissa Phillips

Ink all paper edges.

1 Make card from cardstock. **2** Cut patterned paper to fit card front; adhere. **3** Cut square of die cut paper; adhere. Cut rectangle of patterned paper; adhere. **4** Stamp image on cardstock; cut into rectangle and adhere. Zigzag-stitch border. **5** Stamp sentiment on chipboard tile; ink edges and adhere. Affix stickers. **6** Tie ribbon bow; adhere. Thread button with string; attach to bow.

13 | Floral Friends

Designer: Brandy Jesperson

1 Make card from patterned paper.
2 Punch cardstock and adhere to patterned paper strip. Adhere to card. **3** Wrap ribbon around card front; tie ribbon bow. **4** Apply rub-on to chipboard rectangle. **5** Attach brad to flower; adhere to chipboard rectangle. **6** Adhere piece with foam tape. Adhere rhinestone.

14 | Heartfelt Thank You

Designer: Shanna Vineyard

1 Make card from cardstock. **2** Cut rectangles of patterned and embossed paper; adhere. Stamp sentiment. **3** Create flower, using pattern on p. 178. Stitch stem, leaf, and flower center. Mat flower center with cardstock; adhere to flower with foam tape. Adhere remaining flower pieces.
4 Thread button with floss; tie bow and adhere.

15 | Classic Congrats

Designer: Charity Hassel

1 Make card from cardstock. **2** Cut rectangles of patterned paper and adhere.
3 Adhere trim. Apply rub-on to cardstock; cut out and adhere. **4** Layer flower and sticker together; adhere. **5** Adhere rhinestones.

16 Happy Couple
Designer: Wendy Sue Anderson

5 STEPS

1 Make card from patterned paper. **2** Cut rectangle of cardstock; stitch border. Adhere chipboard figures. *Note: Adhere heads with foam tape.* **3** Wrap ribbon around piece; tie bow and attach tag with string. Adhere piece. **4** Paint chipboard bubble; let dry. Adhere bubbles. **5** Spell "I do" on bubbles with stickers.

17 Cheery Smile
Designer: Heidi Van Laar

1 Emboss front cover of card. Cut rectangles of patterned paper; adhere inside card. *Note: Adhere face down on inside front cover so pattern shows through.* **2** Die-cut scalloped circle from patterned paper; adhere. **3** Die-cut scalloped circle from felt and circle from patterned paper; adhere. **4** Color stickers with marker; spell "Smile" on card. **5** Cut flowers and leaves from patterned paper; pierce holes to create details in leaves. Layer and adhere with foam tape. **6** Thread buttons with ribbon; adhere.

18 Butterfly Birthday Girl
Designer: Betsy Veldman

5 STEPS

1 Make card from cardstock. **2** Cut patterned paper to fit card front; adhere. **3** Cut rectangle of patterned paper; adhere. Cut notched rectangle from vintage book page; adhere. Stitch border. **4** Die-cut butterfly and shadow from cardstock; ink edges and adhere together. Adhere to card. **5** Die-cut sentiment from patterned paper; adhere. Affix sticker.

Be a Millionaire Day

May 20th is Be a Millionaire Day. So celebrate by counting both your financial and spiritual blessings.

---

19 | ## Dreams Come True

Designer: Lea Lawson

1 Make card from cardstock. **2** Cut patterned paper to fit card front; ink edges and adhere. **3** Cut cardstock square; ink edges, apply rub-ons, stamp image. **4** Color image, adhere rhinestones, apply glitter glue. Adhere piece.

---

20 | ## Thanks a Million

Designer: Alicia Thelin

1 Make card from cardstock. **2** Cut strip of patterned paper; adhere. **3** Punch ovals from cardstock; pierce holes to create borders and adhere, two with foam tape. **4** Stamp sentiment on cardstock; cut out, attach brads, and adhere with foam tape. **5** Wrap ribbon around card front; tie knot.

---

21 | ## Bouncy Smile

Designer: Maren Benedict

1 Make card from cardstock. **2** Cut strip of patterned paper; trim one edge, distress lightly, and adhere. **3** Die-cut circles from cardstock and patterned paper; cut into pieces and combine to form one circle. Zigzag-stitch seams and adhere with foam tape. **4** Pierce holes to create bouncing line; spell "Smile" with chipboard letters.

International Wear a Tiara Day

Everyone deserves to be queen for a day, and here's your chance to announce your royalty to the world! International Wear a Tiara Day is celebrated each year on May 24th, so get out your jewel-encrusted crown and wear it with pride.

---

22 **Birthday Stripes**

Designer: Layle Koncar

5 STEPS

1 Make card from patterned paper.
2 Trace journaling die cut on card, adding an additional 1/3" all around; cut out window. **3** Apply rub-on to journaling card; mat with cardstock and adhere inside card with foam tape. **4** Draw border around window on card front.

---

23 **Let's A Go-Go**

Designer: Maren Benedict

5 STEPS

1 Make card from patterned paper. **2** Apply rub-ons. **3** Pierce holes to create border and line behind bicycle. **4** Punch circles from patterned paper; adhere with foam tape. Adhere rhinestones. **5** Punch circle from patterned paper; adhere to chipboard sun with foam tape; adhere sun to card.

---

24 **We Are Royalty**

Designer: Ashley Harris

1 Make card from cardstock. **2** Cut patterned paper slightly smaller than card front; adhere. **3** Cut rectangle of patterned paper; adhere. **4** Print sentiment on cardstock; cut out and adhere. **5** Cut border from die cut paper; adhere. **6** Adhere crown, pearls, and rhinestones.

Memorial Day

Celebrated on the last Monday of May, Memorial Day is a holiday for honoring the brave men and women who died during military service. It was first created to honor only the soldiers killed in the Civil War, but after World War I it grew to commemorate Americans who gave their lives in any war.

---

25 Remember

Designer: Carolyn King

5 STEPS

1 Make card from cardstock; round bottom corners. **2** Cut rectangles of patterned paper; adhere. **3** Punch flourish from patterned paper; adhere. Adhere star with foam tape. **4** Punch rounded rectangle from cardstock; affix sticker and adhere with foam tape. **5** Adhere beads; knot ribbon around card front.

---

26 Teacher, Thank You

Designer: Wendy Sue Anderson

1 Make card from cardstock. **2** Cut square of packaging. **3** Cut rectangle of patterned paper; ink edges. Cut strip of cardstock; trim with decorative-edge scissors and adhere to inked piece. Adhere to square. **4** Create sentiment with stickers and rub-ons. Tie on ribbon. **5** Cut patterned paper to fit tag; adhere. Cut apple from patterned paper; adhere to tag with foam tape. Adhere tag. **6** Mat square with cardstock; adhere to card.

---

27 A Heart-y Thanks

Designer: Carolyn King

5 STEPS

1 Make card from cardstock; round bottom corners. **2** Cut lined paper to fit card front; staple ribbon and adhere. **3** Punch heart from cardstock; adhere. **4** Stamp image on cardstock; color with markers, emboss, trim, and adhere. **5** Apply rub-on; pierce holes to create line.

28 | #1 Teacher

Designer: Maren Benedict

5 STEPS

1 Make card from cardstock. **2** Cut rectangle of patterned paper; cut strip of cardstock; trim with decorative-edge scissors and adhere to piece. **3** Wrap ribbon around piece and knot; adhere piece with foam tape. **4** Cut apple from cardstock; adhere with foam tape. **5** Stamp image and sentiment; color with markers and adhere with foam tape.

29 | Bold, Bright Teacher

Designer: Alli Miles

1 Make card from cardstock. **2** Cut patterned paper to fit card front; adhere. **3** Cut rectangle of patterned paper; adhere. **4** Cut rectangle from die cut paper; adhere. **5** Cut border from patterned paper; adhere. Stamp sentiment. **6** Adhere button to flower. Cut strip of patterned paper; tie knot and adhere to flower. Adhere flower to card.

30 | A Kid with Class

Designer: Jen del Muro

1 Make card from cardstock. **2** Stamp background on cardstock, emboss, mat with cardstock, and adhere. **3** Die-cut scalloped square from cardstock; attach with brads. **4** Die-cut bracketed squares and letters from cardstock. Emboss cardstock squares; emboss. Mat with cardstock and bracketed square; adhere. **5** Die-cut heart from cardstock; adhere with foam tape. **6** Stamp image and sentiment on cardstock. Emboss sentiment, trim, and adhere. Color image with markers; trim and adhere with foam tape. **7** Adhere button and knotted ribbon.

31 **ConGRADulations!** *5 STEPS*

Designer: Charlene Austin

1 Make card from cardstock. **2** Cut patterned paper slightly smaller than card front; adhere. Stitch border. **3** Spell "Congradulations!" with stickers. **4** Stamp image on cardstock; cut out and adhere.

June

Fresh Lemonade

Designer: Wendy Sue Anderson

1 Make card from cardstock. **2** Cut rectangles of patterned paper; adhere.
3 Adhere ribbon over seam. *Note: Leave ½" extra hanging over edge.* **4** Fold over
extra ribbon length; adhere rhinestone. **5** Apply rub-on to sticker; affix sticker. **6** Tie
ribbon bow; adhere flower and rhinestone. Adhere bow to card.

National Cancer Survivors Day

Celebrated on the first Sunday in June, this holiday commemorates all the men, women, and children around the world who have battled cancer and lived to tell about it.

---

1 | **Believe in Your Dreams**

Designer: Stefanie Hamilton

1 Make card from cardstock. **2** Create finished size project in software. **3** Drop in purple paper. Open taupe paper; resize to slightly smaller than project size. Mat with white, add drop shadow, and drag onto project. **4** Add color to butterfly; drag onto project. **5** Drop in stitching, sentiment, ribbon, and rhinestones. **6** Print on cardstock; trim and adhere to card.

2 | **Deer Friend**

Designer: Sherry Wright

1 Make card from cardstock. **2** Cut patterned paper slightly smaller than card front; ink and distress edges and adhere. **3** Adhere trim. Cut rectangle of patterned paper; ink and distress edges and adhere. **4** Cut deer, flowers, and border from patterned paper; distress edges as desired and adhere. *Note: Curl some edges up for dimension.* **5** Spell "Deer" with chipboard letters; apply rub-on and adhere rhinestones.

3 | **A Cupcake Kind of Day!**

Designer: Jen del Muro

1 Make card from cardstock. **2** Cut rectangles of patterned paper; adhere together and mat with cardstock. Adhere. **3** Stamp image on cardstock and patterned paper; trim patterned paper image and adhere to cardstock image. Color, mat with cardstock, and adhere. **4** Cut strip of cardstock; punch edge and adhere. **5** Stamp sentiment on cardstock; trim and adhere. **6** Adhere button and rhinestone. Tie on ribbon.

4 | Hello Friend
Designer: Julia Stainton

5 STEPS

1 Make card from cardstock. **2** Cut rectangles of patterned paper; adhere. **3** Adhere ribbon. **4** Stamp sentiment; adhere rhinestones. **5** Cut out flowers from patterned paper; layer together with foam tape. Adhere to card with foam tape.

Designer Tip

Cut flowers or other images from patterned paper and layer them together with foam tape for dimension and interest.

5 | Good Luck
Designer: Mary MacAskill

5 STEPS

1 Make card from patterned paper. Cover with patterned paper; stitch border. **2** Cut rectangle of patterned paper; adhere. **3** Create sentiment with stickers and rub-ons on patterned paper. Trim piece; wrap ribbon around and tie knot. *Note: Cut slits in piece to accommodate ribbon.* Adhere piece. **4** Apply crown rub-on to cardstock; cut out and adhere with foam tape. Staple card.

6 | Dream Big
Designer: Kristen Swain

5 STEPS

1 Make card from cardstock; stitch border. **2** Cut squares of patterned and die-cut paper; adhere. **3** Adhere acetate journaling box. **4** Apply rub-on to cardstock; trim and adhere. **5** Thread buttons with string; adhere to butterflies. Adhere butterflies.

7	**#1 Coach**	⟨5 STEPS⟩

Designer: Shanna Vineyard

1 Make card from cardstock; stitch border. **2** Cut rectangle of cardstock; mat with patterned paper and stitch border. Adhere with foam tape. **3** Adhere acetate star; apply rub-on. Affix sticker. **4** Spell "Coach" with stickers.

8	**Hit the Road, Jack!**	⟨5 STEPS⟩

Designer: Kimberly Crawford

1 Make card from cardstock; stamp images. **2** Cut strips of patterned paper; adhere together and zigzag-stitch borders. Adhere to card. **3** Stamp images on cardstock. Color scene as desired; round corners and ink edges. Mat with cardstock; ink mat edges and adhere with foam tape. **4** Stamp sentiment on cardstock; round corners, ink edges, and adhere with foam tape. **5** Wrap with string and tie bow.

9	**Dotty Welcome**	⟨5 STEPS⟩

Designer: Julia Stainton

Ink all paper edges.

1 Make card from cardstock. **2** Cut square of cardstock slightly smaller than card front; emboss, using template. **3** Cut rectangle of patterned paper; adhere to embossed piece. Stitch rectangle and adhere piece to card. **4** Stamp image and sentiment on patterned paper; trim and adhere. **5** Adhere trim; knot ribbon through button and attach safety pin. Adhere button.

10 Catch U Later	**11** On the Road Again	**12** Happy Day
Designer: Betsy Veldman	Designer: Kimberly Crawford	Designer: Maren Benedict

10 Catch U Later — Designer: Betsy Veldman

1 Make card from cardstock; paint edges and stitch border. **2** Die-cut wave from patterned paper; adhere. **3** Die-cut catch from patterned paper and adhere. Affix letter sticker. Die-cut "Later" from patterned paper; adhere. **4** Affix sun sticker to cardstock; cut out and adhere. Thread button with string; adhere. **5** Cut strip of patterned paper border; adhere and stitch. Adhere fish to card.

11 On the Road Again — Designer: Kimberly Crawford

1 Make card from cardstock. **2** Cut rectangles of cardstock and patterned paper; adhere together. Wrap ribbon and twine around piece; tie knots. Adhere entire piece with foam tape. **3** Stamp image on cardstock; color with markers, cut out, and adhere with foam tape. **4** Stamp sentiment on cardstock; trim and adhere.

12 Happy Day — Designer: Maren Benedict

1 Make card from cardstock. **2** Cut patterned paper to fit card front; adhere. **3** Paint chipboard letters; let dry and adhere to spell "Day". **4** Apply rub-ons to cardstock; punch and adhere with foam tape to spell "Happy". **5** Wrap ribbon around card front; tie bow.

Flag Day

Held every year on June 14th, Flag Day is a holiday to commemorate the adoption of the United States flag in 1777.

13 **Together**	**14** **Starry Stripes**	**15** **In Sympathy**
Designer: Roree Rumph	Designer: Susan R. Opel	Designer: Angie Hagist

13 Together

Designer: Roree Rumph

1 Make card from cardstock. **2** Cut patterned paper to fit card front; sand edges and adhere. **3** Cut square of patterned paper. Cut strips of cardstock; trim with decorative-edge scissors. Adhere strips to paper square; zigzag-stitch borders and adhere. **4** Cut strip of patterned paper; sand edges and adhere. Affix journaling tile sticker. **5** Lightly ink chipboard figures; adhere. **6** Affix sentiment sticker; adhere button and heart.

14 Starry Stripes

Designer: Susan R. Opel

1 Make card from cardstock. **2** Adhere ribbon, rhinestones, and beads to make stripes. **3** Cut rectangle of cardstock; adhere. **4** Attach brad to chipboard star; adhere with foam tape.

15 In Sympathy

Designer: Angie Hagist

1 Make card from cardstock; round right corners. **2** Ink edges of cloud die cut; adhere. **3** Apply rub-on. **4** Ink edges of tree die cut; adhere trunk. Adhere tree with foam tape.

Father's Day

The third Sunday in June is dedicated to honoring fathers. Created by Sonora Dodd in 1909, it wasn't legitimized until the 1930s, when the Associated Mens Wear Retailers formed a committee to promote the holiday to boost sales.

---

16 | **My Dad Rocks!** | 5 STEPS

Designer: Shanna Vineyard

1 Make card from cardstock. **2** Cut patterned paper slightly smaller than card front; ink edges and adhere. Zigzag-stitch border. **3** Spell "My dad rocks!" with stickers and chipboard star on chipboard tiles. Adhere with foam tape. **4** Adhere chipboard volume meter.

---

17 | **One-of-a-Kind Dad**

Designer: Charlene Austin

1 Make card from cardstock. **2** Cut patterned paper slightly smaller than card front; adhere. **3** Cut rectangle of cardstock; ink edges and adhere. **4** Spell "Dad" with stickers; stamp sentiment. **5** Cut rectangle of cardstock. Cut tie shapes from cardstock and patterned paper; attach brads and adhere to rectangle. Adhere piece to card. **6** Knot ribbon; wrap around card front and adhere.

---

18 | **Happy Father's Day** | 5 STEPS

Designer: Rae Barthel

1 Make card from cardstock. **2** Cut patterned paper slightly smaller than card front; adhere. **3** Cut square of patterned paper; adhere. **4** Cut strips of patterned paper; adhere. **5** Punch circles from patterned paper in varying sizes; apply rub-on to smallest circle. Stack and adhere together and to card with foam tape.

Summer Begins

The first day of summer changes depending on where you live. This is because it's determined by the summer solstice, which is the longest day of the year.

---

19 | **Whooo is the Best Dad Ever?** | 5 STEPS

Designer: Wendy Sue Anderson

1 Make card from cardstock. **2** Cut patterned paper slightly smaller than card front; ink edges and adhere. **3** Cut rectangles of patterned paper; ink edges and adhere together. Wrap twine around piece, and tie knot. Tie on button with cord. Adhere piece to card with foam tape. **4** Apply rub-ons to create sentiment on journaling tile. Adhere.

---

20 | **Love You, Dad** | 5 STEPS

Designer: Layle Koncar

1 Make card from cardstock. **2** Cut patterned paper slightly smaller than card front; adhere. **3** Cut square of patterned paper; mat with cardstock and adhere. **4** Fussy-cut image from patterned paper; adhere. **5** Spell "Love you dad" with stickers. Adhere chipboard heart.

---

21 | **Happy Summer**

Designer: Alli Miles

1 Make card from cardstock; emboss, using template. **2** Cut rectangle of patterned paper; adhere. Zigzag-stitch border. **3** Cut rectangle of patterned paper; mat with cardstock and adhere with foam tape. **4** Affix stickers and adhere ticket. Create "Happy summer" label and affix. **5** Cut strip of patterned paper; adhere. Punch photo corners from patterned paper; adhere. **6** Wrap ribbon around card front; tie knot.

National Pink Day

Each year on June 23rd, the color pink takes its place as the reigning hue of the day. Whether you prefer pink, blush, coral, raspberry, puce, fuchsia, rose, or salmon, it's the ultimate girly color. Celebrate with friends and loved ones by hosting a pink party (think pink food, pink drinks, pink decorations, pink clothing).

---

22 A Flower for You

Designer: Roree Rumph

5 STEPS

1 Make card from cardstock. **2** Cut patterned paper slightly smaller than card front; adhere. **3** Cut flower and leaves from patterned paper; adhere. **4** Cut second flower from patterned paper; attach brad and adhere with foam tape. **5** Wrap ribbon around card front; tie knot.

---

23 Think Pink

Designer: Kim Kesti

5 STEPS

1 Make card from cardstock. **2** Cut patterned paper to fit card front; adhere. **3** Cut strip of patterned paper; adhere. Adhere ribbon. **4** Print sentiment on ticket; cut out and adhere. **5** Adhere flowers, chipboard crown, and rhinestone.

---

24 Bright & Cheery Thanks

Designer: Rae Barthel

5 STEPS

1 Make card from cardstock. **2** Cut patterned paper to fit card front; adhere. **3** Cut rectangles of patterned paper; adhere. **4** Adhere scalloped strip; wrap ribbon around card front and tie bow. **5** Apply rub-on; adhere flowers with foam tape.

25 Twinkle, Twinkle Little Star

Designer: Maren Benedict

1 Make card from cardstock. **2** Cut strip of patterned paper; adhere. **3** Wrap ribbon around card front; tie knot. Adhere trim. **4** Punch stars from patterned paper; attach brads to two stars and adhere with foam tape. **5** Stamp image; color with markers, cut out, and adhere with foam tape. **6** Stamp sentiment.

26 You Are My Sunshine

Designer: Dawn McVey

1 Make card from cardstock. **2** Cut strips of cardstock; adhere. **3** Stamp polka dots; emboss. **4** Cut strip of cardstock; round left corners. Stamp "Sunshine" and write remainder of sentiment. Adhere. **5** Tie ribbon bow; adhere bow and rhinestones. **6** Stamp hearts on cardstock; cut out and adhere with foam tape.

27 Happiness Is You

Designer: Daniela Dobson

1 Make card from cardstock. **2** Cut patterned paper slightly smaller than card front; adhere and stitch border. **3** Adhere journaling card; stamp sentiment. **4** Tie on ribbon. Adhere trim. **5** Adhere patterned paper to chipboard tree; sand edges and adhere. **6** Make butterfly, using pattern on pg. 178. Adhere flowers; adhere butterfly with foam tape.

28   Miss You
5 STEPS

Designer: Dawn McVey

1 Make card from cardstock. **2** Cut rectangle of patterned paper; mat with cardstock and stitch border. Wrap ribbon around piece; tie bow and adhere with foam tape. **3** Die-cut bracketed box from cardstock; stamp sentiment and border. Adhere with foam tape. **4** Thread button with twine; adhere flower and button.

29   Hi, Neighbor
5 STEPS

Designer: Wendy Sue Anderson

1 Wrap string around chipboard house; tie bow and adhere to card with foam tape. Apply glitter glue. **2** Cut cloud shape from cardstock; apply glitter glue and adhere. **3** Spell "Neighbor" with stickers; affix badge.

30   And They Lived
5 STEPS

Designer: Maren Benedict

1 Make card from cardstock. **2** Cut patterned paper to fit card front; distress edges and adhere. *Note: Cut patterned paper at angle.* **3** Apply rub-on; adhere pearls. **4** Distress edges of sentiment label; mat with cardstock and adhere. **5** Knot ribbon on hat pin; adhere.

July

5 STEPS Happy Fourth

Designer: Wendy Sue Anderson

1 Make card from cardstock. **2** Stamp branch. **3** Adhere birds and stars with foam tape. *Note: Do not use foam tape on red bird.* Spell "Happy 4th" with stickers. **4** Adhere ribbon and border. Tie ribbon bow; adhere. Attach flag clip.

Go Green

Canada, Eh?

da rulz

No texting while driving
Turn off phone in restaurants
Be courteous, always

Canada Day
Celebrate Canada's birthday with a barbecue, some music, and fireworks on July 1st.

Cell Phone Courtesy Month
Did you know that July is Cell Phone Courtesy Month? Celebrate by following the simple rules on this card.

1 | Canada, Eh? | 5 STEPS
Designer: Cathy Schellenberg

1 Make card from cardstock. **2** Trim patterned paper slightly smaller than card front and adhere. **3** Create Canada flag with patterned paper strips; mat with black cardstock and adhere. **4** Cut maple leaf from patterned paper, adhere, and outline with pen. **5** Apply scalloped trim rub-on; create sentiment with rub-ons.

2 | Go Green | 5 STEPS
Designer: Teri Anderson

1 Make card from cardstock. **2** Cover with patterned paper. **3** Trim patterned paper slightly smaller than card; round corners; adhere. Trim snail and toadstools from patterned paper and adhere. **4** Print "Go green" on cardstock strip and staple to card.

3 | Da Rulz | 5 STEPS
Designer: Kim Kesti

1 Make card from cardstock. **2** Trim patterned paper slightly smaller than card front and adhere. **3** Cut cell phone from cardstock and adhere with foam tape. Print rules on cardstock, trim, outline, and adhere. Trim phone buttons from cardstock, outline, and adhere. **4** Spell "Da rulz" with stickers.

Fourth of July

The United States' Independence Day is a great holiday to spend time with family and friends. Enjoy the warm summer night with a barbeque and some fireworks.

---

4 | Star-Spangled Day *5 STEPS*

Designer: Kimberly Crawford

1 Make card from patterned paper. **2** Trim and adhere patterned paper pieces. **3** Adhere chipboard circles with foam tape. **4** Affix sticker strip; punch star from patterned paper and adhere. **5** Die-cut and emboss label from cardstock. Stamp sentiment. Adhere with foam tape.

5 | Bright Birthday *5 STEPS*

Designer: Roree Rumph

1 Make card from cardstock. **2** Trim patterned paper, sand edges, adhere, and zigzag-stitch edges. Trim patterned paper strips, sand edges, and adhere. **3** Apply rub-on. Tie ribbon around card front. Affix orange circle sticker. **4** Cover chipboard star with orange paper. Affix red circle sticker. Thread button and adhere. **5** Adhere star with foam tape. Affix candle sticker. Thread button and adhere.

6 | It's a Boy *5 STEPS*

Designer: Maren Benedict

1 Make card from cardstock. **2** Trim patterned paper slightly smaller than card front; adhere and zigzag-stitch edges. **3** Die-cut and emboss circles from cardstock. Mat cream circle with kraft circle, using foam tape. Adhere to card with foam tape. **4** Spell "It's a boy" with rub-ons; add apostrophe with marker. Adhere arrow. **5** Tie ribbon around card front.

7	Sweet Baby Girl	5 STEPS

Designer: Wendy Sue Anderson

1 Make card from cardstock. **2** Trim cardstock piece; trim and adhere patterned paper and stitch edges. **3** Adhere ribbon and trim. Wrap piece with thread, tie through tag and adhere with foam tape. **4** Affix label and spell "Girl" with stickers. Affix elephant and flower stickers. Adhere piece to card.

8	Vintage Friends	5 STEPS

Designer: Maren Benedict

1 Make card from cardstock. **2** Trim patterned paper slightly smaller than card front, distress edges, and adhere. **3** Distress edges of die cut and adhere. Tie ribbon around card front and adhere buttons.

9	BFF	5 STEPS

Designer: Danielle Flanders

1 Make card from cardstock. **2** Trim and adhere patterned paper strips. Adhere ticket die cut. **3** Adhere rickrack. Stamp decorative bracket on transparency sheet, cut out, attach brad, and adhere. **4** Apply rub-on. Tie and adhere ribbon. Thread button with twine and adhere.

10	**Thx**	5 STEPS
	Designer: Alli Miles	

1 Make card from cardstock. **2** Trim patterned paper to fit card front. Trim and adhere patterned paper rectangle. **3** Affix journal sticker. Spell "Thx" with stickers. **4** Tie ribbon around piece and insert pin through bow. Adhere piece to card front.

11	**Thanks for Delivering**	5 STEPS
	Designer: Shanna Vineyard	

1 Make card from cardstock. **2** Trim newspaper slightly smaller than card front; adhere and stitch edges. **3** Cut heart from cardboard, paint, and adhere. Cut newspaper strip; roll. Tie with floss and adhere. Spell "Thanks" with stickers. **4** Print sentiment on cardstock, trim, and adhere with foam tape.

12	**Elephant Love You**	5 STEPS
	Designer: Angie Hagist	

1 Make card from cardstock. **2** Trim curved cardstock strip for grass and adhere. **3** Stamp four elephants on cardstock and color. Add eyelashes with pen. Cut out elephant heads and adhere with foam tape. Adhere elephant bodies to card. Hand-draw bow on cardstock, cut out, and adhere. **4** Attach brads. Hand-draw clouds on cardstock, trim, and adhere. **5** Apply rub-ons.

13 Silly Old Bear

Designer: Maren Benedict

1 Make card from cardstock. **2** Trim patterned paper slightly smaller than card front and adhere. **3** Tie ribbon around card front. Trim sentiment from patterned paper and adhere. **4** Stamp doll and costume on cardstock and color. Cut out; adhere doll; adhere costume with foam tape. **5** Adhere pearls.

14 Have a Sweet Day

5 STEPS

Designer: P. Kelly Smith

1 Make card from cardstock. **2** Trim border from die cut paper and adhere. **3** Cut fruit slices from patterned paper and adhere rhinestones; adhere with foam tape. **4** Spell "Have a sweet day" with stickers.

Designer Tip

If the scale of a patterned paper is too large or busy for your card design, try fussy-cutting out focal images and popping them with foam tape.

15 Polka Dot Hello

5 STEPS

Designer: Kimberly Crawford

1 Make card from cardstock. **2** Adhere patterned paper pieces. Punch cardstock strip; adhere. **3** Affix label and apply rub-on. **4** Adhere flower and adhere badge with foam tape.

16	Birdie Anniversary	5 STEPS

Designer: Kim Moreno

1 Make card from cardstock. **2** Trim patterned paper slightly smaller than card front and adhere. Trim patterned paper, round corners, and adhere. **3** Punch cardstock strip, draw line with pen, and adhere. Trim patterned paper strip and adhere. Adhere rhinestones. **4** Cut peacocks from patterned paper, apply glitter glue, ink edges, and adhere with foam tape. Apply rub-on.

17	Beach Run	5 STEPS

Designer: Maren Benedict

1 Make card from cardstock. **2** Trim patterned paper to fit card front. Affix dots. **3** Trim image from patterned paper and adhere with foam tape. Adhere cardstock strip. Tie ribbon around card front.

18	Crazy	5 STEPS

Designer: Layle Koncar

1 Make card from cardstock. **2** Adhere patterned paper strips. **3** Punch bottom of patterned paper rectangle; adhere. **4** Trim sentiment from patterned paper, mat with cardstock, and adhere.

National Ice Cream Month

The third Sunday of July is National Ice Cream Day. Don't miss out on this opportunity to eat as much ice cream as you want!

Lollipop Day

Lollipop Day is always on July 20th. So celebrate with a sweet card accompanied by a yummy treat!

---

19 | What's the Scoop?

Designer: Betsy Veldman

1 Make card from cardstock. Stamp card front with solid and outline polka dots. Adhere ribbon. **2** Trim and adhere cardstock and patterned paper. Die-cut scalloped trim from cardstock and adhere. **3** Stamp ice cream cone. Cut out and adhere. **4** Die-cut "Scoop?" from cardstock and adhere. **5** Die-cut tag from cardstock and adhere. Stamp "What's the". Thread button with string and adhere. **6** Tie ribbon into knot, trim, and adhere.

20 | Lollipop Love *5 STEPS*

Designer: Anabelle O'Malley

1 Make card from cardstock. Trim bottom of patterned paper rectangle with decorative-edge scissors; stitch to card. **2** Trim patterned paper and cardstock strips with decorative-edge scissors; adhere. **3** Die-cut scalloped circle and circle from patterned paper and cardstock; adhere. Affix rhinestone circle. **4** Tie ribbon bow around lollipop; adhere. **5** Adhere tag and rhinestones.

21 | Bright Friends

Designer: Rae Barthel

1 Make card from cardstock. **2** Mat patterned paper with patterned paper; adhere. **3** Trim frames from patterned paper and embossed cardstock using templates; adhere together. **4** Apply rub-on and adhere piece with foam tape. **5** Tie ribbon bow around front flap. Tie flowers together with cord; adhere. **6** Adhere birds with foam tape.

22 Sweet on You

Designer: Beatriz Jennings

1 Make card from cardstock; paint edges. **2** Zigzag-stitch patterned paper to card front. **3** Paint chipboard circle, sand edges, adhere glitter, and adhere to card. **4** Cut cupcake holder from patterned paper. Stitch and ink edges; punch top. **5** Trim strip of vellum with decorative-edge scissors; adhere. Adhere piece to card. **6** Tie ribbon bow and adhere. Insert brad through flower and adhere. **7** Adhere sweet on you die cut.

23 Pink & Black Birthday

Designer: Rae Barthel

1 Make card from cardstock. **2** Mat patterned paper square with patterned paper; stitch around edges. **3** Trim scalloped edge from cardstock. **4** Trace cardstock onto patterned paper; trim and ink edges; adhere scalloped strips. **5** Adhere border to square; tie on ribbon. **6** Adhere pearls to border and adhere flowers with foam tape; adhere pearls to flower centers with foam tape. **7** Apply rub-on; adhere square to card.

24 Miss You Travel

5 STEPS

Designer: Angie Hagist

1 Make card from cardstock; round right corners. **2** Trim patterned paper and adhere. **3** Cut ribbon and adhere. **4** Adhere accent and create sentiment with stickers.

Designer Tip

Use a thin grid ruler to line up letter stickers before attaching them to the card. Add them to the ruler, so that they hang off the top, and then add them to the project all at once so you'll know that they're even.

25 Friends Forever Flowers

Designer: Alli Miles

5 STEPS

1 Make card from cardstock. 2 Emboss rectangle on card front. 3 Stamp sentiment and flower stems. 4 Adhere buttons.

26 Enjoy the Journey

Designer: Wendy Price

5 STEPS

1 Make card from cardstock. 2 Die-cut cityscape from cardstock and adhere with foam tape. 3 Tie ribbon around card; apply sentiment. 4 Stamp car on cardstock; sketch grid to create taxi. 5 Color image with watercolors; trim and adhere with foam tape.

27 Medallion Thanks

Designer: Betsy Veldman

5 STEPS

1 Make card from cardstock. 2 Trim journaling card and patterned paper; adhere and zigzag-stitch top and bottom edges. 3 Stamp medallion, circle, and sentiment on cardstock; cut out and adhere with foam tape. 4 Stamp circles down center of card; embellish with buttons. 5 Tie ribbon around flower sticker and affix.

28 Polka Dot Floral Hello

Designer: Dawn McVey

1 Make card from cardstock. **2** Trim square piece of vellum. Stamp flowers. **3** Mat stamped piece with patterned paper; adhere with foam tape. **4** Trim strip of cardstock. Stamp sentiment, emboss, and adhere. **5** Thread buttons; adhere.

29 Thanks

Designer: Heidi Van Laar

1 Make card from cardstock; round bottom corners. **2** Trim patterned paper to fit card front; adhere. **3** Trim patterned paper; round bottom corners. Mat with cardstock and adhere. **4** Trim piece of patterned paper. Round bottom corners and use border punch along top edge; adhere. **5** Adhere ribbon. Layer flowers and leaves, tie ribbon bow, and adhere. **6** Affix stickers to spell "Thanks".

Designer Tip

Layering embellishments such as flowers can add a big impact to a simple card.

30 Imagine

Designer: Maren Benedict

1 Make card from cardstock. **2** Die-cut and emboss scalloped square from patterned paper. **3** Tie ribbon around square; knot and adhere with foam tape. **4** Adhere chipboard baseball player and sentiment.

Designer Tip

Embossing the edges of die cut shapes adds interest.

31 Safe Travels

Designer: Becky Olsen

1 Make card from cardstock. **2** Trim patterned paper slightly smaller than card front; adhere. **3** Trim strip of patterned paper; punch edge and adhere. **4** Adhere trim. Thread button with floss; adhere.
5 Trim strip of patterned paper; cut one end to form banner; adhere and roll up end.
6 Affix stickers to spell "Safe travels".

Designer Tip

Use a map for the destination being visited or an older map to reuse paper and help save the environment.

August

Greetings from Camp

Designer: Wendy Sue Anderson

1 Make card from cardstock; adhere patterned paper and stitch edges. **2** Mat journaling card with cardstock. Adhere patterned paper strip with foam tape; tie on cord. **3** Ink edges of patterned paper; adhere. **4** Attach clip and apply rub-on. Affix stickers and attach brad. **5** Adhere panel to card.

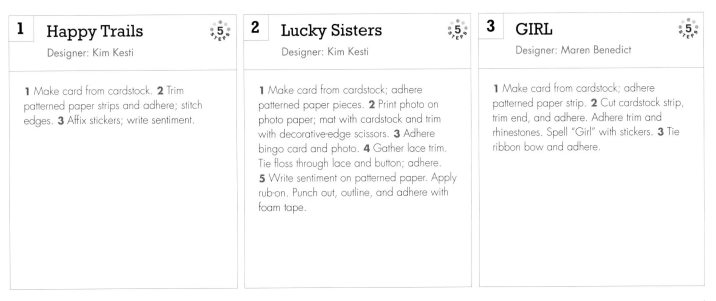

1 | Happy Trails

Designer: Kim Kesti

1 Make card from cardstock. **2** Trim patterned paper strips and adhere; stitch edges. **3** Affix stickers; write sentiment.

2 | Lucky Sisters

Designer: Kim Kesti

1 Make card from cardstock; adhere patterned paper pieces. **2** Print photo on photo paper; mat with cardstock and trim with decorative-edge scissors. **3** Adhere bingo card and photo. **4** Gather lace trim. Tie floss through lace and button; adhere. **5** Write sentiment on patterned paper. Apply rub-on. Punch out, outline, and adhere with foam tape.

3 | GIRL

Designer: Maren Benedict

1 Make card from cardstock; adhere patterned paper strip. **2** Cut cardstock strip, trim end, and adhere. Adhere trim and rhinestones. Spell "Girl" with stickers. **3** Tie ribbon bow and adhere.

4 **Bear Hugs**	**5** **The Earth**	**6** **Great Job!**
Designer: Michele Boyer	Designer: Natasha Trupp	Designer: Mary MacAskill
1 Make card from cardstock. **2** Mat patterned paper with cardstock; adhere patterned paper piece and stitch edges. **3** Adhere patterned paper strip; zigzag-stitch edges. Adhere panel to card. **4** Stamp sign and bear hugs on cardstock. Color and outline image. **5** Stamp bear on cardstock; color, cut out, and adhere to stamped panel with foam tape. Attach brads. **6** Mat stamped panel with cardstock. Adhere to card with foam tape.	**1** Make card from cardstock. **2** Stamp earth on cardstock. Cut out and adhere with foam tape. **3** Stamp sentiment on card.	**1** Make card from cardstock; apply starburst rub-ons. **2** Apply remaining rub-ons to cardstock; cut out and adhere with foam tape.

7	4U	5 STEPS

Designer: Carla Peicheff

1 Adhere patterned paper rectangle to card front. **2** Punch patterned paper piece; adhere. Adhere patterned paper strip. Adhere patterned paper inside card. **3** Adhere ribbon; affix stickers. **4** Adhere flowers and butterfly. Attach brads through button holes; adhere. **5** Adhere rhinestones and pearls.

8	I Read Your Emails	5 STEPS

Designer: Maren Benedict

1 Make card from cardstock; adhere patterned paper. **2** Punch cardstock; adhere with foam tape. **3** Adhere sentiment strip and rhinestones. **4** Tie on ribbon.

9	Birthday Wish	5 STEPS

Designer: Carla Peicheff

1 Die-cut heart and scalloped heart from cardstock. **2** Set eyelet in heart. Adhere patterned paper squares; stitch edges of squares and heart. **3** Affix stickers to spell "Wish". Adhere chipboard star, rhinestones, and metal tag. **4** Place heart on scalloped heart and attach with brad.

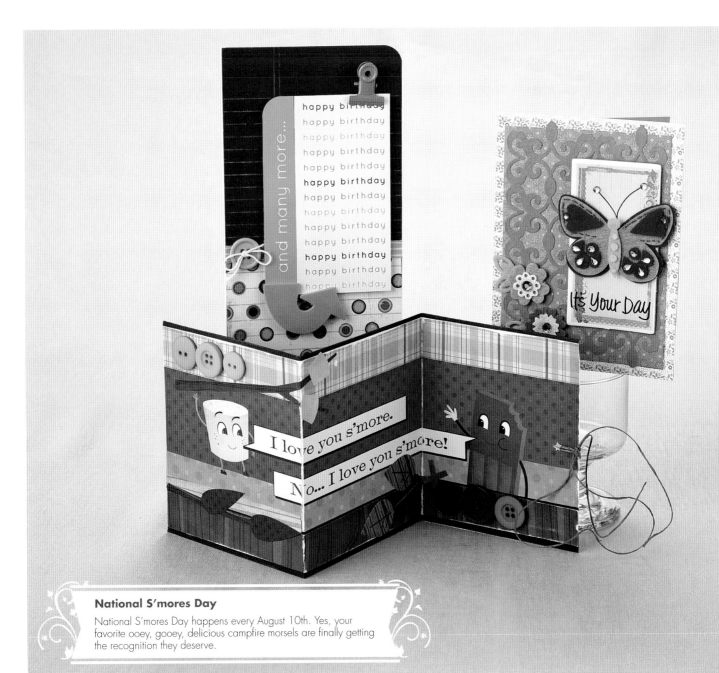

National S'mores Day

National S'mores Day happens every August 10th. Yes, your favorite ooey, gooey, delicious campfire morsels are finally getting the recognition they deserve.

10 Love You S'More	**11** Many More	**12** It's Your Day
Designer: Kim Kesti	Designer: Wendy Sue Anderson	Designer: Anabelle O'Malley
1 Make card from cardstock; adhere patterned paper strips. **2** Affix stickers and adhere buttons. **3** Punch star; tie on raffia.	**1** Make card from cardstock; round right corners. Adhere patterned paper and ribbon. **2** Print "Happy birthday" and "And many more" on cardstock. Trim and adhere together. Round top left corner and adhere with foam tape. **3** Thread button with string and adhere. **4** Attach clip and adhere arrow with foam tape.	**1** Make card from cardstock; adhere patterned paper panels and die cut paper. **2** Adhere journaling tag. Affix stickers. **3** Draw antennae and adhere rhinestones. Apply rub-on.

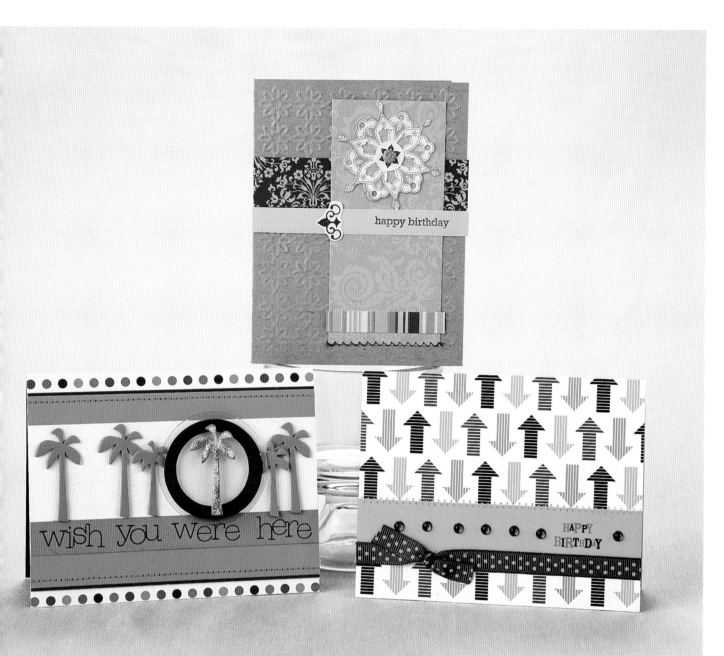

13	**Wish You Were Here**

Designer: Mary MacAskill

1 Make card from cardstock; cover with patterned paper. **2** Layer cardstock panels; stitch edges. **3** Spell sentiment with rub-ons on cardstock strip; adhere to panel. **4** Adhere palm trees to cardstock panel. **5** Cut ring from cardstock; adhere to acrylic circle. Adhere palm tree and apply glitter glue. **6** Adhere circle to cardstock panel with foam tape. Adhere panel to card.

14	**Embossed Birthday**	5 STEPS

Designer: Betsy Veldman

1 Make card from cardstock; emboss. **2** Adhere patterned paper rectangles. **3** Stamp happy birthday on cardstock; trim and adhere. **4** Adhere die cuts and attach brad. Zigzag-stitch edge of patterned paper.

15	**Birthday Arrows**	5 STEPS

Designer: Mary MacAskill

1 Make card from patterned paper. **2** Adhere patterned paper strip; zigzag-stitch top edge. **3** Tie ribbon and adhere. **4** Adhere rhinestones and apply rub-on.

16 Folder of Thanks

Designer: Shanna Vineyard

1 Make card from patterned paper; trim to create tab. **2** Adhere patterned paper strip. **3** Tie ribbon and adhere; attach staples. **4** Trim cardstock with decorative-edge scissors; punch each scallop. Attach brads and adhere. **5** Ink stamp with markers and stamp. **6** Apply rub-on.

17 Pink & Orange Get Well

Designer: Dawn McVey

1 Make card from cardstock; emboss using template. **2** Stamp flower strip and get well soon strip on cardstock strips. Trim cardstock strip with decorative-edge scissors. **3** Stamp heart strip on cardstock; heat-emboss. **4** Layer cardstock strips and adhere. Tie on ribbon. **5** Stamp get well soon circle on cardstock; punch. **6** Stamp heart and flower on cardstock; punch and adhere to larger circles with foam tape. **7** Adhere circles with foam tape. Adhere rhinestones.

18 Arrrgh Birthday

Designer: Teri Anderson

1 Make card from cardstock; adhere patterned paper. **2** Adhere patterned paper behind tag; adhere to card. **3** Stamp skull on cardstock. Cut out and adhere. **4** Stamp arrrgh on sticker; crumple, flatten out, and affix. **5** Stamp another birthday? on cardstock; trim and adhere. Attach staples.

19 | What's Up?

Designer: Laura Williams

1 Make card from cardstock. **2** Stamp hello there repeatedly on cardstock; adhere. **3** Stamp what's up? on cardstock; adhere. **4** Stamp cityscape on transparency sheet; trim. **5** Cut scraps into building shapes and adhere to cardstock; mat with cardstock. Adhere to card. **6** Staple on stamped piece. Color random windows with markers.

20 | Break a Leg

Designer: Susan R. Opel

1 Make card from cardstock; adhere patterned paper and trim. **2** Create sentiment in software; print on photo paper and trim. **3** Adhere sentiment to frame; adhere with foam tape.

21 | You Made My Day Butterfly

Designer: Lea Lawson

1 Make card from cardstock. **2** Round corners and ink edges of patterned paper; adhere. **3** Cover chipboard with patterned paper; sand edges. **4** Punch holes in chipboard; thread ribbon through. Adhere chipboard and ribbon to card. **5** Tie ribbon bow and adhere. **6** Trim butterfly from patterned paper; adhere. **7** Apply rub-ons; adhere rhinestones.

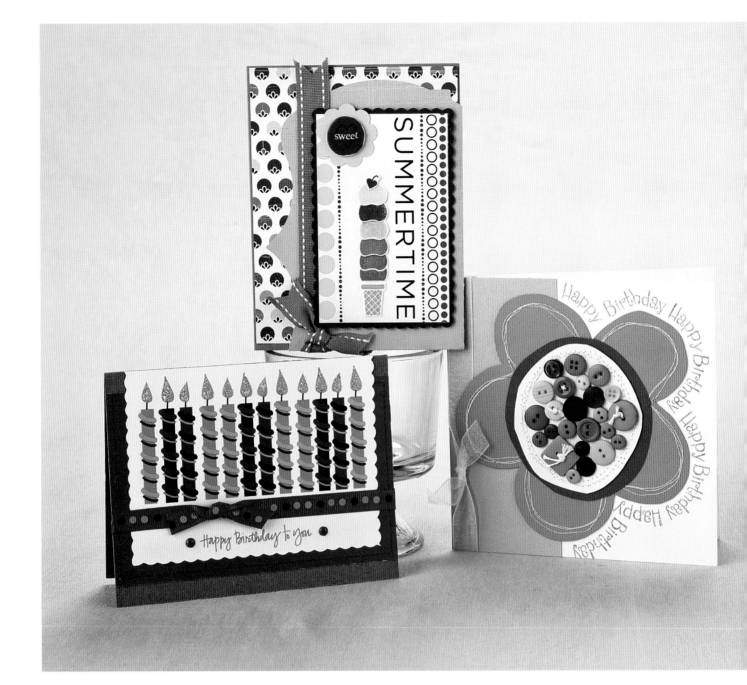

22 Candles

STEPS

Designer: Mary MacAskill

1 Make card from cardstock. **2** Adhere patterned paper and stitch edges. **3** Trim cardstock with decorative-edge scissors; adhere. **4** Apply rub-ons. Tie ribbon and adhere. **5** Apply glitter glue and attach brads.

23 Summertime

Designer: Betsy Veldman

1 Make card from cardstock; adhere patterned paper. **2** Die-cut label from cardstock. Fold over card front edges and adhere. **3** Trim ribbon. Tie and adhere. **4** Trim cardstock with decorative-edge scissors; adhere journaling tag. **5** Stamp ice cream cone repeatedly on cardstock with different inks. Stamp tiny heart. Cut out images and adhere to tag. **6** Die-cut scalloped circle from cardstock; adhere. **7** Adhere chipboard. Adhere panel to card with foam tape.

24 Birthday Buttons

STEPS

Designer: Alisa Bangerter

1 Make card from cardstock; adhere cardstock panel. **2** Cut flower from cardstock. Stitch around petals. Cut cardstock circles and adhere; stitch around center. Adhere flower. **3** Thread several buttons with floss and adhere. **4** Stamp happy birthday on card. Tie on ribbon.

Designer Tip

To make sure the image is placed correctly on the card, bend the stamp on the block each time before stamping the sentiment.

Kiss & Make Up Day

Who doesn't get into an argument occasionally? Well, Kiss and Make Up Day, August 25th, is the perfect excuse to do something special to say you're sorry.

---

25 | **Hi There Cherries**

Designer: Maren Benedict

1 Make card from cardstock. Adhere patterned paper and stitch along bottom edge. **2** Trim vellum and adhere; zigzag-stitch along bottom edge. **3** Tie on ribbon. **4** Stamp cherries on cardstock; color and cut out. **5** Stamp hi there on cardstock piece. Adhere cherries with foam tape. Adhere rhinestone. **6** Die-cut scalloped rectangle from cardstock. Die-cut scalloped rectangle from vellum and stitch. **7** Mat sentiment panel with scalloped rectangles, using foam tape. Adhere to card with foam tape.

26 | **Kiss & Make Up**

Designer: Kim Kesti

1 Make card from cardstock; adhere cardstock panel. **2** Trim patterned paper with decorative-edge scissors; adhere. **3** Punch patterned paper with circle punch; adhere to punched scalloped circle cardstock. Adhere circles to card. Color with marker. **4** Print sentiments on cardstock. Trim and adhere with foam tape. **5** Adhere badge with foam tape. Apply rub-on.

27 | **Almost Human**

Designer: Alicia Thelin

1 Make card from cardstock. **2** Punch cardstock and ruffle edges. Wrap cardstock strip around cardstock; tie on ribbon. Adhere to card. **3** Stamp image twice on cardstock. Cut out rabbit and adhere with foam tape. Punch cardstock circles; adhere. **4** Adhere stamped panel to card.

28	Special Delivery

Designer: Debbie Olson

1 Make card from cardstock; round bottom corners. **2** Round corners of patterned paper strip; sand edges and adhere. **3** Punch patterned paper. Stitch, sand edges, and adhere. **4** Die-cut bracket from patterned paper and chipboard; adhere. **5** Stamp sentiments on cardstock; die-cut and emboss oval frame from piece and chipboard; adhere. Ink edges. **6** Adhere photo behind frame. Adhere to bracket label. **7** Adhere bracket, ribbon, and threaded buttons. **8** Die-cut and emboss tag from cardstock. Stamp special delivery. Thread tag; adhere.

29	Gingham Get Well

Designer: Rae Barthel

1 Make card from cardstock. **2** Ink patterned paper edges and adhere. **3** Trim patterned paper and adhere. Adhere rhinestones. **4** Tie on ribbon and spell sentiment with stickers.

30	Believe in Yourself

Designer: Julie Campbell

1 Make card from cardstock. **2** Sand edges of cardstock panel. Adhere trim. **3** Sand edges of patterned paper; mat with cardstock. Adhere to cardstock panel. **4** Peel top layer from cardboard; apply rub-on. Tie on twine. Adhere to cardstock panel. **5** Die-cut and emboss oval from cardstock; stamp tree and emboss. Adhere with foam tape. **6** Cut end off pin and adhere heart. Adhere cardstock panel to card.

31 | Baby Butterflies

Designer: Maren Benedict

5 STEPS

1 Make card from cardstock; round bottom corners. **2** Round bottom corners of patterned paper; adhere. **3** Adhere tag, trim, butterflies, and rhinestones. **4** Tie ribbon bow and adhere.

September

thank you
very much

Thank You Very Much

Designer: Wendy Sue Anderson

1 Make card from cardstock. **2** Trim patterned paper to fit card front, stitch edges, and adhere. **3** Adhere patterned paper strips. **4** Trim patterned paper, emboss, and stitch edges; adhere. **5** Affix sticker to cardstock, trim, and adhere using foam tape. **6** Thread buttons and adhere. Apply rub-on sentiment.

1 | Back to School Apple

Designer: Charity Hassel

5 STEPS

1 Make card from patterned paper.
2 Trim patterned papers and adhere. Trim patterned paper strip and adhere. 3 Adhere die cut trim and ribbon. Thread button and adhere. 4 Adhere chipboard apple. Apply parenthesis rub-on. 5 Apply rub-on sentiment.

2 | School Days

Designer: Danielle Flanders

1 Make card from cardstock; paint edges.
2 Trim patterned paper and adhere. Tie ribbon and adhere; stitch paper edges.
3 Affix border sticker. 4 Adhere patterned paper behind chipboard negative; adhere to card. 5 Apply rub-on to date sticker and affix.
6 Thread buttons with twine and adhere.

Designer Tip

Using the negative space from chipboard letters is a thrifty and stylish way to get the most out of your product.

3 | Touch Lives Forever

Designer: Kimberly Crawford

1 Make card from cardstock. 2 Trim patterned paper, mat with cardstock and adhere. 3 Die-cut label shapes from cardstock and adhere. 4 Trim cardstock, stamp sentiment, and adhere. 5 Tie ribbon bow and adhere. Adhere buttons. 6 Trim apple shape from patterned paper and adhere using foam tape.

Designer Tip

Using white ink on black paper and cardstock gives a great chalkboard-feel to any teacher-inspired project.

4 | Much Appreciated

Designer: Ashley C. Newell

1 Die-cut and emboss card from cardstock. **2** Trim cardstock strip and adhere. Stamp sentiment. **3** Trim cardstock and adhere. Stamp flower solids and then outlines. Stamp dots. **4** Tie ribbon and adhere. **5** Stamp flower solid and outline on cardstock, trim, and attach brad; adhere using foam tape. **6** Punch circles from cardstock and adhere.

5 | Hi Flower

Designer: Teri Anderson

1 Make card from cardstock. **2** Trim patterned paper, round left corners, and adhere. **3** Die-cut "Hi" from cardstock and adhere to tag; adhere piece. **4** Adhere die cut.

6 | So Stylish

Designer: Kristen Swain

1 Make card from cardstock. **2** Trim patterned paper and adhere. Trim cardstock rectangle and adhere. **3** Trim cardstock strip, attach brads, and adhere. Trim patterned paper and adhere. **4** Tie twine around front flap. **5** Trim leaves from patterned paper and adhere. Adhere die cuts using foam tape; adhere pearls. *Note: Bend petal edges up.* **6** Apply rub-on to cardstock; trim with decorative-edge scissors and adhere using foam tape.

Labor Day

Send a "labor of love" to a friend on Labor Day, which is always celebrated on the first Monday in September. Labor Day originated in 1882 in honor of the contributions made by working citizens for the growth of the country.

International Literacy Day

Share your love of reading on International Literacy Day, September 8th!

National Grandparents Day

Show the special grandparents in your life how much you care by sending them a card on National Grandparents Day, which is celebrated every year on the first Sunday after Labor Day.

---

7 ### Heartfelt Flag

Designer: Charlene Austin

1 Make card from cardstock; ink edges. **2** Apply happy rub-on and spell "Labor day" with rub-ons. **3** Trim cardstock strips and adhere to paper. Trim cardstock square and adhere to piece. Die-cut and emboss heart from piece; adhere. **4** Punch stars from cardstock; adhere.

8 ### Read, Read, Read

Designer: Kim Moreno

1 Make card from cardstock. **2** Trim patterned paper, round right corners, and adhere. **3** Trim patterned paper strips with border punches and adhere. Trim patterned paper strip and adhere. **4** Punch circles, wrap string, and tie through button. **5** Spell "Read read read" with stickers.

9 ### Happy Grandparents Day

Designer: Wendy Sue Anderson

1 Make card from cardstock. **2** Trim patterned paper and adhere. Trim cardstock strips and adhere. Trim cardstock strips, punch edges, and adhere. **3** Trim cardstock panel and adhere. Adhere ribbon. **4** Thread buttons with twine and adhere. Adhere twine around edges of panel. **5** Write "Happy grandparents day" with pen. Draw picture.

Designer Tip

Have a child draw a small picture on the front of your card for an extra personal touch!

Patriot Day

Honor your country on Patriot Day, every September 11th, with a thoughtful card.

10	Miss You Butterflies	5 STEPS

Designer: Rae Barthel

1 Make card from cardstock. Trim patterned paper and adhere. **2** Trim patterned paper square, mat with patterned paper, and adhere. **3** Trim patterned paper piece. Trim patterned paper strips and adhere to piece; affix scalloped border stickers. Tie ribbon around piece and adhere piece. **4** Spell "Miss you" with stickers. **5** Thread raffia through buttons; adhere using foam tape.

11	America the Beautiful	5 STEPS

Designer: Julie Campbell

1 Make card from cardstock. Cut square from denim and adhere; stitch edges. **2** Trim patterned paper, stitch edges, attach eyelets, and adhere. **3** Die-cut circles from patterned paper and denim. Layer pieces and stitch edges. **4** Die-cut star from patterned paper, stitch edges, and adhere using foam tape. **5** Stamp sentiment and trace with gel pen. Adhere rhinestones.

Designer Tip

Recycle an old pair of jeans by using scrap pieces of denim on your next paper project!

12	Dots & Flowers Thank You	5 STEPS

Designer: Heidi Van Laar

1 Make card from cardstock. **2** Trim patterned paper and adhere. **3** Trim patterned paper, affix border sticker, and adhere. **4** Stitch yellow ribbon with floss and adhere. Spell "Thank you" with stickers. **5** Adhere cardstock flower using foam tape. Attach brad to flowers and adhere.

Designer Tip

To spice up a plain piece of ribbon, stitch along the edges with embroidery floss.

13	Classy	5 STEPS
	Designer: Susan R. Opel	

1 Make card from cardstock. **2** Trim cardstock and adhere. **3** Trim diamond shapes from cardstock and adhere. **4** Spell "Classy" with stickers. **5** Adhere rhinestones.

14	Thanks Apples	5 STEPS
	Designer: Dawn McVey	

1 Make card from cardstock. **2** Trim cardstock strip, punch edge, and adhere. **3** Trim cardstock and adhere. Adhere rhinestones. Tie ribbon around front flap. **4** Stamp apples patterns and apple outlines on cardstock. Trim stamped images and adhere using foam tape. **5** Stamp thank you on cardstock, punch, and adhere using foam tape.

15	You Are a Peach
	Designer: Dawn McVey

1 Make card from cardstock; round bottom corners. **2** Stamp grid and flower; emboss. **3** Trim strip of cardstock and create scalloped edge using slit punch; adhere. Trim strip of cardstock and adhere. **4** Tie ribbon around front flap. **5** Stamp "Peach" on cardstock and write "You are a" with marker. Punch sentiment and adhere using foam tape. **6** Punch butterfly from cardstock and adhere; adhere rhinestone.

16 | Happy Anniversary

Designer: Ashley C. Newell

1 Make card from cardstock; emboss, using template. **2** Tie ribbon around front flap. Stamp sentiment. **3** Die-cut scalloped square from cardstock; adhere using foam tape. Affix rhinestone sticker. **4** Stamp swirled heart on cardstock, trim, and adhere using foam tape. **5** Adhere felt flower. Tie floss through button and adhere. **6** Stamp small heart on cardstock, heat-emboss, and adhere using foam tape.

17 | Birthday Rainbow

Designer: Heidi Van Laar

1 Make card from cardstock. **2** Cut cardstock to fit card front. Trim patterned paper, round corners, and score along lines; adhere. Tie ribbon around piece and adhere. **3** Punch circle from patterned paper and adhere behind button. Thread button with floss and adhere. **4** Trim patterned paper, round left corners, and stitch edges with floss; mat with cardstock and adhere using foam tape. **5** Fussy-cut bird and rainbow from patterned paper, stitch with floss, and adhere using foam tape. **6** Stamp sentiment.

18 | Shabby Birthday

Designer: Beatriz Jennings

Ink all edges.

1 Make card from cardstock. **2** Trim patterned paper and adhere. **3** Trim patterned paper, adhere, and zigzag-stitch edges. **4** Adhere rickrack. Thread buttons with floss and adhere. **5** Apply rub-on to sticker and affix. **6** Tie ribbon bow and adhere. Attach brad to flower and adhere.

International Talk Like a Pirate Day

Get out your paper-crafting booty and send a treasure-filled greeting on International Talk Like a Pirate Day—every year on September 19th!

---

19 | Yo Matey

Designer: Kim Hughes

Ink all edges.

1 Make card from cardstock; cover with patterned paper. **2** Stamp sentiment along edge. **3** Tie trim around front flap. Thread button with twine and adhere. **4** Trim patterned paper and tear edge. Stamp parrot, yo matey, and diamond. Draw line and fill in hat shape using marker. Adhere piece to card using foam tape. **5** Punch circle from patterned paper. Stamp skull on cardstock, trim, and adhere using foam tape; color with marker and adhere piece.

20 | 5th Birthday

Designer: Shanna Vineyard

1 Make card from patterned paper. Draw lines around edges with marker. **2** Trim patterned paper pieces and adhere. Draw lines on edges of top piece. **3** Tie ribbon around front flap. **4** Trim cardstock, apply rub-on, and adhere using foam tape. **5** Cut circle from patterned paper using template; adhere. Draw lines around circle. **6** Adhere chipboard number.

21 | Choo Choo

Designer: Maren Benedict

1 Make card from cardstock. **2** Trim patterned paper strips and adhere. **3** Punch circles from cardstock and adhere. Stitch across circles. **4** Trim patterned paper, adhere to chipboard tag, and adhere tag with foam tape. Stamp sentiment on cardstock, trim, and adhere to tag. **5** Tie ribbon around front flap. **6** Stamp train on cardstock, color with markers, and trim; adhere using foam tape.

Autumn Begins

The first day of Autumn falls on the 22nd or 23rd of September, so celebrate the new season with a festive card!

---

22 Autumn

Designer: Beatriz Jennings

1 Make card from patterned paper; round right corners. **2** Trim patterned paper, round right corners, and adhere. Zigzag-stitch edge. **3** Trim ribbon and adhere. **4** Trim shapes from die cut paper and adhere. Apply rub-on. **5** Adhere flower. Thread button with twine, tie, and adhere.

---

23 Hi Fall

Designer: Laura Williams

1 Make card from patterned paper. **2** Stamp trees on cardstock, trim and punch; adhere red tree. **3** Adhere cardstock behind orange and yellow trees; adhere using foam tape. **4** Spell "Hi fall" with stickers on cardstock. Trim and sand edges; adhere.

---

24 Bling Flowers With Gratitude

Designer: Gretchen Clark

1 Make card from cardstock. **2** Trim cardstock and mat with cardstock. Stamp sentiment. **3** Stamp stem. Stamp flower solids and flower outlines. **4** Apply glitter glue. Tie ribbon around piece and adhere using foam tape.

25 | ## Oh Deer
Designer: Melissa Phillips

1 Make card from cardstock; emboss. Round bottom corners. **2** Cut cardstock piece; stamp deer and grass. Embellish with glitter glue and adhere. Stitch top edge. **3** Trim patterned paper strip with decorative-edge scissors; adhere. Affix sticker and adhere patterned paper strip. **4** Paint chipboard bookplate; apply glitter. Stamp sentiment on cardstock; trim and adhere behind bookplate. Tie on ribbon and adhere. **5** Punch butterfly from patterned paper; adhere. Adhere rhinestone. Thread button with twine; adhere.

26 | ## Love You Forever
Designer: Dawn McVey

1 Make card from cardstock; ink edges. **2** Stamp sentiment. **3** Trim cardstock, stamp grid and medallions. Tear edge; stitch edges and adhere. **4** Tie ribbon around front flap and adhere. **5** Die-cut bird from cork and adhere using foam tape.

27 | ## Blooming Flower
Designer: Anabelle O'Malley

1 Make card from cardstock; round corners. **2** Trim packaging. Punch edge of cardstock strip; adhere. Tie ribbon around piece and adhere. **3** Apply rub-ons to tag. Tie ribbon through tag and adhere. **4** Insert pin through knot. **5** Adhere rhinestones. Adhere flower.

28	With Sympathy Branches	5 STEPS

Designer: Dawn McVey

1 Make card from cardstock. **2** Trim cardstock strips and adhere; stitch. Trim cardstock strip and punch edge. **3** Trim cardstock, stamp sentiment, branches, and leaves; mat with cardstock and adhere punched strip. Tie ribbon around piece and adhere using foam tape. **4** Adhere rhinestones.

29	Leafy Birthday

Designer: Betsy Veldman

1 Make card from cardstock. **2** Trim patterned paper rectangles, mat with cardstock, and adhere. **3** Adhere ribbon. **4** Affix sticker to cardstock, trim, and apply rub-on; adhere with foam tape. **5** Tie ribbon bow and adhere. **6** Cut out leaf shapes from felt, stitch with floss, and adhere. Thread button with floss and adhere.

30	Wishing You Well

Designer: Ashley C. Newell

1 Make card from cardstock. **2** Trim cardstock, stamp grass, and adhere ribbon; adhere. **3** Stamp bird on cardstock, trim, and adhere using foam tape. **4** Die-cut and emboss oval and scalloped oval from cardstock. **5** Stamp sentiment on oval. Adhere to scalloped oval with foam tape; adhere piece to card with foam tape. **6** Adhere pearls.

October

⁙5⁙ Eek

Designer: Wendy Sue Anderson

1 Make card from cardstock. **2** Cut patterned paper to fit card front. Punch edge of patterned paper strip; ink edge and adhere. **3** Adhere button, tie ribbon around piece, and affix star sticker. **4** Cut label shape from patterned paper; emboss. Ink edges and adhere. **5** Adhere piece to card. Affix remaining stickers.

World Card Making Day

The first Saturday in October is World Card Making Day, a day set aside for celebrating the creativity of handmade cards and the personal connection they create among friends and family. To find out more, visit *www.WorldCardMakingDay.com*.

1

Birthday Countdown

Designer: Mary MacAskill

1 Make card from cardstock. Stitch line. 2 Apply number rub-ons. 3 Adhere plastic and chipboard labels. 4 Apply happy birthday rub-on. 5 Adhere rhinestones.

Designer Tip

Use stamps instead of rub-ons, varying the ink color for a different look.

2

Butterfly Thanks

Designer: Mary MacAskill

1 Make card from cardstock; round corners. 2 Round corners of patterned paper; stitch edges and adhere. 3 Punch centers from flowers on patterned paper; adhere. 4 Stamp sentiment. 5 Make tag from cardstock; stamp flourish. Adhere ribbon, attach eyelet, and tie on twine. Adhere with foam tape. 6 Stamp butterfly on cardstock, trim, and color with pencils. Adhere buttons; adhere butterfly with foam tape.

3

World Card Making Day

Designer: Kim Kesti

1 Make card from cardstock. 2 Punch scalloped squares from cardstock; adhere. 3 Print logo on photo paper; trim and mat with cardstock. 4 Staple ribbon loop to piece; adhere with foam tape.

World Smile Day

Share a smile with someone today, because the first Friday in October is World Smile Day. Harvey Ball created the smiley face in 1963, and an official celebration was launched in 1999 to honor this familiar symbol.

4   Earthy Thank You

Designer: Kimberly Crawford

1 Make card from cardstock; stamp small flower randomly. **2** Stamp Four Leaf Grid on cardstock strip; mat with cardstock and adhere. **3** Stamp vines, woodgrain, and flowers on cardstock; trim. **4** Adhere stamped pieces to card. Thread wood buttons with twine; adhere all buttons.

Designer Tip

Stamp and cut different combinations of images and colors. Have fun rearranging them in a layout until you find one you really like.

5   Reasons to Smile

Designer: Alicia Thelin

1 Make card from cardstock. **2** Stamp and emboss butterfly on cardstock. Trim to square, round corners, and adhere with foam tape. **3** Stamp sentiment on cardstock; punch circle. **4** Tie on ribbon. Adhere sentiment piece with foam tape. **5** Adhere button.

6   Sustaining Hope

Designer: Debbie Olson

1 Make card from cardstock; round right corners. **2** Trim gold cardstock panel; round right corners. **3** Stamp and emboss vines. Outline edges with paint pen. **4** Stamp and emboss sentiment on cardstock strip. Score lines at top and bottom edges; outline edge with paint pen. **5** Punch piece; tie ribbon through and around panel. Adhere to panel with foam tape. **6** String beads on stick pin; insert. Adhere panel.

7 | ### What's Buggin' You? ⁵STEPS
Designer: Susan R. Opel

1 Make card from cardstock. **2** Cut cardstock piece and adhere to card. **3** Print sentiment on cardstock; trim and adhere. **4** Emboss "Buggin'". **5** Adhere bug, ribbon and rhinestones.

Designer Tip

Susan's clever use of heat embossing on the sentiment gives a custom look to otherwise plain print.

8 | ### Sparkle Thank You ⁵STEPS
Designer: Rae Barthel

1 Make card from cardstock. Adhere cardstock. **2** Adhere patterned paper and border; adhere rhinestones. **3** Punch two circles from patterned paper; double-mat with punched cardstock circles. Adhere rhinestones and adhere with foam tape. **4** Apply rub-on to cardstock; punch into circle. Mat with punched cardstock circle and adhere rhinestones. Adhere to card with foam tape.

9 | ### Shine! ⁵STEPS
Designer: Roree Rumph

1 Make card from cardstock. **2** Adhere patterned papers; round corners. **3** Adhere ribbon at seam. Stitch with floss. **4** Cut circles from patterned paper; adhere and attach brads. **5** Cover chipboard star with cardstock; stitch edge. Spell "Shine!" with rub-ons and attach brad. Adhere with foam tape.

Designer Tip

Turn this card on its side and adjust the direction of the rub-on sentiment for a different look.

10	Love Me	5 STEPS

Designer: Maren Benedict

1 Make card from cardstock; round bottom corners. **2** Cut heart from patterned paper; adhere. Adhere rhinestone heart. **3** Stamp sentiment; color hearts with marker. Apply glitter glue to hearts. **4** Tie on ribbon.

11	Retro Thank You	5 STEPS

Designer: Rae Barthel

1 Make card from cardstock; round bottom corners. **2** Round bottom corners of patterned paper; adhere piece and cardstock strip. **3** Stamp sentiment on cardstock; punch oval. Ink edges. **4** Adhere rhinestones; adhere piece to card.

12	Owl Thank You

Designer: Daniela Dobson

1 Make card from cardstock. **2** Ink edges of patterned paper; adhere. **3** Stitch edge of journaling card with floss; adhere. **4** Stamp leafy branch and sentiment; color letters. **5** Stamp branch on cardstock; trim and adhere. **6** Apply rub-on to patterned paper; trim. Adhere using foam tape. **7** Adhere buttons.

Designer Tip

Instead of stitching, pierce holes and connect with a white gel pen.

Canadian Thanksgiving

Canada celebrates its national Thanksgiving Day the second Monday of October. Create a simple card to let your loved ones know how grateful you are for their support.

---

13 | Birthday Star

Designer: Mary MacAskill

1 Make card from cardstock; round corners. **2** Round corners of cardstock rectangle. Stamp flourish; adhere. **3** Stamp and emboss stars on patterned paper. Punch border on strip of patterned paper. Zigzag-stitch to embossed piece. Adhere piece to card. **4** Apply sentiment rub-on. Tie ribbon; adhere. **5** Cut circles from vellum and cardstock; adhere together. Cut circle ring from cardstock; adhere over vellum; adhere to card. **6** Adhere chipboard star. Thread buttons with floss; adhere.

14 | Cornucopia of Gratitude

Designer: Alice Golden

1 Make card from cardstock. **2** Layer ribbon; adhere to patterned paper. Adhere piece to card. **3** Die-cut and emboss label from cardstock. Stamp sentiment; ink edges. Adhere to card with foam tape. **4** Color sticker with markers; adhere. **5** Tie ribbon bow; adhere.

15 | Pineapple Thanks

Designer: Julie Masse

1 Make card from cardstock; adhere patterned paper. **2** Die-cut square and scalloped square from cardstock. Layer and adhere together. **3** Stamp pineapple. Stamp "Thanks". **4** Punch slot in piece. Tie on ribbon. **5** Adhere with foam tape.

National Breast Cancer Awareness Month

October is National Breast Cancer Awareness Month (NBCAM), which is celebrating 25 years of promoting breast cancer awareness.

National Chocolate Cupcake Day

October 18th is National Chocolate Cupcake Day. Brighten someone's day with a handmade card and chocolate cupcake!

16 Delicate Thank You
Designer: Sherry Wright

5 STEPS

1 Make card from cardstock; cover with patterned paper. 2 Ink edges of patterned paper piece; adhere. 3 Trim flowers and leaves from patterned paper; adhere. 4 Apply frame rub-on to cardstock; trim, ink edges, and adhere. Apply sentiment and swirl rub-ons. 5 Adhere butterfly die-cut. Adhere rhinestones.

17 Strength
Designer: Melissa Phillips

5 STEPS

Ink edges of all cut paper and stickers.

1 Make card from cardstock; round bottom corners. 2 Adhere patterned paper and rickrack. 3 Punch edge of cardstock strip; adhere to patterned paper piece. Adhere to card. 4 Tie knot in ribbon; adhere. Adhere flowers and affix strength sticker. 5 Paint chipboard wings. Sand edges, apply glitter, and adhere to card. Affix sentiment sticker. Thread button with string; adhere.

18 Chocolate Cupcake Day
Designer: Wendy Sue Anderson

5 STEPS

1 Make card from cardstock. Cut and adhere patterned papers. 2 Punch edge of patterned paper strip; adhere. Adhere ribbon. Tie on ribbon. 3 Stamp cupcake liner three times on cardstock. Stamp and emboss frosting three times. 4 Trim cupcakes; adhere sequins and beads. Adhere, using foam tape for middle cupcake. 5 Print sentiment on cardstock, trim, and make into tag with rim. Adhere beads and chipboard heart. Adhere to card. *Note: Use WordArt function in software to create circle text shape.*

19 Chocolate Cake Birthday

Designer: Tanis Giesbrecht

1 Make card from cardstock. **2** Sand edges of patterned paper rectangle; adhere to card. **3** Cut rectangle of patterned paper; sand edges. Mat with cardstock, sand edges and adhere. **4** Trim and adhere ribbon. **5** Stamp banner and cake on cardstock; color with markers. Trim; mat cake with cardstock. **6** Adhere cake to cardstock rectangle; mat with cardstock, sand edges, and adhere. Adhere banner.

20 Leaf Gratitude

Designer: Ashley C. Newell

1 Make card from cardstock. **2** Adhere cardstock rectangle and patterned paper square. **3** Stamp sentiment on cardstock; trim and adhere, using foam tape under part. **4** Tie ribbon; adhere. Adhere felt leaf.

Designer Tip

Try stamping words in a sentiment separately, using different ink colors or paper. Add dimension by adhering one or two words with foam tape.

21 Striped Thank You

Designer: Roree Rumph

1 Make card from cardstock. **2** Trim two pieces of patterned papers, one to fit card front; sand edges and adhere. **3** Affix label stickers and floral journaling tag. **4** Adhere flowers and buttons; stitch with floss. **5** Spell "Thank you" with stickers.

Designer Tip

Hand stitching is a fun technique that will add texture and give your project a handmade feel.

National Mammography Day

National Mammography Day is always the third Friday in October. Send this card to all of your female friends and family as a reminder to get their annual mammograms.

---

22 | **Breast Wishes** | *5 STEPS*

Designer: Ashley Harris

1 Make card from cardstock. **2** Trim two pieces of patterned paper to fit card front and inside of card; adhere. **3** Make bra from patterned paper, following pattern on p. 178. Embellish with trim, ribbon and rhinestone; adhere. **4** Print sentiments on cardstock; adhere to front and inside of card.

Simple Sentiment

The inside of this card says, "Let's keep it that way. Get your mammogram today!"

---

23 | **Congratulations Bouquet**

Designer: Maren Benedict

1 Make card from cardstock. **2** Stamp two flowers on cardstock. Cut out and embellish with marker. Attach brads and adhere with foam tape. **3** Stamp flower twice on cardstock. Cut out center of second flower and adhere with foam tape. **4** Stamp sentiment above middle flower. **5** Stitch stems. **6** Cut slits in card front; tie ribbon through slits.

---

24 | **Hot Dawg** | *5 STEPS*

Designer: Becky Olsen

1 Make card from cardstock. **2** Trim patterned paper to fit card front; adhere. **3** Stamp dog image repeatedly on cardstock; emboss. Trim and adhere. **4** Trim two strips of patterned paper. Adhere larger one, then smaller one over paper seams; adhere trim. **5** Spell sentiment with stickers.

Designer Tip

Use stamps to create customized colors and backgrounds in lieu of patterned paper.

25	Thanks Coach

Designer: Lisa Dorsey

1 Make card from cardstock. 2 Trim patterned paper to fit card front; adhere. Draw border with marker. 3 Adhere ribbon. 4 Paint edges of chipboard circle; let dry. 5 To create soccer ball, find soccer ball image on internet. Resize to fit on chipboard circle and reverse print on back of white cardstock; cut sections apart. Using black sections as a template, trace on patterned paper. Ink all edges and adhere pieces to chipboard circle; adhere to card. 6 Create star using software. Print on cardstock; trim, ink edges and adhere with foam tape.

26	Haunt Couture	5 STEPS

Designer: Betsy Veldman

1 Make card from cardstock; ink edges. 2 Trim patterned paper to fit card front; adhere at angle and trim excess. 3 Adhere journaling tag; tie and adhere ribbon. 4 Stamp Witch Shoes and sentiment on cardstock; color. Punch out corners, ink edges, and mat with cardstock. 5 Attach brads to corners; adhere piece to card. Tie button with raffia and adhere.

27	Boo!	5 STEPS

Designer: Angie Hagist

1 Make card from cardstock. 2 Spell "Boo" with stickers. 3 Adhere two sets of eye die cuts with foam tape. 4 Apply eye rub-ons randomly.

Designer Tip

You can vary the look of the eyes by rubbing some of them upside down.

28	Beware

Designer: Stefanie Hamilton

1 Make card from cardstock. **2** Open a 4" x 6" canvas in software; open digital elements. **3** Drag and drop yellow paper onto upper portion of canvas. Drop torn edge onto bottom edge; add drop shadow. **4** Drag and drop green paper along lower portion of canvas. **5** Drop in candelabra, sentiment, and frame. **6** Print on cardstock and adhere to card front.

29	Bejeweled Halloween

Designer: Kim Moreno

1 Make card from cardstock. **2** Trim cardstock to fit card front; tear edges and adhere. **3** Adhere patterned paper square. Draw border around edges with pen; adhere rhinestones. **4** Trim strip of patterned paper and mat with cardstock; adhere. **5** Cut sentiment from patterned paper. Adhere rhinestones and adhere to card with foam tape.

30	Trick or Treat

Designer: Sherry Wright

1 Make card from cardstock. **2** Trim patterned paper to fit card front; adhere. **3** Trim two pieces of patterned paper. Mat smaller with larger. Ink and distress edges; adhere. **4** Trim two pieces of rickrack; accent with glitter glue and adhere. **5** Affix owl sticker to chipboard circle. Distress and ink edges; accent with glitter glue and adhere. **6** Adhere chipboard sentiment; accent with glitter glue.

Halloween

Halloween falls on October 31st each year. Send out this card on All Hallows' Eve and your friends will surely think it's a treat and not a trick!

---

31 | **Pumpkin Patch**

Designer: Beatriz Jennings

5 STEPS

1 Make card from cardstock. **2** Trim two pieces of patterned paper to fit card front; ink edges, adhere, and stitch edges. **3** Affix sticker; stitch edges. **4** Tie bow and adhere. Thread twine through button and tie bow; adhere. **5** Adhere trim. Thread twine through buttons; adhere.

November

5 STEPS Fall Blessings

Designer: Wendy Sue Anderson

1 Make card from cardstock. **2** Stitch edges of patterned paper; adhere. **3** Cut patterned paper block; adhere patterned paper strip and zigzag-stitch seam. Affix blessings tab sticker. **4** String tags on yarn and tie to block. Mat block with cardstock and adhere to card. **5** Spell "Fall" with stickers; affix asterisk.

| **1** | **Birthday Wish Ticket** | **2** | **Offbeat Birthday** | **3** | **Newsprint Thank You** |

1 Birthday Wish Ticket

Designer: Sherry Wright

1 Make card from cardstock; cover with cardstock. **2** Distress and ink edges of book page; adhere. Adhere fabric strip. **3** Cut patterned paper, distress and ink edges, and tie on ribbon. Adhere. *Note: Trim ribbon with decorative-edge scissors.* **4** Distress and ink edges of patterned paper piece; adhere. Apply rub-on. **5** Distress and ink edges of wish ticket; adhere. **6** Cover button shell with fabric; adhere to card. Adhere rhinestone.

2 Offbeat Birthday

Designer: Courtney Kelley

1 Make card from cardstock. Sand edges of patterned paper; adhere. **2** Cut patterned paper strip, sand edges, and adhere. **3** Sand edges of flower sticker; affix. Attach brads. **4** Zigzag-stitch with floss. **5** Spell "Birthday" with stickers.

3 Newsprint Thank You

Designer: Dawn McVey

1 Make card from cardstock. Punch edge of card front; ink edges. **2** Stamp grid and medallions on cardstock; tear edge and adhere. **3** Stamp sentiment and finials on card. Tie on ribbon. **4** Die-cut flowers from book page; ink edges and adhere. **5** Adhere flowers. Thread buttons with twine; adhere.

4	**Always**	5 STEPS

Designer: Maren Benedict

1 Make card from cardstock. **2** Adhere patterned paper strip. Tie on ribbon. **3** Cut always label from patterned paper; adhere with foam tape. Adhere flourishes. **4** Punch two flowers from patterned paper; distress edges. Layer, attach brad, and adhere with foam tape.

5	**Autumn Glow Birthday**	5 STEPS

Designer: Rae Barthel

1 Make card from cardstock. Adhere patterned paper. **2** Cut patterned paper piece. Adhere patterned paper strip. Mat with cardstock. **3** Adhere paper border. Apply rub-on. **4** Adhere piece to card.

Designer Tip

Mat patterned paper with black cardstock to create a bold, framed effect.

6	**Simply Red**	5 STEPS

Designer: Maren Benedict

1 Make card from cardstock; round bottom corners. **2** Cut patterned paper strip, round bottom corners, and adhere. **3** Adhere lace trim. Tie on ribbon. **4** Layer flowers, attach brad, and adhere.

7 | Layered Hello

Designer: Kimberly Moreno

1 Make card from cardstock. **2** Cut patterned paper slightly smaller; ink edges and adhere. **3** Cut patterned paper strips, punch edges, layer, and adhere. *Note: Bend edges up slightly for added dimension.* Ink card edges. **4** Tie on ribbon. Thread button with string and adhere. **5** Cut heart from patterned paper; ink edges. Mat with cardstock, ink edges, and adhere with foam tape. Fussy-cut leaves from patterned paper; adhere. **6** Stamp hello on cardstock piece; ink edges and adhere. Adhere epoxy dots.

8 | Blessing

Designer: Alice Golden

1 Make card from cardstock. Adhere slightly smaller patterned paper piece. **2** Die-cut and emboss scalloped rectangle from cardstock. Stamp sentiment and adhere with foam tape. **3** Tie ribbon bow. Tie floss around bow and adhere to card. Adhere flower. **4** Thread buttons with floss and adhere.

Designer Tip

Alice carefully cut this sentiment stamp apart to make it easier to stamp in different colors. You can also use stamping markers to color the stamp instead of cutting it.

9 | For You

Designer: Danielle Flanders

1 Make card from patterned paper. Adhere cardstock piece. **2** Cut patterned paper square; stitch and distress edges. Cut circle from patterned paper; adhere. Adhere piece with foam tape. **3** Affix frame sticker to chipboard; trim. Tie on ribbon and adhere with foam tape. **4** Spell "For you" with stickers. Adhere rhinestone. Affix make a wish sticker to chipboard; trim and adhere. **5** Apply rub-on.

Veterans Day

Held on November 11th, the anniversary of the end of World War I, this special holiday exists to honor all the men and women who have served the country in the military, whether in war or peacetime. Let your favorite veteran, or currently serving soldier, know how much you appreciate their service and sacrifice with a heartfelt card.

---

10 Welcome to the Neighborhood

Designer: Nicole Maki

Ink all patterned paper edges.

1 Make card from cardstock. **2** Cut patterned paper block; adhere patterned paper and zigzag-stitch seams. **3** Cut patterned paper strip; round right corners. Punch scalloped circle from cardstock and trim with circle cutter to create ring. Place ring over strip and adhere. **4** Mat block with patterned paper; trim with decorative-edge scissors and adhere. **5** Thread button with ribbon and adhere.

11 Freedom

Designer: Alli Miles

1 Make card from cardstock. Cover with patterned paper. **2** Cut patterned paper pieces, layer, and adhere together. **3** Adhere ribbon end behind layered paper; adhere to card. Tie button to ribbon with twine; adhere with foam tape. **4** Stamp Freedom on cardstock; trim and adhere. **5** Stamp Proud Eagle on cardstock; trim, color, and adhere with foam tape.

12 Simply Marvelous

Designer: Maren Benedict

1 Make card from cardstock. Adhere slightly smaller cardstock piece. **2** Adhere patterned paper piece. Adhere chipboard clouds and airplane. **3** Apply rub-on to cardstock; trim, mat with cardstock, and adhere with foam tape. **4** Tie on ribbon and attach colored brads. **5** Punch airplane image from patterned paper. Adhere to brad and cover with epoxy brad top. Adhere brad to ribbon.

13 Adore U
Designer: Sherry Wright

1 Make card from cardstock. Cover with patterned paper. **2** Trim bingo card; distress edges and adhere. **3** Stitch and distress edges of patterned paper piece; adhere. Distress edges of patterned paper piece; tie on ribbon and adhere. *Note: Trim ribbon with decorative-edge scissors.* **4** Stamp circle border and "U" on patterned paper; trim, distress edges, and adhere with foam tape. **5** Fussy-cut berries from patterned paper; adhere.

14 Flourish of Thanks
Designer: Charity Hassel

1 Make card from cardstock. **2** Adhere patterned paper and cardstock. Affix border and flourish stickers. **3** Stamp flourishes on cardstock; trim and adhere. Affix large medallion sticker. **4** Stamp flower four times on cardstock to make large flower; trim and adhere. **5** Affix small medallion sticker and adhere button. Apply rub-on.

15 Botanical Birthday Wishes
Designer: Alli Miles

1 Make card from acrylic sheet. **2** Adhere patterned paper inside card. **3** Stamp floral stems and dragonfly on cardstock; trim. Ink piece and adhere. Stamp sentiment on patterned paper; trim, round corners, and adhere. **4** Sand buttons, thread with twine, and adhere.

16 You are So Thoughtful

Designer: Mary MacAskill

1 Make card from cardstock. Cover with patterned paper. **2** Mat patterned paper with cardstock; trim with decorative-edge scissors. Zigzag-stitch seam and adhere. **3** Stamp sentiment; heat-emboss. **4** Cover chipboard frame with patterned paper; stitch edges. Dry-emboss cardstock; adhere behind frame. Adhere frame to card. **5** Adhere chipboard butterflies. Thread buttons with floss; adhere. Adhere ribbon bow.

17 Blue & Green Thinking of You

Designer: Alice Golden

1 Make card from cardstock. **2** Cut patterned paper slightly smaller than card front. Knot and adhere ribbon. Adhere piece to card. **3** Stamp sentiment on cardstock; trim. Stamp again on cardstock; trim and adhere to first image with foam tape. **4** Attach brads. Adhere piece with foam tape.

18 Elegant Best Friends

Designer: Maren Benedict

1 Make card from cardstock. **2** Adhere cardstock and patterned paper. Adhere ribbon over seam. **3** Adhere chipboard label with foam tape. Tie on ribbon. **4** Adhere rhinestones.

19	**Thinking of You**
	Designer: Ashley C. Newell

1 Make card from cardstock. Adhere slightly smaller cardstock piece. **2** Die-cut circles from patterned paper and cardstock; adhere. **3** Ink chipboard bird and branch; adhere. Cover bird wing with cardstock; stamp circles heart and adhere. **4** Apply rub-on. Adhere pearls.

20	**Red & Black**
	Designer: Maren Benedict

1 Make card from cardstock. **2** Stamp flower and flourishes on cardstock; trim. Mat with cardstock. **3** Tie on ribbon. Adhere piece to card with foam tape.

21	**Vintage Make a Wish**
	Designer: Melanie Douthit

Ink all paper edges.

1 Make card from cardstock. **2** Cut patterned paper; stitch edges. Double-mat with patterned paper and cardstock; adhere. **3** Adhere rickrack. Tie on ribbon. Thread button with twine and adhere. **4** Die-cut circles and scalloped circle from cardstock; layer and adhere together. **5** Apply rub-on and glitter glue to die cut piece. Adhere piece with foam tape.

22 | Thanks Leaves

Designer: Teri Anderson

5 STEPS

1 Make card from cardstock. Cover with patterned paper and round top corners.
2 Fussy-cut leaves from patterned paper; adhere. Adhere patterned paper strips. **3** Apply rub-on. Punch circles from patterned paper; adhere.

23 | Grateful Wreath

Designer: Ashley C. Newell

5 STEPS

1 Make card from cardstock. Cut cardstock, tear bottom edge, and adhere. **2** Cut cardstock, tear bottom edge, and adhere cardstock piece. **3** Stamp grateful on piece; tie on ribbon, and adhere with foam tape. **4** Stamp Rose Hip Wreath on cardstock; fussy-cut. Accent with glitter glue and adhere with foam tape.

24 | November

Designer: Betsy Veldman

5 STEPS

1 Make card from cardstock. **2** Cut patterned paper pieces; ink edges and adhere. **3** Stamp circle tag and sentiment on cardstock; trim and adhere with foam tape. Thread button with twine; adhere. Tie on ribbon. **4** Ink edges of calendar card; color. Attach bookplate with brads and adhere with foam tape.

Thanksgiving

The fourth Thursday in November is often the holiday celebrated with family gathered for a huge turkey feast and watching football. Share the true spirit of Thanksgiving and express your gratitude to your loved ones with a thoughtful card filled with appreciation.

---

25 | **So Thankful**

Designer: Kristen Swain

1 Make card, following pattern on p. 178. **2** Cut patterned paper slightly smaller than card front; adhere. **3** Cut swirl from transparency sheet, outline with marker, and adhere to patterned paper strip. Adhere to card. **4** Spell "So thankful" with stickers. **5** Cut cardstock square, stitch edges, and mat with felt. Adhere square to card and tie on ribbon. **6** Adhere felt leaves. Thread button with twine and adhere.

---

26 | **Grateful Silhouette** 🟡5 STEPS

Designer: Ashley C. Newell

1 Make card from cardstock. Stamp grateful. **2** Stamp leaf twice on cardstock; trim and mat with cardstock. **3** Adhere matted piece to cardstock. Tie on ribbon and adhere with foam tape.

---

27 | **Thank You So Much** 🟡5 STEPS

Designer: Charlene Austin

1 Make card from cardstock; round right corners. **2** Adhere patterned paper. Adhere trim. **3** Apply rub-on. **4** Cut flowers from patterned paper; mat with cardstock and adhere with foam tape.

Designer Tip

Pop the pattern from your favorite paper by cutting elements out and adhering with foam tape.

28 Princess for a Day	**29** Red Medallion Thanks	**30** Warm Wishes
Designer: Dawne Ivey	Designer: Melissa Phillips	Designer: Mary MacAskill

28 Princess for a Day

Designer: Dawne Ivey

1 Make card from cardstock. **2** Cut patterned paper, punch top corners, and adhere. **3** Adhere acrylic frame; apply rub-on. **4** Punch cardstock strip, adhere, and spell sentiment with stickers. **5** Cover chipboard crowns with glitter; layer and adhere. Adhere rhinestones.

29 Red Medallion Thanks

Designer: Melissa Phillips

1 Make card from cardstock, adhere patterned paper strip, and round bottom corners. **2** Trim ribbon and adhere. **3** Stamp and emboss medallion on cardstock. Punch with scalloped circle and adhere. **4** Stamp finial and thank you; adhere button.

30 Warm Wishes

Designer: Mary MacAskill

1 Make card from cardstock. Adhere patterned paper strip. **2** Cut cardstock piece. Stamp Old Letter Writing with watermark ink; apply chalk while wet. Adhere to card. **3** Affix sticker. Apply rub-on. **4** Adhere trim and tie on ribbon. Thread buttons with floss; adhere. **5** Stamp Old Letter Writing on cardstock with watermark ink; apply chalk while wet. Cut into circle. **6** Stamp tree on transparency sheet; cut to fit cardstock circle and adhere. Detail with paint and glitter glue. **7** Adhere with foam tape.

December

Joy Defined

Designer: Wendy Sue Anderson

1 Make card from cardstock; emboss card front. **2** Stitch edges of patterned paper; adhere. **3** Punch edge of patterned paper strip; adhere inside card. **4** Affix stickers. Adhere ribbon. Punch snowflakes from cardstock and adhere. **5** Tie ribbon bow and adhere. Thread button with yarn; adhere.

---

1 | Classic Congrats ⟨5 STEPS⟩

Designer: Rae Barthel

1 Make card from cardstock. **2** Adhere patterned paper and border. **3** Tie on ribbon; apply rub-on and adhere rhinestones.

Designer Tip

Use rhinestones for a fast and easy way to brighten up a plain ribbon.

---

2 | Celtic Friend ⟨5 STEPS⟩

Designer: Melanie Douthit

Ink all paper edges.

1 Make card from cardstock; round bottom corners. **2** Cut patterned paper; round bottom corners. Adhere patterned paper strip. Punch edge of cardstock strip; adhere. Mat piece with cardstock and adhere. **3** Tie on ribbon. Thread button with twine, tie bow, and adhere. **4** Stamp friend on cardstock; punch into oval. Double-mat with punched cardstock oval and scalloped oval; adhere with foam tape.

---

3 | Wings to the Heart ⟨5 STEPS⟩

Designer: Alli Miles

1 Make card from cardstock. **2** Cut patterned paper pieces; layer and adhere. Stamp sentiment. **3** Die-cut and emboss label from cardstock; adhere with foam tape. **4** Die-cut and emboss circle from cardstock; ink edges and adhere with foam tape. **5** Adhere wings and affix heart. Adhere ribbon.

4 Cold Outside	**5** Vintage Christmas	**6** Believe in Joy
Designer: Julie Masse	Designer: Beatriz Jennings	Designer: Carla Peicheff
1 Make card from cardstock. Apply snowflake rub-ons. **2** Cut cardstock square; round corners. Apply sentiment rub-on. Tie on trim and adhere. **3** Die-cut and emboss rectangle from patterned paper. Mat with rectangle die-cut from cardstock and adhere with foam tape. **4** Stamp deer on cardstock, color, and cut out. Adhere with foam tape and adhere rhinestone.	**1** Make card from cardstock. Cover with patterned paper and ink edges. **2** Ink edges of patterned paper piece; adhere and zigzag-stitch edge. **3** Adhere label and trim. **4** Tie ribbon bow; adhere. Thread button with string and adhere.	**1** Make card from cardstock; ink edges. **2** Trim die cut paper to fit card front; adhere. Adhere rhinestones. **3** Adhere ribbon loops to tag; adhere. Spell "Joy" with stickers. **4** Apply glitter to chipboard snowflake; adhere. Tie button with twine and adhere.

7 Gift at Christmas	**8** Merry Christmas Leaves	**9** Three Trees Christmas
Designer: Beatriz Jennings	Designer: Rebecca Oehlers	Designer: Maren Benedict
1 Make card from cardstock. **2** Cut patterned paper, ink edges, and adhere. Zigzag-stitch top edge. **3** Sand edges of sticker; affix. Adhere trim, stitch, and adhere buttons. **4** Tie ribbon around card front and through snowflake. Adhere snowflake and tie bow. Thread button with string and adhere.	**1** Make card from cardstock. Stamp leafy branch twice. **2** Adhere cardstock and patterned paper strips; stitch along seam. Adhere ribbon and tie on ribbon. **3** Stamp sentiment; emboss. **4** Stamp leafy branch on cardstock; trim leaves and adhere with foam tape. **5** Color pearls with marker; adhere.	**1** Make card from cardstock. **2** Cut patterned paper piece and strip. Lightly ink edges, adhere, and stitch edges. Stamp sentiment; emboss. **3** Die-cut and emboss oval from cardstock; stamp trees and ink edges. **4** Die-cut scalloped oval from cardstock; adhere stamped piece with foam tape. Adhere to card with foam tape. **5** Adhere rhinestones and tie on ribbon.

Hanukkah

For eight days, the Festival of Lights is celebrated in remembrance of the Maccabees and the rededication of the Temple in Jerusalem in the second century BC. There was only enough oil to light the Temple's flame for one day, but a miracle occurred, and the oil burned a full eight days. A joyful celebration marked by lighting candles each night, enjoying games and good meals with family and friends, Hanukkah falls anywhere from the end of November to nearly the end of December, because it is determined by the Hebrew calendar rather than the Gregorian.

---

10 Happy Hanukkah

Designer: Betsy Veldman

1 Make card from cardstock. **2** Cut patterned paper, ink edges, and adhere. Apply rub-on. **3** Cut cardstock piece; trim with decorative-edge scissors and ink edges. Stamp menorah and sentiment. Tie on ribbon and adhere with foam tape. **4** Adhere rhinestones and insert pins. **5** Stamp stars on cardstock; emboss. Trim and adhere with foam tape.

11 Menorah Card

Designer: Nichole Heady

1 Make card from cardstock. **2** Stamp medallion on cardstock. Draw border using paint pen. Adhere to base. **3** Stamp menorah on cardstock and outline with paint pen. Adhere to cardstock. **4** Stamp sentiment, round bottom corners, and adhere with foam tape.

12 Festival of Lights

Designer: Stefanie Hamilton

1 Make card from cardstock. **2** Open finished size project in software. Open digital elements. **3** Drag and drop patterned paper onto project. Drop in photo; add drop shadow. **4** Adjust color on wire to yellow and drop in wire twice. Drop in sentiment. **5** Print on cardstock; trim and adhere to card.

13	**'Tis the Season**	5 STEPS

Designer: Beatriz Jennings

1 Make card from cardstock. **2** Cover card with patterned paper. Cut wavy patterned paper strips; ink edges and adhere. Stitch edges. **3** Adhere chipboard star, keyhole, and rhinestone. **4** Apply rub-on. Adhere trim. Tie ribbon bow and adhere.

14	**Winter Wonderland**	5 STEPS

Designer: Maren Benedict

1 Make card from cardstock. **2** Cut patterned paper strips, adhere, and zigzag-stitch. Tie on ribbon. **3** Stamp trees on cardstock; color, trim, and mat with cardstock. Adhere with foam tape. **4** Thread buttons and adhere. **5** Trim sentiment card, attach brads, and adhere with foam tape.

15	**Christmas Reindeer**	5 STEPS

Designer: Ivanka Lentle

1 Make card from cardstock. **2** Cut patterned paper square, ink edges. Mat with patterned paper and adhere. **3** Emboss cardstock piece; double-mat with cardstock and patterned paper; adhere. **4** Affix reindeer and adhere flourish. **5** Apply rub-on to ribbon; tie on card. Adhere flower. Tie cord bow; adhere. Adhere button.

Designer Tip

To create a unique sentiment or accent, apply rub-ons to sheer ribbon.

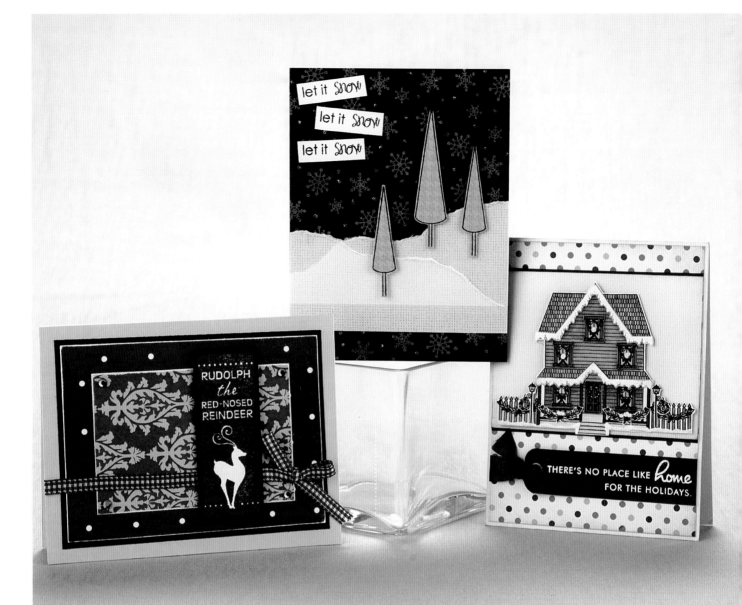

16 Rudolph the Reindeer

Designer: Laura Williams

5 STEPS

1 Make card from cardstock; cover with cardstock. **2** Cut patterned paper, sand edges, mat with cardstock, and adhere. **3** Cut patterned paper, sand edges, and adhere. Adhere rhinestones. **4** Tie ribbon and adhere. **5** Stamp Rudolph on cardstock; trim. Mat with cardstock and adhere with foam tape.

17 Houndstooth Trees

Designer: Kimberly Crawford

5 STEPS

1 Make card from cardstock. **2** Stamp snowflakes randomly on card front; accent with glitter glue. **3** Tear strips of vellum; adhere and accent with glitter glue. **4** Stamp Fine Houndstooth Scrapblock on cardstock with watermark ink. Stamp trees on piece; cut out and adhere with foam tape. **5** Stamp sentiment three times on cardstock; trim and adhere. Adhere rhinestones.

Designer Tip

Create your own patterned paper using stamps. It never runs out!

18 Home for the Holidays

Designer: Debbie Olson

5 STEPS

1 Make card from cardstock. **2** Ink edges of patterned paper panel. Cut cardstock; ink edges. Mat with cardstock and adhere. **3** Stamp sentiment on cardstock; emboss. Trim, round left corners, and attach eyelet. Tie on ribbon; adhere ribbon and sentiment. **4** Stamp house and fences on cardstock; color and trim. Stamp remaining images on cardstock; color and trim. *Note: Punch centers of lamppost wreaths.* Assemble scene and adhere to card with foam tape. **5** Accent with gel pens and liquid appliqué.

Winter Begins

It's time to pull out your wonderful sweater collection and bring the coats out of storage—winter is officially here! Though the date shifts between December 21st and December 22nd, the beginning of winter gives you a great reason to create fun cards for those you love.

---

19 Merry Wishes

Designer: Gretchen Clark

1 Make card from cardstock. **2** Cut cardstock panel. Adhere cardstock and patterned paper pieces. **3** Stamp sentiment, tie on ribbon, and adhere to card. **4** Stamp deer on cardstock; punch into circle. Mat with scalloped circle punched from cardstock. **5** Attach brad to piece and adhere with foam tape.

20 Snowflake Joy

Designer: Heidi Van Laar

1 Cut patterned paper; adhere inside. Adhere patterned paper strip inside. **2** Stamp Tiny Snowflake randomly on card front. **3** Cut cardstock piece; score diamond pattern. Sand, stitch, and mat with cardstock. Score mat edge. **4** Wrap piece with twine; adhere. **5** Adhere patterned paper behind large acrylic snowflake; trim. Layer snowflakes; adhere. **6** Punch patterned paper circle; adhere behind button. Tie twine bow, adhere, and adhere button with foam tape. **7** Adhere patterned paper behind acrylic letters; trim and adhere to spell "Joy".

21 Soft Snow

Designer: Maren Benedict

1 Make card from cardstock. **2** Adhere patterned paper and cardstock pieces; zigzag-stitch seams. **3** Cut patterned paper piece; adhere. Cut out sentiment from card and adhere with foam tape. **4** Layer and tie on ribbon and twine.

Festivus

Do you remember the Seinfeld episode where George's dad carries around the Festivus pole? He created Festivus as an alternative holiday in response to the commercialization of Christmas. Festivus is celebrated on December 23rd. The holiday includes practices such as the "Airing of Grievances" and performing "Feats of Strength."

---

22 'Tis the Season to be Jolly

Designer: Maren Benedict

1 Make card from cardstock. **2** Adhere patterned paper piece. **3** Apply rub-ons. Tie on ribbon.

Designer Tip

You can soften loud patterned paper with a touch of satin ribbon and some white space.

23 Happy Festivus

Designer: Laura O'Donnell

1 Make card from cardstock. **2** Stamp gnomes on cardstock; color and trim. **3** Write "Happy Festivus" on flag. Adhere gnomes to card.

24 Birthday Trees

Designer: Julie Masse

1 Make card from cardstock. **2** Stamp Stripes on card front; stamp sentiment. **3** Die-cut and emboss rectangle from cardstock. Mat with scalloped rectangle die-cut cardstock. **4** Stamp Itsy Bitsy Giggles on matted piece and on patterned papers. Trim patterned paper images and adhere. Adhere piece to card. **5** Tie on thread.

Christmas

Christmas is celebrated all over the world, religiously and secularly. Whether you honor the birth of the Christ child, or focus on the magic of Santa Claus, there are unlimited opportunities for card making and gift giving at the "most wonderful time of the year".

Kwanzaa

This seven-day celebration of values and principles runs from December 26th to January 1st. The principles of Kwanzaa are uplifting and beautiful: unity, self-determination, collective work and responsibility, cooperative economics, purpose, creativity, and faith.

25 Christmas Tickets

Designer: Mary Jo Johnston

1 Make card from cardstock. **2** Cut patterned paper slightly smaller than card front; ink edges and adhere. **3** Print tickets on cardstock, cut out, trim with decorative-edge scissors, and adhere. **4** Attach brad.

26 Happy Kwanzaa

Designer: Layle Koncar

1 Make card from patterned paper. **2** Print candles on cardstock; trim, mat with patterned paper, and adhere. **3** Spell sentiment with stickers. Draw outline with pen.

27 Simple Hi

Designer: Ashley C. Newell

1 Make card from cardstock. **2** Adhere ribbon. **3** Stamp hi on cardstock; emboss. Trim and mat with cardstock using foam tape. **4** Adhere piece with foam tape. Adhere rhinestones.

| 28 | Beep! Beep! | 29 | New Year Clock | 30 | Party Like it's 1999 |

28 Beep! Beep!

Designer: Maren Benedict

1 Make card from cardstock. **2** Cut patterned paper pieces; adhere. **3** Cut cardstock strip; adhere. Adhere narrow cardstock strip; punch cardstock circles and adhere. **4** Stamp car on cardstock and patterned paper; trim. Color windows, wheels, and bumper of cardstock image. Adhere patterned paper car over image with foam tape. Adhere to card. **5** Stamp sentiment and swirl on cardstock; punch into circle. Mat with punched cardstock circle and adhere with foam tape.

29 New Year Clock

Designer: Heidi Van Laar

1 Make card from cardstock; adhere slightly smaller cardstock piece. **2** Cut patterned paper rectangle; mat with patterned paper and adhere. **3** Cut cardstock strip, round corners, and adhere. Die-cut cardstock circle; adhere. **4** Adhere flourishes and spell sentiment with stickers. **5** Cut cardstock to fit behind clock face; attach pieces and clock hands with brad. Adhere with foam tape.

30 Party Like it's 1999

Designer: Charlene Austin

1 Make card from cardstock. Apply rub-ons. **2** Cover chipboard party with glitter; adhere. **3** Stamp "Like it's" on card; affix numbers. **4** Stamp "Happy new year" on cardstock; trim, ink edges, and adhere. **5** Affix rhinestones. Ink card edges.

New Year's Eve

December 31st, the last day of the year, is a great time to look back at all that the previous twelve months have brought you and yours. Make fun craft projects to help remember the good things, and let the bad things wash away with the singing of "Auld Lang Syne".

---

31 | **Bubbly New Year**

Designer: Maren Benedict

1 Make card from cardstock. **2** Cut cardstock strip, punch edge, and adhere. Stitch edge. **3** Stamp goblet with bubbles on tag. Stamp sentiment on cardstock; trim and adhere. Accent stamped bubbles with paint; let dry. **4** Adhere tag to card. Tie on ribbon; insert pin.

Must Have Tools

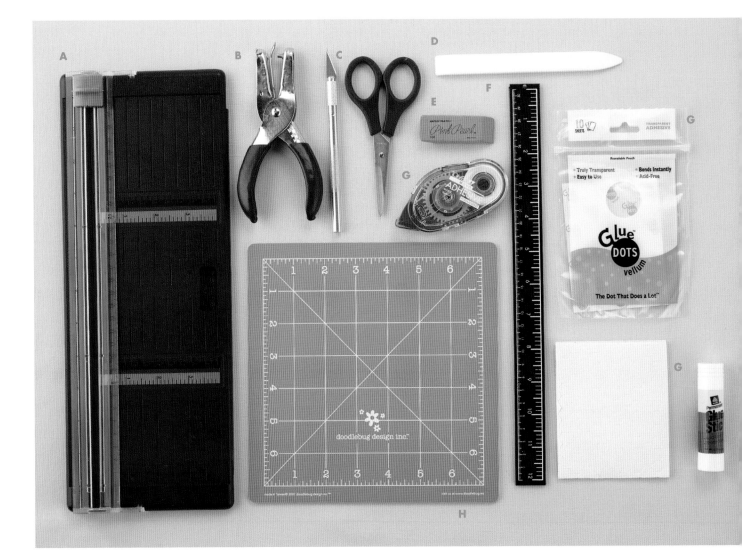

It only takes a few essential tools to get started making your very own beautiful cards.

A   Paper trimmer. Neatly and accurately cut what you need from large or small pieces of paper with a trimmer.

B   Hole punch. A basic circle punch creates perfect holes for setting eyelets or threading ribbon.

C   Sharp scissors and craft knife. In order to make exact and intricate cuts, super sharp scissors or a craft knife should do the trick.

D   Bone folder. This versatile tool can score lines, smooth folds, and even apply rub-ons.

E   Eraser. Easily clean up pencil marks with a simple eraser.

F   Ruler. Waste not with a ruler. You'll cut precisely and save paper when you measure carefully.

G   Adhesive. With a variety of adhesives at your fingertips (like glue stick, foam tape, adhesive dots, and an adhesive runner) you'll be prepared to adhere anything to any surface.

H   Non-stick self-healing cutting mat. Preserve your tabletop from nicks and messes with a cutting mat. It's not only a safe place to cut with a craft knife; it will also make cleaning up a snap!

Keep It Organized

Save time by gathering all of your crafting supplies in one easy to find spot. With everything organized, you'll be making card magic before you know it!

A Use vertical magazine holders to keep tons of ideas at your fingertips.

B Wrap ribbon around wooden clothespins and store in large clear containers to add a bit of color to the room.

C Store rubber stamps in one spot — they'll be easy to find and serve as a decorative element as well.

D Scour the hardware store for clever storage solutions.

E Display your creations on the wall and celebrate your creativity!

Color Wheel Creativity

Take the guesswork out of creating a unified color scheme with the color wheel. Since its creation, the color wheel has been studied by artists and scientists alike. The fascination with this artistic tool lies in the way it organizes colors around a circle, showing relationships between hues considered to be complementary, analogous, and triadic.

Primary Colors
The primary colors are red, yellow, and blue. These three colors cannot be mixed by any combination of any other pigments.

Secondary Colors
Orange, green, and purple are the secondary colors, and are created by mixing any two of the primary colors.

Tertiary Colors
Tertiary colors like yellow-orange, red-orange, yellow green, blue-green, blue-violet, red-violet are created by mixing a primary color and a secondary color.

Analogous Color
Any three colors which are next to each other on the color wheel, i.e. red-violet, red, red-orange.

Complementary Colors
Any two colors which appear directly accross from each other, i.e. blue and orange.

Split Complementary Colors
One color and the two colors next to the color directly across from it, i.e. orange, blue-violet, and blue-green.

Scrumptious Sketches

Jumpstart your creativity with these simple sketches.

Cards by Occasion

Supplies

January

Page 7
Let It Snow
Designer: Wendy Sue Anderson

SUPPLIES: *Cardstock:* (white) *Patterned paper:* (Stripes from Snowed In collection, FulFilled from French Flea Market collection) My Mind's Eye *Chalk ink:* (Chestnut Roan) Clearsnap *Accents:* (white snowflake circle, brown swirl die cuts) My Mind's Eye; (snowflake brad, woven snowflakes) Making Memories *Rub-ons:* (let it snow, winter) Crate Paper *Fibers:* (red ribbon) Offray **Finished size: 5½" x 4¼"**

Page 8
Thanks a Bunch
Designer: Melanie Douthit

SUPPLIES: All supplies from Stampin' Up! unless otherwise noted. *Cardstock:* (kraft, Very Vanilla) *Patterned paper:* (blue flower print, polka dots from Baja Breeze Designer Series collection) *Rubber stamp:* (thanks a bunch from A Little Somethin' set) *Dye ink:* (Chocolate Chip) *Accents:* (blue felt flower); (blue button) no source *Fibers:* (cream ribbon); (jute twine) no source *Adhesive:* (foam tape) *Die:* (scalloped circle) Provo Craft *Tools:* (die cut machine) Provo Craft; (doily border punch) Martha Stewart Crafts **Finished size: 5½" x 4¼"**

Together Forever
Designer: Melissa Phillips

SUPPLIES: *Cardstock:* (kraft, Vintage Cream) Papertrey Ink *Patterned paper:* (Courage) Melissa Frances *Clear stamps:* (large, tiny flowers from With Sympathy set, congratulations from Around & About Sentiments set) Papertrey Ink *Dye ink:* (Old Paper) Ranger Industries *Pigment ink:* (Vintage Cream) Papertrey Ink *Specialty ink:* (Aqua Mist hybrid) Papertrey Ink *Embossing powder:* (clear) Ranger Industries *Accents:* (green patterned tag, vintage pearl brad) Melissa Frances; (pink pearls) Kaisercraft; (white tag) Creative Imaginations; (green acrylic button) *Stickers:* (together forever tag, date prompt label, scalloped circle sentiment) Melissa Frances *Fibers:* (cream ribbon) Papertrey Ink; (hemp twine) *Adhesive:* (foam tape) *Tools:* (heart scalloped border punch) Martha Stewart Crafts **Finished size: 5¼" x 3¾"**

Backwards in Heels
Designer: Melissa Phillips

SUPPLIES: *Cardstock:* (hot pink) Bazzill Basics Paper *Patterned paper:* (Suzanne, Charlotte, Bianca) Melissa Frances *Dye ink:* (Old Paper) Ranger Industries *Paint:* (off-white) Delta *Accents:* (white, pink glitter flowers) Melissa Frances; (green rhinestones) Kaisercraft; (pink pearl button) *Rub-ons:* (crown, decorative swirl) Melissa Frances *Sticker:* (quote) Melissa Frances *Fibers:* (yellow crocheted trim) Prima; (blue ribbon, pink floss, hemp twine) *Tool:* (scalloped edge punch) Martha Stewart Crafts **Finished size: 4" x 5¾"**

Page 9
To You from Me
Designer: Dawn McVey

SUPPLIES: All supplies from Stampin' Up! unless otherwise noted. *Cardstock:* (Kiwi Kiss, Rose Red, Regal Rose, Whisper White) *Patterned paper:* (floral from Kiwi Kiss Designer Series collection, blue polka dot from Pacific Point collection) *Rubber stamp:* (sentiment from Best Yet set) *Pigment ink:* (Rose Red) *Accents:* (clear rhinestones) Mark Richards *Fibers:* (green striped ribbon) *Adhesive:* (foam tape) no source *Tools:* (slit punch; 1¾", 1³⁄₈" circle punches) **Finished size: 4¼" x 5½"**

Happy Bird Day!
Designer: Ashley Harris

SUPPLIES: *Cardstock:* (Bubble Blue, white) Bazzill Basics Paper *Patterned paper:* (Close the Loop from Office Lingo collection) Pink Paislee; (Tea Cups from Spring & Summer collection) American Crafts; (Baby's Breath, Tiny Tantrum from Baby Powder collection) Imaginisce *Rubber stamps:* (Schoolbook Serif alphabet) Stampin' Up! *Clear stamp:* (birds from Tags & Words set) Heidi Grace Designs *Solvent ink:* (Jet Black) Tsukineko *Chalk ink:* (Ice Blue) Clearsnap *Accent:* (chipboard house) Maya Road *Rub-on:* (happy day) Melissa Frances *Adhesive:* (foam tape) *Tool:* (scalloped edge punch) Fiskars **Finished size: 5" square**

Hello Birdie
Designer: Kalyn Kepner

SUPPLIES: *Cardstock:* (white) Bazzill Basics Paper *Patterned paper:* (Hey Foxy, Mushroom Fancy from Twitterpated collection) Imaginisce; (Good Morning from Everyday collection) American Crafts *Chalk ink:* (blue) *Stickers:* (rhinestone bird) Imaginisce; (Daiquiri alphabet) American Crafts *Fibers:* (orange polka dot ribbon) *Adhesive:* (foam tape) *Tools:* (decorative-edge scissors, corner rounder punch) **Finished size: 6" x 5¼"**

Page 10
Medical Thanks
Designer: Ashley C. Newell

SUPPLIES: *Cardstock:* (kraft, Ripe Avocado, Dark Chocolate) Papertrey Ink *Vellum:* (Linen) Papertrey Ink *Clear stamps:* (sentiment from Out on a Limb Sentiments set; circles, solid hearts from Heart Prints set) Papertrey Ink; (stethoscope from Doctor Doctor set) Madison Avenue Stamps *Dye ink:* (Chocolate Chip) Stampin' Up! *Watermark ink:* Tsukineko *Embossing powder:* (clear) *Accent:* (green pearl) Queen & Co. *Fibers:* (brown ribbon) Papertrey Ink *Adhesive:* (foam tape) **Finished size: 4¼" x 5½"**

Wood Grain Thanks
Designer: Ashley C. Newell

SUPPLIES: *Cardstock:* (kraft, white) Papertrey Ink; (blue) Stampin' Up! *Clear stamps:* (leaves from Beautiful Blooms set, thank you from Remember set)

Papertrey Ink *Dye ink:* (Kiwi Kiss) Stampin' Up!; (black) Close To My Heart *Fibers:* (white ribbon) Michaels *Template:* (Distressed Stripes embossing) Provo Craft *Tool:* (embossing machine) Provo Craft **Finished size: 4¼" x 5½"**

Thinking of You Friend
Designer: Wendy Sue Anderson

SUPPLIES: *Cardstock:* (lime green) Die Cuts With a View *Patterned paper:* (Quarter Shot, Raspberry Creme, Mintberry Crush from MochaChica collection) Cornish Heritage Farms *Clear stamp:* (Tree) Imaginisce *Solvent ink:* (Mellow Mint) Tsukineko *Accent:* (peach polka dot button) O'Scrap! *Rub-on:* (thinking of you) K&Company *Stickers:* (peach alphabet) EK Success *Fibers:* (tan gingham ribbon, jute twine) *Tool:* (decorative-edge scissors) Fiskars **Finished size: 4¼" square**

Page 11
Bambino
Designer: Melissa Phillips

SUPPLIES: *Cardstock:* (Cream Puff) Bazzill Basics Paper *Patterned paper:* (Xavier, Wyatt from Hush a Bye collection) Melissa Frances *Clear stamp:* (large motif from Baroque set) Melissa Frances *Dye ink:* (Walnut Stain) Ranger Industries *Pigment ink:* (Copper) Clearsnap *Paint:* (off-white) Delta *Accents:* (resin keyhole) Melissa Frances; (chipboard house) Maya Road; (clear rhinestones) Kaisercraft; (clear mica flakes) Martha Stewart Crafts; (cream button) *Rub-on:* (crown) Melissa Frances *Stickers:* (baby date label, bambino tag) Melissa Frances *Fibers:* (cream ribbon) Wrights; (hemp twine) Darice; (yellow rickrack) *Other:* (vintage sheet music) **Finished size: 4½" x 5¼"**

Forever Begins Now
Designer: Julia Stainton

SUPPLIES: *Cardstock:* (white) Prism *Rubber stamps:* (sentiment from Wedding Centers set, A Perfect Yellow Rose) Cornish Heritage Farms *Dye ink:* (Tuxedo Black) Tsukineko *Pigment ink:* (Smokey Gray) Tsukineko *Accents:* (white flower) Prima; (pearl-head stick pin) *Fibers:* (white ribbon) May Arts *Tool:* (scoring tool) Scor-Pal Products **Finished size: 4¼" square**

Husband & Wife
Designer: Melissa Phillips

SUPPLIES: *Cardstock:* (Fairy Tale Pink Medium) WorldWin *Patterned paper:* (floral, striped, blue and white swirls from Girly Girl collection) Melissa Frances *Dye ink:* (Old Paper) Ranger Industries *Paint:* (off-white) Delta *Accents:* (clear rhinestones, iridescent glitter) Doodlebug Design; (cream flower) *Rub-on:* (husband and wife) Melissa Frances *Stickers:* (cake sign) Melissa Frances *Fibers:* (blue ribbon) May Arts *Adhesive:* (foam tape) *Tools:* (doily border punch, butterfly punch) Martha Stewart Crafts **Finished size: 4½" x 5¼"**

Cow Jumped Over the Moon
Designer: Maren Benedict

SUPPLIES: *Cardstock:* (Spring Rain, white) Papertrey Ink *Patterned paper:* (Tweedle Dee from Storytime collection) Cosmo Cricket *Rubber stamps:* (cow, sentiment, moon & star from In the Nursery set) Lizzie Anne Designs *Dye ink:* (Tuxedo Black) Tsukineko *Color media:* (assorted markers, glitter pen) Copic Marker *Fibers:* (black striped ribbon) Offray; (black rickrack) May Arts *Adhesive:* (foam tape) **Finished size: 4¼" x 5½"**

Page 18
All Star Birthday
Designer: Betsy Veldman

SUPPLIES: *Cardstock:* (True Black, Aqua Mist, Summer Sunrise, Raspberry Fizz, Plum Pudding, white) Papertrey Ink *Patterned paper:* (flowers from Black & White Basics collection) Papertrey Ink *Clear stamps:* (Fresh Alphabet set; sentiment circle, star from Around & About Sentiments set) Papertrey Ink *Pigment ink:* (Fresh Snow) Papertrey Ink *Specialty ink:* (Raspberry Fizz, Summer Sunrise, True Black hybrid) Papertrey Ink *Accents:* (clear rhinestone) Kaisercraft; (star loop brad) Karen Foster Design *Fibers:* (black gingham ribbon) Papertrey Ink *Adhesive:* (foam tape) *Template:* (Decorative Circles embossing) Provo Craft *Die:* (star) Provo Craft *Tools:* (1", ¾" circle punches) EK Success; (decorative-edge scissors; die cut, embossing machines) Provo Craft **Finished size: 7" x 3½"**

February

Page 19
True Romance Awaits
Designer: Wendy Sue Anderson

SUPPLIES: All supplies from Making Memories unless otherwise noted. *Patterned paper:* (Sampler, Kraft Cherry Blossom, Kraft Heart Brocade, Red Glitter from Love Notes collection) *Accents:* (tag die cut, ticket, red glitter heart brads, metal sentiment charm) *Stickers:* (Love Notes alphabet) *Fibers:* (red striped ribbon) *Adhesive:* (foam tape) no source *Dies:* (heart, scalloped heart frame) *Tools:* (die cut machine) Making Memories; (dotted scallop border punch) Fiskars **Finished size: 5¼" x 4"**

Page 20
XOXO Buttons
Designer: Rebecca Oehlers

SUPPLIES: *Cardstock:* (Raspberry Fizz, Dark Chocolate, Pure Poppy, Berry Sorbet, white) Papertrey Ink *Clear stamps:* (hearts, XOXO from Heart Prints set) Papertrey Ink *Specialty ink:* (Raspberry Fizz, Pure Poppy, Berry Sorbet, Dark Chocolate hybrid) Papertrey Ink *Accents:* (small buttons) SEI; (large buttons) BasicGrey *Fibers:* (white string) *Adhesive:* (foam tape) *Tools:* (scoring tool) Scor-Pal Products; (1¼" circle, heart punches) EK Success; (rounded rectangle, corner rounder punches) Stampin' Up! **Finished size: 5½" square**

Groundhog Day
Designer: Teri Anderson

SUPPLIES: *Cardstock:* (white) *Patterned paper:* (woodgrain, animals, green plaid, brown stripe from The Green Stack pad) Die Cuts With a View *Fibers:* (jute twine) DC&C *Font:* (CK Tipsy) www.scrapnfonts.com **Finished size: 4¼" square**

Kiss Me
Designer: Julia Stainton

SUPPLIES: *Cardstock:* (kraft) *Rubber stamps:* (Distressed Grid Scrapblock; sentiment from The Birds and the Bees set) Cornish Heritage Farms *Specialty ink:* (Burnt Umber, black hybrid) Stewart Superior Corp. *Accents:* (silver, red heart brads) Making Memories **Finished size: 5¼" square**

Page 21
Heart Possibilities
Designer: Melissa Phillips

SUPPLIES: *Cardstock:* (kraft) Papertrey Ink *Patterned paper:* (Abigail, Bianca, Chelsey) Melissa Frances *Clear stamps:* (stars from Background Basics: Stars set, sentiment from Heart Prints Sentiments set, flourish from Recipe Box Label set) Papertrey Ink *Dye ink:* (Old Paper) Ranger Industries *Pigment ink:* (Copper) Clearsnap *Specialty ink:* (Dark Chocolate hybrid) Papertrey Ink *Paint:* (off-white) Delta *Accents:* (pink glitter chipboard heart) Melissa Frances; (pink rhinestones) Kaisercraft; (chipboard frame) Maya Road; (white glitter) Doodlebug Design; (pink, white buttons) *Stickers:* (date scalloped circle) Melissa Frances *Fibers:* (cream ribbon) Wrights; (brown/white twine) Martha Stewart Crafts **Finished size: 5¼" x 3¾"**

Thank You So Very Much Butterfly
Designer: Betsy Veldman

SUPPLIES: *Cardstock:* (white, Aqua Mist) Papertrey Ink *Patterned paper:* (Breeze from Blue Hill collection) Crate Paper; (Isn't She Lovely from Sweet Baby Girl collection) My Mind's Eye *Specialty paper:* (Gossip White Lace from Pop Culture collection) KI Memories *Clear stamps:* (circle, straight sentiments from Around & About Sentiments set; decorative circle from Simply Stationery set) Papertrey Ink *Specialty ink:* (Sweet Blush, Dark Chocolate hybrid) Papertrey Ink *Accent:* (butterfly appliqué) KI Memories *Fibers:* (aqua stitched ribbon) Papertrey Ink; (jute twine) The Beadery *Adhesive:* (foam tape) *Tools:* (scalloped circle punch) EK Success; (decorative-edge scissors) Provo Craft **Finished size: 5½" x 4¼"**

Love is All You Need
Designer: Anabelle O'Malley

SUPPLIES: *Cardstock:* (white) *Patterned paper:* (Cream Sweet Pea from French Sweet Pea collection) Creative Imaginations; (Glitter Dots Pink from Garden Party collection) Making Memories *Dye ink:* (Antique Linen) Ranger Industries *Specialty ink:* (Vintage Pink shimmer spray) Tattered Angels *Accents:* (chipboard swirl) Fancy Pants Designs; (chipboard heart frame) Doodlebug Design; (pink rhinestones) Darice; (glitter flower, tag die cuts) Making Memories *Stickers:* (lined heart, polka dot scalloped heart) Creative Imaginations *Font:* (Amazone BT) www.fontstock.net *Adhesive:* (foam tape) **Finished size: 4¼" x 5½"**

Page 22
Hello Flower
Designer: Kim Moreno

SUPPLIES: *Cardstock:* (brown) Core'dinations; (pink) Bazzill Basics Paper *Patterned paper:* (Old Fashioned, Affection, All Dolled Up, Beau from Rue collection) Dream Street Papers *Chalk ink:* (brown) Clearsnap *Color medium:* (brown marker) American Crafts *Accents:* (blue rhinestone brad) Creative

Imaginations; (pink felt, paper flowers) Making Memories *Stickers:* (Loopy Lou alphabet) Doodlebug Design *Tools:* (corner rounder, spiral binding punches) Stampin' Up! **Finished size: 3¾" x 6"**

Live the Life
Designer: Jessica Witty

SUPPLIES: *Cardstock:* (white, gray) *Clear stamps:* (damask from Baroque set) Melissa Frances; (sentiment from Out on a Limb Sentiments set) Papertrey Ink *Dye ink:* (Certainly Celery, Going Gray) Stampin' Up! *Accents:* (clear rhinestones) Kaisercraft *Adhesive:* (foam tape) *Die:* (label) Spellbinders *Tool:* (die cut/embossing machine) Spellbinders **Finished size: 4½" square**

Just For You
Designer: Melissa Phillips

SUPPLIES: *Cardstock:* (Vintage Cream, Lavender Moon) Papertrey Ink *Patterned paper:* (Tea Box Lacework from Lotus collection) K&Company *Clear stamps:* (reeds, tops from With Sympathy set; sentiment from Men of Life set) Papertrey Ink *Specialty ink:* (True Black, Spring Moss hybrid) Papertrey Ink *Accents:* (clear rhinestones) Doodlebug Design *Fibers:* (cream ribbon) Papertrey Ink *Adhesive:* (foam tape) *Template:* (Swiss Dots embossing) Provo Craft *Tools:* (corner rounder punch) Marvy Uchida; (circle cutter) Fiskars; (butterfly punch) Martha Stewart Crafts; (embossing machine) Provo Craft **Finished size: 3¾" x 5¼"**

Page 23
S.W.A.K.
Designer: Julie Masse

SUPPLIES: *Cardstock:* (kraft, Dark Chocolate, Aqua Mist, Summer Sunrise, Raspberry Fizz, White Shimmer) Papertrey Ink *Clear stamps:* (sentiment, envelope, hearts from Sealed With a Kiss set) Paper Pretties *Dye ink:* (Tuxedo Black) Tsukineko *Watermark ink:* Tsukineko *Embossing powder:* (white) Stampin' Up! *Color medium:* (red marker) Copic Marker *Accents:* (flower button) Stampin' Up!; (pink heart brad) *Adhesive:* (foam tape) *Die:* (heart) Spellbinders *Tools:* (die cut/embossing machine) Spellbinders **Finished size: 4¾" square**

Sweetie
Designer: Mary MacAskill

SUPPLIES: *Cardstock:* (white, kraft) *Patterned paper:* (lined from Ledger Collection pad, White Mini Dot from Kraft Paper collection) Making Memories *Rubber stamps:* (Sweetie, Three Stitched Hearts) Hero Arts *Clear stamp:* (flourish from Pollen Dust set) Fancy Pants Designs *Dye ink:* (Cranberry) Close To My Heart *Watermark ink:* Tsukineko *Embossing powder:* (Chocolate Bliss) Gel-a-tins; (clear) Stampendous! *Color medium:* (red chalk) Craf-T Products *Accents:* (iridescent glitter glue) Ranger Industries; (brown glitter button) Chatterbox; (brown button) The Paper Studio *Fibers:* (jute twine, tan floss) *Adhesive:* (foam tape) *Tools:* (dotted scalloped border punch) Fiskars **Finished size: 4¼" x 5½"**

Be Mine
Designer: Ashley C. Newell

SUPPLIES: *Cardstock:* (Dark Chocolate, Raspberry Fizz) Papertrey Ink; (Kiwi Kiss) Stampin' Up! *Vellum:* (Linen) Papertrey Ink *Clear stamps:* (hearts, sentiment from Heart Prints set) Papertrey Ink *Dye ink:* (Chocolate Chip) Stampin' Up! *Watermark ink:* Tsukineko *Embossing powder:* (clear) Stampendous! *Fibers:* (pink ribbon) Papertrey Ink *Adhesive:* (foam tape) *Tools:* (scalloped edge punch) Stampin' Up! **Finished size: 4¼" x 5½"**

Page 24
My Funny Valentine
Designer: Maren Benedict

SUPPLIES: *Cardstock:* (Sweet Blush) Papertrey Ink *Patterned paper:* (Togetherness, Journal Cards from Chemistry collection) Cosmo Cricket *Accents:* (clear rhinestone heart) Me & My Big Ideas *Fibers:* (pink ribbon) Papertrey Ink *Adhesive:* (foam tape) **Finished size: 4¼" x 5½"**

Be My Valentine
Designer: Sherry Wright

SUPPLIES: *Cardstock:* (light green) *Patterned paper:* (Full Moon Dots, Wood Fern, Lacework from Lotus Tea Box collection) K&Company *Chalk ink:* (Lipstick Red) Clearsnap *Accents:* (magenta flower) Prima; (clear rhinestones, magenta brad) Queen & Co. *Rub-ons:* (be my valentine) Melissa Frances; (glitter flower) K&Company **Finished size: 5¼" square**

Many Thanks
Designer: Anabelle O'Malley

SUPPLIES: *Cardstock:* (pink) *Patterned paper:* (Love Note from Hello Beautiful collection; Drizzle, Pokee Dot from Raspberry Truffle collection) Webster's Pages *Clear stamp:* (sentiment from 3 Step School Days set) Kitchen Sink Stamps *Color medium:* (brown marker) Marvy Uchida *Paint:* (Light Ivory) Delta *Accents:* (pink rhinestones) Darice *Stickers:* (chipboard circle, tag) BasicGrey; (hot pink epoxy circles) Kaisercraft *Fibers:* (ivory trim) Webster's Pages *Tool:* (decorative-edge scissors) **Finished size: 4" x 6½"**

Page 25
Swirly Hi
Designer: Daniela Dobson

SUPPLIES: *Cardstock:* (white) *Patterned paper:* (Kettle, Ladybug from Urban Prairie collection) BasicGrey *Rubber stamps:* (flower from Floral Accent set, branch from Branches set) Hero Arts *Clear stamp:* (tree from Love That set) Hero Arts *Solvent ink:* (Jet Black) Tsukineko *Chalk ink:* (red) Clearsnap *Color medium:* (red, green pencils) Prismacolor *Accents:* (clear buttons) Maya Road; (green brads) BasicGrey; (white swirl border) Bazzill Basics Paper *Stickers:* (Getty alphabet) American Crafts *Adhesive:* (foam tape) *Template:* (Swiss Dots embossing) Provo Craft *Tool:* (embossing machine) Provo Craft **Finished size: 4" x 6"**

Celebrate
Designer: Melanie Douthit

SUPPLIES: *Cardstock:* (white, red) *Patterned paper:* (Sneaky, I {Heart} You from MJ collection) Dream Street Papers *Paint:* (white, red) Plaid *Accents:*

(chipboard star, star frames) Everlasting Keepsakes; (white glitter) Doodlebug Design; (white button) *Rub-ons:* (celebrate) Imaginisce *Sticker:* (label) Luxe Designs *Fibers:* (red gingham ribbon, jute twine) *Tool:* (dotted scalloped border punch) Fiskars **Finished size: 5½" x 4"**

Pink Birthday
Designer: Daniela Dobson

SUPPLIES: *Cardstock:* (white) *Patterned paper:* (Big Dot from Paperie Rouge collection, pink ticket from Paperie Rouge collection notebook) Making Memories *Dye ink:* (Pine Cone) Bazzill Basics Paper *Accents:* (white flower border) Bazzill Basics Paper; (pink flower) Prima; (pink felt flower) Making Memories; (pink, clear heart rhinestones) *Rub-ons:* (happy birthday) American Crafts; (branch, flower) BasicGrey **Finished size: 4" x 5½"**

Page 26
Best Friends
Designer: Maren Benedict

SUPPLIES: *Cardstock:* (Dark Chocolate) Papertrey Ink *Patterned paper:* (Monday, Elements from Girl Friday collection) Cosmo Cricket *Rub-on:* (best friends) Cosmo Cricket *Fibers:* (brown trim) Cosmo Cricket *Adhesive:* (foam tape) **Finished size: 5½" x 4¼"**

Love Your Pet
Designer: Becky Olsen

SUPPLIES: *Patterned paper:* (Boardwalk, Carbonation from Snorkel collection) Cosmo Cricket; (Plie Dancing Daisies from Penny Lane collection) My Mind's Eye *Clear stamp:* (dog from Cutie Pet-Tootie set) Cornish Heritage Farms *Color medium:* (brown, red pencils) Prismacolor *Stickers:* (Rockabye alphabet) American Crafts *Fibers:* (green ribbon) Making Memories *Adhesive:* (foam tape) *Other:* (dog biscuit) **Finished size: 4" x 6"**

Grateful For You Friend
Designer: Melissa Phillips

SUPPLIES: *Cardstock:* (Vintage Cream, Dark Chocolate) Papertrey Ink *Clear stamps:* (flower, sentiments from Friends 'Til the End set) Papertrey Ink *Pigment ink:* (Vintage Cream) Papertrey Ink *Specialty ink:* (Dark Chocolate, Raspberry Fizz hybrid) Papertrey Ink *Embossing powder:* (clear) *Accents:* (pink rhinestone) Doodlebug Design; (pink glitter glue) Ranger Industries *Fibers:* (pink ribbon) Papertrey Ink *Tools:* (corner rounder) Marvy Uchida **Finished size: 5¼" x 3¾"**

Page 27
You're So Sweet
Designer: Mary MacAskill

SUPPLIES: *Cardstock:* (white, black, pink) Bazzill Basics Paper *Patterned paper:* (Gumdrops, Mintstix from Winterfresh collection) Heidi Swapp *Clear stamps:* (Rustic alphabet) Close To My Heart *Watermark ink:* Tsukineko *Embossing powder:* (Bubble Gum Yum!) Gel-a-tins *Accents:* (clear button) Autumn Leaves; (chipboard cherries) Heidi Swapp *Fibers:* (pink string) *Font:* (AL Uncle Charles) www.twopeasinabucket.com *Software:* (word processing) Microsoft *Tools:* (dotted scalloped border punch) Fiskars; (circle cutter) Creative Memories; (corner rounder punch) Marvy Uchida **Finished size: 4" x 9"**

Black & Pink I Do
Designer: Susan R. Opel

SUPPLIES: *Cardstock:* (black, hot pink) Die Cuts With a View *Patterned paper:* (Grey Damask from Love Letters collection) Little Yellow Bicycle *Accents:* (black chipboard glitter frame) American Crafts; (transparent damask) Little Yellow Bicycle; (pink flower) Heidi Swapp *Stickers:* (Black Tie alphabet) American Crafts *Adhesive:* (foam tape) *Tool:* (border punch) Martha Stewart Crafts **Finished size: 4" x 6"**

Be Yourself Flower
Designer: Charity Hassel

SUPPLIES: *Cardstock:* (kraft) *Patterned paper:* (Orange You Beautiful from Hello Beautiful collection) Webster's Pages *Stickers:* (felt leaves, flower) Chatterbox *Rub-on:* (be yourself) My Mind's Eye *Other:* (woodgrain contact paper) Home Depot **Finished size: 4¼" x 6"**

Page 28
Heartfelt Love
Designer: Melissa Phillips

SUPPLIES: *Cardstock:* (kraft, Vintage Cream) Papertrey Ink *Patterned paper:* (Pink Polka die cut from Sweet Pea collection) Creative Imaginations *Clear stamp:* (polka dot heart from Heart Prints set) Papertrey Ink *Dye ink:* (Walnut Stain) Ranger Industries *Specialty ink:* (Raspberry Fizz hybrid) Papertrey Ink *Accents:* (pink pearls) Kaisercraft; (pink button) BasicGrey *Fibers:* (pink ribbon) Papertrey Ink; (twine) *Adhesive:* (foam tape) *Template:* (Argyle embossing) Provo Craft *Tools:* (scalloped square punch) Marvy Uchida; (embossing machine) Provo Craft; (decorative-edge scissors) **Finished size: 3¾" x 3½"**

Always & Forever
Designer: Charlene Austin

SUPPLIES: *Cardstock:* (Dark Chocolate) Papertrey Ink; (Shimmery White) Stampin' Up! *Accents:* (rhinestone hearts) Glitz Design; (pink rhinestone) Darice *Rub-on:* (always and forever) All My Memories *Fibers:* (cream ribbon) May Arts *Adhesive:* (foam tape) **Finished size: 5½" square**

Little Prince
Designer: Heidi Van Laar

SUPPLIES: *Cardstock:* (black) *Patterned paper:* (black gingham) Making Memories *Accents:* (crown, little prince label die cuts) Teresa Collins Designs; (blue rhinestones) Me & My Big Ideas *Fibers:* (black gingham ribbon) Offray; (blue ribbon) Lion Ribbon *Dies:* (circle, scalloped circle) Spellbinders *Tools:* (die cut machine) Spellbinders; (decorative-edge scissors, decorative corner punch) Fiskars *Other:* (blue houndstooth card) Teresa Collins Designs **Finished size: 5½" x 4¼**

Sweetie Pi
Designer: Julie Campbell

SUPPLIES: *Cardstock:* (kraft, Suede Brown Dark) Prism *Patterned paper:* (Garden Chair from Daydream collection; Walk in the Park from Detours collection) October Afternoon; (Crimson Dots from Blue Boutique collection) Sassafras Lass *Clear stamp:* (dashed circle from Borders & Corners {Circle} set) Papertrey Ink *Solvent ink:* (Timber Brown) Tsukineko *Accent:* (chipboard pi sign) BasicGrey *Stickers:* (Poolside alphabet) American Crafts; (red felt heart, blue beaded felt strip) Chatterbox *Adhesive:* (foam tape) *Die:* (circle) Spellbinders *Tools:* (dotted scalloped border punch) Fiskars; (die cut/embossing machine) Spellbinders **Finished size: 7" x 4"**

Lucky
Designer: Alli Miles

SUPPLIES: *Cardstock:* (white) Papertrey Ink; (light green, green, dark green) Core'dinations *Patterned paper:* (green polka dot) *Rubber stamps:* (clover, lucky from Sweet Spring set) Cornish Heritage Farms *Pigment ink:* (Pitch Black) Ranger Industries *Accent:* (resin crown) Melissa Frances *Adhesive:* (foam tape) *Dies:* (labels) Spellbinders *Tools:* (die cut/embossing machine) Spellbinders; (corner rounder punch) EK Success **Finished size: 6" x 3"**

Page 36
Lucky Friend
Designer: Betsy Veldman

SUPPLIES: *Cardstock:* (white) Papertrey Ink; (green) Bazzill Basics Paper *Patterned paper:* (Night Owl from Vintage Moon collection) Pink Paislee; (Nothing to Lose from Hugs-n-Kisses collection) Dream Street Papers; (green polka dot) *Clear stamp:* (polka dot heart from Heart Prints set) Papertrey Ink *Dye ink:* (Certainly Celery) Stampin' Up! *Accent:* (orange glitter brad) Doodlebug Design *Adhesive:* (foam tape) *Font:* (Arial) Microsoft *Die:* (lucky) Provo Craft *Tools:* (die cut machine) Provo Craft; (flower punch) EK Success **Finished size: 4¼" x 5½"**

Kiss Shamrock
Designer: Shanna Vineyard

SUPPLIES: *Cardstock:* (kraft, white) *Accents:* (green glitter) Martha Stewart Crafts; (white button) Creative Café *Stickers:* (Daiquiri alphabet) American Crafts *Fibers:* (green polka dot ribbon) Making Memories; (white floss) *Other:* (cardboard) **Finished size: 5½" square**

Happy Everything
Designer: Melissa Phillips

SUPPLIES: *Cardstock:* (Raspberry Fizz, Spring Moss, white) Papertrey Ink *Patterned paper:* (Adirondack from Poppy collection) SEI; (glitter floral from Bumblebee Paper Potpourri pad) Doodlebug Design *Clear stamps:* (sentiment, hearts, circle from Around & About Sentiments set; polka dots from Polka Dot Basics set) Papertrey Ink *Pigment ink:* (Fresh Snow) Papertrey Ink *Specialty ink:* (Raspberry Fizz, True Black hybrid) Papertrey Ink *Accents:* (green chipboard flower button) Making Memories; (green button) *Fibers:* (black polka dot ribbon) Papertrey Ink; (white string) *Adhesive:* (foam tape) *Tools:* (corner rounder punch) Marvy Uchida; (circle cutter) Fiskars; (1³⁄₈" circle punch) *Other:* (dimensional glaze) Ranger Industries **Finished size: 4½" square**

Page 37
Spring
Designer: Courtney Kelley

SUPPLIES: *Cardstock:* (brown) *Patterned paper:* (Walk in the Park, Garden Path, Dirt Roads from Detours collection; Freshly Mown Lawn from Daydream collection) October Afternoon *Accents:* (chipboard butterfly) Heidi Swapp; (chipboard flowers) Fancy Pants Designs; (assorted brads) Queen & Co. *Stickers:* (Poolside alphabet) American Crafts *Fibers:* (pink floss) DMC *Tool:* (decorative-edge scissors) Fiskars **Finished size: 5½" x 4¼"**

Spring Time
Designer: Danni Reid

SUPPLIES: *Cardstock:* (white) *Accents:* (orange printed, green polka dot flowers; orange flower stick pins) Making Memories; (green button) *Stickers:* (orange alphabet) Rose Moka; (Chloe's Closet Cork alphabet) Making Memories *Rub-on:* (clock) Imaginisce *Fibers:* (green polka dot ribbon) Making Memories *Adhesive:* (foam tape) *Template:* (Swiss Dots embossing) Provo Craft *Tools:* (embossing machine) Provo Craft; (doily border punch) Fiskars; (corner rounder punch) **Finished size: 4" x 6"**

Beloved
Designer: Beatriz Jennings

SUPPLIES: *Cardstock:* (teal) Bazzill Basics Paper *Patterned paper:* (Checkered Tablecloth from Picnic/Family Reunion collection) Karen Foster Design; (Peacefulness from Inspired collection) Webster's Pages *Vellum:* (polka dot) Hot Off The Press *Dye ink:* (Old Paper) Ranger Industries *Accents:* (journaling card) Webster's Pages; (clear glitter) Martha Stewart Crafts; (chipboard heart negative) Heidi Swapp; (white pearls) *Fibers:* (white ribbon) *Die:* (flower) Provo Craft *Tools:* (die cut machine, decorative-edge scissors) Provo Craft **Finished size: 4¾" x 5½"**

Page 38
Smiles & Giggles
Designer: Danni Reid

SUPPLIES: *Cardstock:* (white) *Patterned paper:* (Sprinkled, Sugary Love from Sunshine Lollipop collection) Sassafras Lass *Accents:* (chipboard bee, flower frame) BasicGrey; (white button) Creative Café; (white flower; pink, blue rhinestones) *Rub-on:* (smiles & giggles) Melissa Frances *Fibers:* (hemp twine) Darice; (pink ribbon) *Template:* (Swiss Dots embossing) Provo Craft *Tools:* (embossing machine) Provo Craft; (corner rounder punch) **Finished size: 5" square**

Many Thanks
Designer: Danni Reid

SUPPLIES: *Cardstock:* (white) *Patterned paper:* (Crunching Leaves from Weathervane collection) October Afternoon; (Unexpected from Offbeat collection) BasicGrey *Accent:* (white pearl) Martha Stewart Crafts *Rub-ons:* (many thanks) Deja Views; (heart) Pink Paislee *Sticker:* (heart badge) American Crafts *Fibers:* (green striped ribbon) American Crafts; (hemp twine) Darice *Adhesive:* (foam tape) *Template:* (Swiss Dots embossing) Provo Craft *Tools:* (embossing machine) Provo Craft; (eyelet border punch) Martha Stewart Crafts *Other:* (black wire) **Finished size: 4" x 6"**

Get Well Soon
Designer: Sherry Wright

SUPPLIES: *Cardstock:* (green) Prism; (white) *Patterned paper:* (Sitting Room from Victoria collection) Jenni Bowlin Studio *Rubber stamps:* (Get Well Soon!, Simple Berry Branch, Scroll Wording Frame) DRS Designs *Chalk ink:* (Chestnut Roan) Clearsnap *Specialty ink:* (Twilight shimmer spray) Tattered Angels *Accents:* (green rhinestones) Queen & Co.; (butterfly) *Fibers:* (green ribbon) Offray *Adhesive:* (foam tape) **Finished size: 5½" x 4¾"**

Page 39
Tulip Hi
Designer: Teri Anderson

SUPPLIES: *Cardstock:* (white) Bazzill Basics Paper *Patterned paper:* (Cucumber Sandwiches from Spring & Summer collection) American Crafts *Accents:* (pink, yellow tulip stick pins) Fancy Pants Designs *Stickers:* (Sotheby's alphabet) American Crafts *Fibers:* (pink ribbon) Offray *Tools:* (corner rounder punch) Marvy Uchida; (1¾" circle punch) Fiskars **Finished size: 3½" x 6"**

Celebrate Life
Designer: Melissa Phillips

SUPPLIES: *Cardstock:* (Cream Puff) Bazzill Basics Paper *Patterned paper:* (I Walk For, Joanne) Melissa Frances *Dye ink:* (Old Paper) Ranger Industries *Accents:* (celebrate life die cut, white chipboard glitter heart) Melissa Frances; (yellow flower, white button, pink rhinestones, white pearls) Melissa Frances *Sticker:* (crown) Melissa Frances *Fibers:* (beige ribbon) Wrights; (pink floss) *Tools:* (embossing border punch) Fiskars; (corner rounder punch) **Finished size: 4¾" x 3¾"**

Pink Floral Sympathy
Designer: Jennifer Hansen

SUPPLIES: *Cardstock:* (white) *Patterned paper:* (Cherie from Chocolat collection) SEI *Accents:* (pink corduroy brads) Imaginisce *Rub-ons:* (Simply Sweet alphabet) Doodlebug Design *Stickers:* (floral journaling, pink/brown strip) SEI **Finished size: 5½" x 4"**

Page 40
Thoughts & Prayers
Designer: Sherry Wright

SUPPLIES: *Cardstock:* (gray) *Patterned paper:* (blue/green scrolls, monochromatic green, floral lace from Lotus Faded China pad) K&Company *Rub-on:* (sentiment) Melissa Frances *Fibers:* (off-white ribbon) Offray *Adhesive:* (foam tape) **Finished size: 5" square**

Quote of the Day
Designer: Shanna Vineyard

SUPPLIES: *Cardstock:* (white) *Patterned paper:* (Sophisticated from Splendid collection) Fancy Pants Designs *Pigment ink:* (Midnight Black) Tsukineko *Rub-on:* (journaling block) Kaisercraft *Stickers:* (Fashion Script alphabet) Pink Paislee *Fibers:* (black polka dot ribbon) *Adhesive:* (foam tape) *Tool:* (decorative-edge scissors) **Finished size: 7" x 5"**

Happily Ever After
Designer: Wendy Sue Anderson

SUPPLIES: *Patterned paper:* (Glitter Dot from Wedding collection; teal glimmer dot, silver brocade from Shimmer collection) Making Memories *Accent:* (white heart stick pin) Making Memories *Rub-on:* (happily ever after) American Crafts *Fibers:* (white scalloped trim, teal polka dot ribbon) American Crafts; (silver ribbon) **Finished size: 5¼" x 5½**

Page 41
Husband Birthday
Designer: Betsy Veldman

SUPPLIES: *Cardstock:* (brown) Bazzill Basics Paper; (cream, blue) *Patterned paper:* (Oxford Stripe from Lotus Faded China collection) K&Company; (Marjoram from Dill Blossom collection) SEI *Clear stamps:* (husband from Men of Life set, happy birthday from Birthday Basics set, decorative bracket from Simply Stationery set) Papertrey Ink *Chalk ink:* (Charcoal) Clearsnap *Accent:* (chipboard sentiment circle) Scenic Route *Fibers:* (green ribbon) Papertrey Ink *Adhesive:* (foam tape) *Tool:* (1¾" circle punch) **Finished size: 4¼" x 5½"**

April
Page 42
Happy Easter
Designer: Wendy Sue Anderson

SUPPLIES: *Cardstock:* (white) *Patterned paper:* (Easter Eggs, Easter Stripe, Artisan die cut from Flower Patch collection) Making Memories; (Hot Chicks from For Peeps Sake collection) Imaginsce *Accent:* (yellow chipboard flower with green button) Making Memories *Stickers:* (Tiny Alpha alphabet) Making Memories *Fibers:* (green felt trim) Making Memories; (yellow daisy ribbon) **Finished size: 6" x 5"**

Page 43
Prank Me
Designer: Teri Anderson

SUPPLIES: *Cardstock:* (white) WorldWin *Patterned paper:* (Ethel Dartsmith, Lucy Hootski, Pearl Bobbinhauser from Craft Fair collection) American Crafts *Stickers:* (Rockabye alphabet) American Crafts *Fibers:* (green stitched ribbon) Die Cuts With a View *Font:* (Century Gothic) Microsoft *Tool:* (1¾" circle punch) Fiskars **Finished size: 4¼" x 5½"**

Right Now
Designer: Jessica Witty

SUPPLIES: *Patterned paper:* (Petticoat from Urban Prairie collection) BasicGrey *Specialty paper:* (Faded China Acanthus die cut from Lotus collection) K&Company *Dye ink:* (Black Soot) Ranger Industries *Accents:* (clear rhinestones) Kaisercraft; (black butterfly die cut) K&Company *Stickers:* (celebrate, right now) Creative Café *Tool:* (corner rounder punch) **Finished size: 5½" x 4¼"**

Snail Hello
Designer: Mary MacAskill

SUPPLIES: *Cardstock:* (cream, yellow) *Patterned paper:* (green ledger, yellow polka dots from Sweet Baby kit) American Crafts *Sticker:* (snail epoxy) Creating Keepsakes *Rub-on:* (hello!) American Crafts *Tools:* (assorted circle, corner rounder punches) **Finished size: 5½" x 4¼"**

Page 44
Elegant Anniversary
Designer: Teri Anderson

SUPPLIES: *Cardstock:* (white) WorldWin *Patterned paper:* (Discretion from Prudence collection) Crate Paper *Accents:* (white pearl brad) Oriental Trading Co.; (flourish, frame die cuts) Crate Paper *Rub-on:* (happy anniversary) Deja Views *Fibers:* (cream ribbon) May Arts **Finished size: 4¼" square**

Matthew 17:20
Designer: Julie Masse

SUPPLIES: *Cardstock:* (brown) *Patterned paper:* (Rain Showers, Skipping Stones, Flower Beds from Spring Fling collection) Pink Paislee *Specialty paper:* (photo) *Rubber stamp:* (Move Mountains) Unity Stamp Co. *Dye ink:* (Rich Cocoa, Bamboo Leaves) Tsukineko *Color medium:* (brown colored pencil) Prismacolor *Accents:* (brass brads) Stampin' Up!; (brass flower buckle) We R Memory Keepers *Digital element:* (blue bracket frame from Bright Colorful Brackets kit) www.shabbymissjenndesigns.com *Fibers:* (cream trim) Melissa Frances *Software:* (photo editing) *Tool:* (decorative-edge scissors) **Finished size: 5½" square**

Spread Your Wings
Designer: Jessica Witty

SUPPLIES: *Cardstock:* (white) *Rubber stamps:* (Stipple Butterfly; medium butterfly from Botanicals set) Stampin' Up! *Clear stamps:* (sentiment from Birds of a Feather set) Papertrey Ink; (small butterfly from Backyard Dwellers set) Hanna Stamps *Dye ink:* (Soft Sky) Stampin' Up! *Chalk ink:* (Dark Brown) Clearsnap *Accent:* (butterfly die cut) B. Shackman *Die:* (label) Spellbinders *Tool:* (die cut machine) Spellbinders **Finished size: 3¾" square**

Page 45
Take a Load Off
Designer: Ashley Harris

SUPPLIES: *Cardstock:* (white) Bazzill Basics Paper; (Lip Gloss) American Crafts *Patterned paper:* (Birds of a Feather from Happy Bird-Day collection) Three Bugs in a Rug; (Gladys Pauline from Forever Family collection) Dream Street Papers *Accents:* (pink rhinestones) Kaisercraft *Font:* (American Typewriter) www.myfonts.com *Tool:* (1" circle punch) **Finished size: 4¼" x 6"**

Welcome Baby
Designer: Betsy Veldman

SUPPLIES: *Cardstock:* (kraft, Spring Moss) Papertrey Ink *Patterned paper:* (Word from Everyday collection) American Crafts; (Words from Christmas collection) Heidi Grace Designs *Paint:* (white) Plaid *Accents:* (blue starburst die cut) Scenic Route; (yellow, green, pink buttons) Autumn Leaves, BasicGrey *Adhesive:* (foam tape) *Template:* (embossed scalloped border) Provo Craft *Dies:* (owl, branch, welcome baby) Provo Craft *Tool:* (die cut/embossing machine) Provo Craft **Finished size: 4¼" x 5½"**

Hey, Chickie
Designer: Julie Campbell

SUPPLIES: *Cardstock:* (Vintage Cream) Papertrey Ink *Patterned paper:* (Myrrh from Dill Blossom collection) SEI *Rubber stamps:* (sentiment, chick with egg from Hey Chickie set) Cornish Heritage Farms *Dye ink:* (Walnut Stain) Ranger Industries *Pigment ink:* (Onyx Black) Tsukineko *Color media:* (assorted markers, colored pencils) Prismacolor *Accent:* (blue button) BasicGrey *Fibers:* (white ribbon) Stampin' Up! *Adhesive:* (foam tape) *Other:* (dimensional glaze) Ranger Industries **Finished size: 5½" x 4¼"**

Page 46
Worthy is the Lamb
Designer: Lea Lawson

SUPPLIES: *Cardstock:* (blue, white) *Patterned paper:* (Iced Cappy, Cocomocha from MochaChica collection) Cornish Heritage Farms; (brown with blue swirls) *Chalk ink:* (Dark Brown) Clearsnap *Accents:* (clear, blue rhinestones) Doodlebug Design *Sticker:* (clear rhinestone cross) Me & My Big Ideas *Font:* (AmazeD) www.bayfonts.com *Die:* (bracket) Provo Craft *Tools:* (die cut machine) Provo Craft; (decorative-edge scissors) *Other:* (cream felt) **Finished size: 5½" square**

Hoppy Easter
Designer: Sherry Wright

SUPPLIES: *Cardstock:* (red, cream) *Patterned paper:* (Say Timber from Woodland Whimsy collection) Sassafras Lass *Rubber stamps:* (hoppy Easter, scalloped border from Easter set) Paper Salon *Chalk ink:* (Lipstick Red, Lime Pastel) Clearsnap *Fibers:* (tan trim, green raffia) *Adhesive:* (foam tape) **Finished size: 5" x 6"**

Easter Eggs
Designer: Maren Benedict

SUPPLIES: *Cardstock:* (kraft) Papertrey Ink *Patterned paper:* (Isabel, Clementine, Avery, Ella from Honey Pie collection) Cosmo Cricket *Rubber stamp:* (Hoppy Easter) Lizzie Anne Designs *Dye ink:* (Antique Linen) Ranger Industries; (Tuxedo Black) Tsukineko *Color medium:* (pink, green markers) Copic Marker *Accents:* (chipboard eggs) Cosmo Cricket; (white flock) Stampendous! *Fibers:* (pink stitched ribbon) Papertrey Ink **Finished size: 8" x 4¼"**

Page 47

Scrabble Congrats
Designer: Kim Kesti

SUPPLIES: *Cardstock:* (green, black) Bazzill Basics Paper *Patterned paper:* (Good Fortune, Origami from Fortune Cookie kit) Studio Calico *Accents:* (white staples) *Font:* (Impact) Microsoft *Other:* (Scrabble tiles, score sheet) **Finished size: 7" x 4½"**

Grow a Friend
Designer: Dawn McVey

SUPPLIES: *Cardstock:* (Pure Poppy, Spring Moss, Ripe Avocado) Papertrey Ink *Patterned paper:* (Atypical, Casual from Offbeat collection) BasicGrey *Clear stamps:* (snail, sentiment from Forest Friends set) Papertrey Ink *Specialty ink:* (Ripe Avocado, Dark Chocolate hybrid) Papertrey Ink *Sticker:* (brown rickrack) BasicGrey *Fibers:* (red stitched ribbon) Papertrey Ink *Adhesive:* (foam tape) **Finished size: 4¼" x 5½"**

R-r-r-rev My Motor
Designer: Beth Opel

SUPPLIES: *Cardstock:* (green) Bazzill Basics Paper *Patterned paper:* (Night Life from All Dressed Up collection) Die Cuts With a View *Transparency sheet:* 3M *Digital element:* (motorcycle) www.googleimages.com *Rub-ons:* (Lauren alphabet) American Crafts *Stickers:* (Polar Alpha alphabet) Arctic Frog *Software:* (photo editing) *Other:* (cream card) American Crafts **Finished size: 5½" x 4"**

Page 48

Enjoy Life
Designer: Carla Peicheff

SUPPLIES: *Cardstock:* (white) *Patterned paper:* (Rain Boots, Paper Lanterns, Garden Chair from Daydream collection) October Afternoon *Accents:* (blue journaling tag) October Afternoon; (white, pink pearls; pink rhinestone, flowers) Kaisercraft; (white chipboard life) Top Line Creations; (white flower) Prima *Stickers:* (Tiny Alpha alphabet) Making Memories *Fibers:* (pink ribbon) Stampin' Up! *Tools:* (butterfly punch) Martha Stewart Crafts; (scalloped border punch) Stampin' Up! **Finished size: 5½" x 4¼"**

Blah. Blah. Blah.
Designer: Teri Anderson

SUPPLIES: *Cardstock:* (white, light blue, blue) WorldWin *Accent:* (pewter brad) Bazzil Basics Paper *Font:* (CK Typewriter) www.scrapnfonts.com *Software:* (word processing) *Tool:* (corner rounder punch) Marvy Uchida **Finished size: 4¼" x 5½"**

High Five
Designer: Wendy Sue Anderson

SUPPLIES: *Cardstock:* (white, tan) *Patterned paper:* (Long Time No See, What's Shakin'? from Everyday collection) American Crafts; (Jack Stripe from Animal Crackers collection) Making Memories *Accents:* (tan chipboard hand) American Crafts; (pink clip, safety pin; silver 5) Making Memories *Stickers:* (Smokey Joe's alphabet) American Crafts *Fibers:* (aqua stitched ribbon) American Crafts *Tool:* (2¼" circle punch) **Finished size: 7" x 4¼"**

Page 49

Dreamer Butterfly
Designer: Roree Rumph

SUPPLIES: *Cardstock:* (orange) *Patterned paper:* (Larkspur, Meadow, Papillon from Beau Jardin collection) Tinkering Ink *Accents:* (black buttons) Autumn Leaves *Rub-on:* (dare to dream) Deja Views *Fibers:* (green, black floss) DMC *Dies:* (flower, circle) Provo Craft *Tool:* (die cut machine) Provo Craft **Finished size: 5½" diameter**

Style
Designer: Dawne Ivey

SUPPLIES: *Cardstock:* (black, white) Bazzill Basics Paper *Accents:* (blue, red rhinestones) Offray; (butterfly die cuts) K&Company *Rub-on:* (flourished style) BasicGrey *Templates:* (Swiss Dots, Allegro embossing) Provo Craft *Tools:* (die cut/embossing machine) Provo Craft; (scalloped square punch) The Paper Studio **Finished size: 4" square**

Lavender Sympathies
Designer: Rae Barthel

SUPPLIES: *Cardstock:* (Lavender) Die Cuts With a View *Patterned paper:* (Purple Majesty from Reflections of Nature collection) Webster's Pages *Accents:* (yellow die cut tag) K&Company; (white pearls) Kaisercraft; (purple, green silk flowers) Michaels; (clear button) *Rub-on:* (our deepest sympathies) Melissa Frances *Fibers:* (green ribbon) Offray **Finished size: 6" x 4"**

Page 50

Happy Earth Day
Designer: Nicole Maki

SUPPLIES: *Cardstock:* (Lakeshore, white) Bazzill Basics Paper *Patterned paper:* (distressed orange, distressed green, ledger from Wild Saffron pad) K&Company *Rubber stamps:* (Earth Topiary, Cathrine's Bow, Happy Earth Day) Just Johanna Rubber Stamps *Dye ink:* (black, brown) *Color medium:* (assorted colored pencils) Prismacolor *Adhesive:* (foam tape) *Tool:* (water brush) **Finished size: 4¼" x 5½"**

Mushroom Hi
Designer: Sherry Wright

SUPPLIES: *Cardstock:* (tan, red) Prism *Patterned paper:* (Over the Rainbow from Happy Place collection) Sassafras Lass *Clear stamps:* (frogs, mushroom from Ribbit set) Pink Persimmon *Chalk ink:* (black) Clearsnap *Color media:* (white gel pen) Ranger Industries; (green, pink markers) Copic Marker *Accents:* (chipboard ring) Technique Tuesday; (chipboard mushroom) Sassafras Lass *Stickers:* (Fashion Script alphabet) Pink Paislee **Finished size: 5½" square**

Happy Arbor Day
Designer: Susan R. Opel

SUPPLIES: *Cardstock:* (blue, green, brown) Die Cuts With a View *Patterned paper:* (Pop from Backyard collection) American Crafts *Accents:* (light green, dark green brads) Making Memories; (green pearl brads) *Stickers:* (Chalkboard alphabet) Jenni Bowlin Studio; (Cookie Cutter alphabet) KI Memories *Adhesive:* (foam tape) *Die:* (tree) QuicKutz *Tool:* (die cut machine) QuicKutz **Finished size: 6" x 5"**

Page 51

Toadstool Thanks
Designer: Dawn McVey

SUPPLIES: *Cardstock:* (kraft, white, Dark Chocolate) Papertrey Ink *Patterned paper:* (pink/white floral from Raspberry Fizz Mix collection) Papertrey Ink *Clear stamps:* (snail, mushrooms, thanks from Forest Friends set) Papertrey Ink *Dye ink:* (Tempting Turquoise) Stampin' Up! *Specialty ink:* (Raspberry Fizz, Dark Chocolate, Ripe Avocado hybrid) Papertrey Ink *Accents:* (brown flower) Bazzill Basics Paper; (small, medium brown pearls) Kaisercraft *Fibers:* (pink ribbon) Papertrey Ink *Adhesive:* (foam tape) *Tool:* (scalloped border punch) Stampin' Up! **Finished size: 5½" x 4¼"**

Krafty Love
Designer: Wendy Price

SUPPLIES: *Cardstock:* (kraft, white) Prism *Rubber stamp:* (flower from Le Jardin) Lizzie Anne Designs *Dye ink:* (red) Ranger Industries *Color medium:* (red, pink colored pencils) *Sticker:* (epoxy love) Provo Craft *Adhesive:* (foam tape) *Tool:* (water brush) **Finished size: 3" x 3¾"**

You're the Best Birds
Designer: Rae Barthel

SUPPLIES: *Cardstock:* (black large scallop) Bazzill Basics Paper *Patterned paper:* (Poolside Houndstooth from Paperie collection) Making Memories *Rub-ons:* (birds) Maya Road; (you're the best) Melissa Frances *Fibers:* (black striped ribbon, black floss) *Adhesive:* (foam tape) *Template:* (chipboard bracket) Maya Road *Tool:* (1½" circle punch) **Finished size: 5¾" square**

Page 52

Vintage Kiss Me
Designer: Anabelle O'Malley

SUPPLIES: *Cardstock:* (white) Bazzill Basics Paper *Patterned paper:* (Love Dots from Irresistible collection; Cupid Straight Arrows from Quite Smitten collection) My Mind's Eye *Dye ink:* (Antique Linen) Ranger Industries *Accents:* (heart die cut, tan button) My Mind's Eye; (pink glitter glue) Ranger Industries; (kiss ticket, pink flowers) Caramelos *Rub-ons:* (Mini Simply Sweet alphabet) Doodlebug Design *Fibers:* (pink trim) Making Memories; (tan ribbon) **Finished size: 5" square**

Butterfly Hello
Designer: Beatriz Jennings

SUPPLIES: *Cardstock:* (white) *Patterned paper:* (Capri from Chloe Marie collection) Daisy D's; (Roundtable Scallop from Office Lingo collection) Pink Paislee *Clear stamps:* (flourish from Swirls set) Autumn Leaves; (hello from Gracious Greetings set) Close To My Heart *Dye ink:* (Old Paper) Ranger Industries; (black) Clearsnap *Accents:* (white glitter) Martha Stewart Crafts; (green flower die cut) Daisy D's; (purple brad) Making Memories; (cream flowers, white chipboard butterfly) *Fibers:* (pink tulle) **Finished size: 3¾" x 5½"**

Simply Fabulous Friend
Designer: Kristen Swain

SUPPLIES: *Cardstock:* (white, black) Bazzill Basics Paper *Patterned paper:* (Style from Crate avenue collection) Crate Paper; (Worn Blue Grid Background) Scenic Route; (ledger pinked from Noteworthy collection notebook) Making Memories *Stickers:* (pink felt bird) Martha Stewart Crafts; (Vintage alphabet) Me & My Big Ideas; (Tiny Alpha alphabet) Making Memories *Fibers:* (pink stitched ribbon) Anna Griffin; (black/cream striped ribbon) BoBunny Press *Tool:* (scalloped circle punch) **Finished size: 4½" x 7"**

May
Page 53
Do What You Love
Designer: Wendy Sue Anderson

SUPPLIES: *Cardstock:* (white) *Patterned paper:* (Breeze, Sky from Blue Hill collection) Crate Paper; (Love Free Bird from Free Bird collection) My Mind's Eye *Chalk ink:* (Chestnut Roan) Clearsnap *Accents:* (flower, sentiment die cuts) My Mind's Eye *Fibers:* (white crocheted trim, jute twine) *Adhesive:* (foam tape) *Tool:* (corner rounder punch) **Finished size: 5½" x 4¼"**

Page 54
Springy Hello
Designer: Jen del Muro

SUPPLIES: *Cardstock:* (kraft) Papertrey Ink; (Basic Black, Whisper White) Stampin' Up! *Patterned paper:* (Bushels of Fun from Christmas 2008 collection) American Crafts *Rubber stamps:* (tree, flower from Spring Trees set; sentiment from Mocha Chica set; Writing Paper Scrapblock) Cornish Heritage Farms *Pigment ink:* (Graphite Black) Tsukineko *Color medium:* (red, green, brown markers) Copic Marker *Accent:* (red heart brad) Making Memories *Fibers:* (green ribbon) Provo Craft *Template:* (Swiss Dots embossing) Provo Craft *Tools:* (flourish border punch) Martha Stewart Crafts; (flourish square punch) Stampin' Up! **Finished size: 5½" square**

Welcome Home
Designer: Heidi Van Laar

SUPPLIES: *Cardstock:* (Java, white) Bazzill Basics Paper *Patterned paper:* (Cozy Home, Picking Pumpkins, Chilly Mornings from Weathervane collection) October Afternoon *Clear stamp:* (sentiment from Greetings set) Heidi Grace Designs *Chalk ink:* (Chestnut Roan) Clearsnap *Stickers:* (Giggles alphabet) American Crafts *Fibers:* (brown ribbon) Michaels; (cream floss) DMC *Adhesive:* (foam tape) *Dies:* (scalloped circle, circle) Spellbinders *Tools:* (die cut/embossing machine) Spellbinders; (corner rounder punch) EK Success; (decorative-edge scissors) Fiskars *Other:* (brown felt) **Finished size: 5½" x 4¼"**

S is for School
Designer: Kim Moreno

SUPPLIES: *Cardstock:* (Poinsettia) Core'dinations *Patterned paper:* (Make a Wish, XOXO from Everyday Celebrations collection) Dream Street Papers *Accents:* (red brads) American Crafts *Stickers:* (sentiment, school border) 7gypsies *Fibers:* (black string) *Tools:* (decorative-edge scissors) Fiskars; (⅛" circle punch) **Finished size: 3¼" x 5½"**

Page 55
Take Care
Designer: Teri Anderson

SUPPLIES: *Cardstock:* (white) WorldWin *Patterned paper:* (Lime from Lemon Grass collection, Virtue from Prudence collection) Crate Paper *Accents:* (sentiment, frame die cuts) Crate Paper *Fibers:* (brown ribbon) May Arts **Finished size: 4¼" x 5½"**

Happy Cinco de Mayo
Designer: Kim Kesti

SUPPLIES: *Cardstock:* (Blue Calypso, Twig, Apricot, Red Rock) Bazzill Basics Paper *Specialty ink:* (red spray) Maya Road *Stickers:* (pinwheel border) BasicGrey *Fibers:* (teal pompom trim) *Adhesive:* (foam tape) *Dies:* (Rollerskate Skinnimini alphabet) QuicKutz *Tool:* (die cut machine) QuicKutz **Finished size: 7" x 4¾"**

Love You, Grandson
Designer: Betsy Veldman

SUPPLIES: All supplies from Papertrey Ink unless otherwise noted. *Cardstock:* (Spring Rain, kraft, white) *Patterned paper:* (stripe, polka dots from Men of Life collection) *Clear stamps:* (sentiments, ship from Men of Life set) *Pigment ink:* (Fresh Snow) *Specialty ink:* (Spring Rain, Pure Poppy hybrid) *Accents:* (red journaling card) Creative Imaginations; (blue duck stick pin) Fancy Pants Designs *Fibers:* (red ribbon) *Adhesive:* (foam tape) no source *Tool:* (scalloped punch) Stampin' Up! **Finished size: 4¼" x 5½"**

Page 56
Little Sprout
Designer: Kristen Swain

SUPPLIES: *Cardstock:* (olive green, white) Die Cuts With a View; (white flower embossed from Hannah collection) Anna Griffin *Patterned paper:* (Green Paisley from Maime collection) Anna Griffin *Accents:* (white, yellow buttons) Darice; (white pearls) Michaels *Rub-on:* (sentiment) Plaid *Sticker:* (felt peapod) Anna Griffin *Fibers:* (white string) The Beadery *Tool:* (decorative-edge scissors) Fiskars **Finished size: 5¾" x 5½"**

Greatest Teacher
Designer: Maren Benedict

SUPPLIES: *Cardstock:* (Dark Chocolate) Papertrey Ink *Patterned paper:* (Louie, Jack from Night Light collection; Crunching Leaves from Weathervane collection) October Afternoon *Clear stamps:* (Small Typewriter alphabet) Stampendous! *Dye ink:* (Tuxedo Black) Tsukineko *Accents:* (white, red, green buttons) Buttons Galore & More *Stickers:* (Loopy Lou alphabet) Doodlebug Design *Fibers:* (red stitched ribbon) *Adhesive:* (foam tape) *Tool:* (decorative-edge scissors) *Other:* (acetate) Stampin' Up! **Finished size: 4¼" x 5½"**

My Amazing Mother
Designer: Alicia Thelin

SUPPLIES: All supplies from Stampin' Up!. *Cardstock:* (Chocolate Chip, Baja Breeze, Garden Green, Pumpkin Pie, Real Red, Whisper White) *Rubber stamps:* (amazing, large flower, small flower, hummingbird from Pretty Amazing set; to my from Wonderful Favorites set; mother from Everyday Flexible Phrases set) *Dye ink:* (Pumpkin Pie) *Pigment ink:* (Whisper White) *Embossing powder:* (white) *Color medium:* (Real Red, Garden Green markers) *Accent:* (red brad) *Fibers:* (red ribbon) *Adhesive:* (foam tape) *Tools:* (¹/₁₆" circle punch, ¾" circle punch, circle cutter) **Finished size: 4¼" x 5½"**

Page 57
A Mother Understands
Designer: Wendy Sue Anderson

SUPPLIES: *Cardstock:* (cream) Canson *Patterned paper:* (Coriander from Dill Blossom collection) SEI *Dye ink:* (Soft Sand) Stewart Superior Corp. *Accents:* (orange flower button, yellow polka dot flower) Doodlebug Design *Rub-on:* (sentiment) K&Company *Fibers:* (cream crocheted trim) Making Memories; (rust ribbon) SEI; (jute twine) **Finished size: 4½" x 6"**

Wonderfully Sweet
Designer: Melissa Phillips

SUPPLIES: *Cardstock:* (light sage) Bazzill Basics Paper *Patterned paper:* (Sweater Weather from Weathervane collection) October Afternoon; (Bouquet of Bliss from Fawnd of You, Too collection) Sassafras Lass; (Endeared from Sugared collection) BasicGrey *Clear stamp:* (roses from Love Blooms set) Sweet 'n Sassy Stamps *Dye ink:* (Old Paper) Ranger Industries *Specialty ink:* (Berry Sorbet hybrid) Papertrey Ink *Color medium:* (black pen) *Accents:* (large pink, green rhinestones) Heidi Swapp; (small pink rhinestones) Kaisercraft; (chipboard rectangle) My Mind's Eye *Rub-ons:* (sentiments) BasicGrey *Sticker:* (cupcake) Martha Stewart Crafts *Fibers:* (blue polka dot ribbon) Offray; (cream sequined trim) Maya Road *Adhesive:* (foam tape) *Tool:* (corner rounder punch) Marvy Uchida **Finished size: 5" x 4½"**

Floral Love
Designer: Melissa Phillips

SUPPLIES: *Cardstock:* (Hazel) Bazzill Basics Paper *Patterned paper:* (Sweater Weather from Weathervane collection) October Afternoon; (Endeared from Sugared collection) BasicGrey; (You & Me from Anniversary collection) Karen Foster Design *Specialty paper:* (Cream Doily die cut from Antique Cream collection) Creative Imaginations *Clear stamps:* (roses, sentiment from Love Blooms set) Sweet 'n Sassy Stamps *Dye ink:* (Walnut Stain) Ranger Industries *Specialty ink:* (Berry Sorbet, True Black hybrid) Papertrey Ink *Accents:* (chipboard journaling tile) My Mind's Eye; (white pearls) Martha Stewart Crafts; (blue button) *Stickers:* (pink daisies) Martha Stewart Crafts *Fibers:* (pink ribbon) Offray; (white string) **Finished size: 5" square**

Page 58

Floral Friends
Designer: Brandy Jesperson

SUPPLIES: *Cardstock:* (yellow) *Patterned paper:* (Drip, Baa from Backyard collection) American Crafts *Accents:* (yellow felt flower, brown chipboard rectangle) American Crafts; (pink flower brad) Making Memories; (clear rhinestone) *Rub-on:* (sentiment) American Crafts *Fibers:* (green ribbon) American Crafts *Adhesive:* (foam tape) *Tool:* (scalloped border punch) EK Success **Finished size: 5½" x 4"**

Heartfelt Thank You
Designer: Shanna Vineyard

SUPPLIES: *Cardstock:* (Kiwi Kiss) Stampin' Up!; (Flourish Impressions embossed) Doodlebug Design; (white) *Patterned paper:* (polka dot from Bella Rose collection, pink floral from Sweet Always collection) Stampin' Up! *Rubber stamp:* (Written Thank You) Hero Arts *Dye ink:* (Kiwi Kiss) Stampin' Up! *Accent:* (pink button) *Fibers:* (white floss) *Adhesive:* (foam tape) *Other:* (pink felt) **Finished size: 5" x 7"**

Classic Congrats
Designer: Charity Hassel

SUPPLIES: *Cardstock:* (green polka dot embossed) Bazzill Basics Paper; (white) Prism *Patterned paper:* (Rim Frost from Alpine Frost collection) SEI; (script) *Specialty paper:* (Poolside Flocked Brocade from Paperie collection) Making Memories *Accents:* (light blue rhinestones) KI Memories; (pink flower) *Rub-on:* (sentiment) American Crafts *Sticker:* (flower) SEI *Fibers:* (blue scalloped trim) SEI **Finished size: 4¾" x 6"**

Page 59

Happy Couple
Designer: Wendy Sue Anderson

SUPPLIES: *Cardstock:* (white stripe embossed) Lasting Impressions for Paper *Patterned paper:* (Tea Pot from Spring & Summer collection) American Crafts *Paint:* (light blue) Making Memories *Accents:* (chipboard word bubbles) American Crafts; (chipboard figures) Creating Keepsakes; (heart tag) Doodlebug Design *Stickers:* (Just My Type alphabet) Doodlebug Design *Fibers:* (white ribbon) American Crafts; (white string) *Adhesive:* (foam tape) **Finished size: 7" x 5"**

Cheery Smile
Designer: Heidi Van Laar

SUPPLIES: *Patterned paper:* (Ocean Dot from Double Dot collection) BoBunny Press; (Funky Flowers, Flowery Fields, Candy Stripe from Day Dream collection) My Mind's Eye *Color medium:* (pink marker) Sanford *Accents:* (orange buttons) *Stickers:* (Daiquiri alphabet) American Crafts *Fibers:* (red ribbon) Offray *Adhesive:* (foam tape) *Template:* (Swiss Dots embossing) Provo Craft *Dies:* (scalloped circles, circle) Spellbinders *Tool:* (die cut/embossing machine) Spellbinders *Other:* (frosted acrylic card) SheetLoad ShortCuts; (red felt) **Finished size: 4¼" x 5 1/2"**

Butterfly Birthday Girl
Designer: Betsy Veldman

SUPPLIES: *Cardstock:* (cream, yellow) Prism *Patterned paper:* (Pot of Gold from Happy Place collection) Sassafras Lass; (Lucy from Playful Petals collection) Daisy Bucket Designs; (red weave) *Chalk ink:* (brown) *Sticker:* (felt flower) K&Company *Dies:* (butterfly, sentiment) Provo Craft *Tool:* (die cut machine) Provo Craft *Other:* (vintage book page) **Finished size: 4¼" x 5½"**

Page 60

Dreams Come True
Designer: Lea Lawson

SUPPLIES: *Cardstock:* (white) Bazzill Basics Paper *Patterned paper:* (Promises from Happy Place) Sassafras Lass *Rubber stamp:* (rainbow from Little Gal set) Cornish Heritage Farms *Solvent ink:* (Jet Black) Tsukineko *Chalk ink:* (Charcoal) Clearsnap *Color medium:* (colored pencils) Heidi Swapp *Accents:* (blue, red, orange, green rhinestones) Doodlebug Design; (iridescent glitter glue) Ranger Industries *Rub-ons:* (dotted border) Creative Imaginations; (sentiment) Urban Lily **Finished size: 3" square**

Thanks a Million
Designer: Alicia Thelin

SUPPLIES: All supplies from Stampin' Up!. *Cardstock:* (Brilliant Blue, Whisper White) *Patterned paper:* (polka dot from Bashful Blue Designer Series collection) *Rubber stamp:* (sentiment from Quirky Quips set) *Dye ink:* (Kiwi Kiss) *Accents:* (blue brads) *Fibers:* (green striped ribbon) *Adhesive:* (foam tape) *Tool:* (scalloped oval punch) **Finished size: 4¼" x 5½"**

Bouncy Smile
Designer: Maren Benedict

SUPPLIES: *Cardstock:* (Summer Sunrise, white) Papertrey Ink *Patterned paper:* (Beach Towel from Snorkel collection) Cosmo Cricket *Accents:* (chipboard letters) Cosmo Cricket *Adhesive:* (foam tape) *Die:* (circle) Provo Craft *Tool:* (die cut machine) Provo Craft **Finished size: 5½" x 4¼"**

Page 61

Birthday Stripes
Designer: Layle Koncar

SUPPLIES: *Cardstock:* (red) Bazzill Basics Paper *Patterned paper:* (Bandwidth from Cogsmo collection) Cosmo Cricket *Color medium:* (black pen) *Accent:* (journaling die cut) Cosmo Cricket *Rub-on:* (sentiment) Scenic Route *Adhesive:* (foam tape) **Finished size: 5" square**

Let's A Go-Go
Designer: Maren Benedict

SUPPLIES: *Cardstock:* (Lemon Tart) Papertrey Ink *Patterned paper:* (Umbrellas from Snorkel collection) Cosmo Cricket *Accents:* (chipboard sun) Cosmo Cricket; (red, yellow, green, blue rhinestones) My Mind's Eye *Rub-ons:* (bicycle, sentiment) Cosmo Cricket *Adhesive:* (foam tape) *Tools:* (assorted circle punches) Stampin' Up! **Finished size: 5½" x 4¼"**

We Are Royalty
Designer: Ashley Harris

SUPPLIES: *Cardstock:* (French Vanilla) Bazzill Basics Paper *Patterned paper:* (Poolside Big Dot from Paperie collection) Making Memories; (Make a Wish from Cupcake collection) BasicGrey *Specialty paper:* (Die-Cut Bird Brocade from Flower Patch collection) Making Memories *Accents:* (resin crown) Melissa Frances; (white pearls) The Paper Studio; (blue rhinestones) Kaisercraft *Fonts:* (Scriptina) www.dafont.com; (Times New Roman) Microsoft **Finished size: 5½" x 4¼"**

Page 62

Remember
Designer: Carolyn King

SUPPLIES: *Cardstock:* (white) Gina K Designs *Patterned paper:* (striped, red crackle from USA Page Kit) The Paper Studio *Accents:* (chipboard star) Heidi Swapp; (silver beads) Michaels *Sticker:* (sentiment) The Paper Studio *Fibers:* (white ribbon) May Arts *Adhesive:* (foam tape) *Tools:* (flourish punch) EK Success; (rounded rectangle punch) Stampin' Up!; (corner rounder punch) **Finished size: 4½" x 5½"**

Teacher, Thank You
Designer: Wendy Sue Anderson

SUPPLIES: *Cardstock:* (Maraschino) Bazzill Basics Paper; (white stripe embossed) Lasting Impressions for Paper; (blue) *Patterned paper:* (Gazebo, Fruit Stand from Detours collection) October Afternoon; (red polka dot) Making Memories *Chalk ink:* (Chestnut Roan) Clearsnap *Accents:* (round metal-rimmed tag) Making Memories *Rub-ons:* (Rue alphabet) American Crafts *Stickers:* (Daiquiri alphabet) American Crafts *Fibers:* (multi-stripe ribbon) *Adhesive:* (foam tape) *Tool:* (decorative-edge scissors) *Other:* (green polka dot packaging) Making Memories **Finished size: 4¾" square**

A Heart-y Thanks
Designer: Carolyn King

SUPPLIES: *Cardstock:* (white) Gina K Designs; (Ruby Red) Stampin' Up! *Paper:* (loose-leaf lined) *Rubber stamp:* (book with apple) Dollar Tree Stores *Dye ink:* (Tuxedo Black) Tsukineko *Watermark ink:* Tsukineko *Embossing powder:* (clear) *Color medium:* (assorted markers) Copic Marker *Accents:* (silver staples) *Rub-on:* (sentiment) Scenic Route *Fibers:* (black gingham ribbon) Stampin' Up! *Adhesive:* (foam tape) *Tools:* (heart punch) Marvy Uchida; (corner rounder punch) Creative Memories **Finished size: 3½" x 4½"**

Page 63

#1 Teacher
Designer: Maren Benedict

SUPPLIES: *Cardstock:* (Spring Moss, white) Papertrey Ink *Patterned paper:* (Lessons from Jacks World collection) Cosmo Cricket *Rubber stamps:* (chalkboard, sentiment from School Days set) Lizzie Anne Designs *Dye ink:* (Tuxedo Black) Tsukineko *Color medium:* (assorted markers) Copic Marker *Fibers:* (green stitched ribbon) Papertrey Ink *Adhesive:* (foam tape) *Tool:* (decorative-edge scissors) **Finished size: 4¼" x 5½"**

Bold, Bright Teacher
Designer: Alli Miles

SUPPLIES: *Cardstock:* (white) Papertrey Ink *Patterned paper:* (Apple Delight from Happy Place collection) Sassafras Lass *Specialty paper:* (Hopscotch die cut from Pop Culture collection) KI Memories *Clear stamp:* (sentiment from Teacher's Apple set) Papertrey Ink *Specialty ink:* (True Black hybrid) Papertrey Ink *Accents:* (burgundy flower) Prima; (tan button) Making Memories **Finished size: 4¼" x 5½"**

A Kid with Class
Designer: Jen del Muro

SUPPLIES: *Cardstock:* (white) Papertrey Ink; (Garden Green, Only Orange, Night of Navy, Summer Sun) Stampin' Up! *Rubber stamps:* (sentiment, worm from Making the Grade set; AlphaNumber Backgrounder) Cornish Heritage Farms *Pigment ink:* (Graphite Black) Tsukineko *Watermark ink:* Tsukineko *Embossing powder:* (white, clear) Stampin' Up! *Color medium:* (assorted markers) Copic Marker *Accents:* (yellow button, silver brads) *Fibers:* (red gingham ribbon) Hobby Lobby *Adhesive:* (foam tape) *Template:* (Swiss Dots embossing) Provo Craft *Dies:* (scalloped square, heart, bracketed square) Spellbinders; (Red Tag Sale alphabet) Provo Craft *Tool:* (die cut/embossing machine) Spellbinders **Finished size: 5" square**

Page 64
ConGRADulations!
Designer: Charlene Austin

SUPPLIES: *Cardstock:* (Chocolate Chip) Stampin' Up!; (white) *Patterned paper:* (Graph from Wild Saffron collection) K&Company *Rubber stamp:* (graduation cap from U R A Hoot set) Cornish Heritage Farms *Solvent ink:* (Jet Black) Tsukineko *Stickers:* (Playroom alphabet) American Crafts **Finished size: 8¾" x 3¾"**

June
Page 65
Fresh Lemonade
Designer: Wendy Sue Anderson

SUPPLIES: *Cardstock:* (white) *Patterned paper:* (Rose McGrain, Sophia Tuckett from Craft Fair collection) American Crafts *Accents:* (yellow flower, gray rhinestones) Making Memories *Rub-on:* (sentiment) Crate Paper *Sticker:* (lemonade journaling box) American Crafts *Fibers:* (yellow gingham ribbon) Offray **Finished size: 3¾" x 6½"**

Page 66
Believe in Your Dreams
Designer: Stefanie Hamilton

SUPPLIES: *Cardstock:* (white) Creative Memories *Digital elements:* (butterfly from Spring Wings Brushes and Stamps kit) www.designerdigitals.com; (sentiment from Moments of Special kit; taupe paper from Today I Am Thankful kit; purple paper from Delight Wings 'n Things kit; rhinestones from Your Heart kit; stitching from Flutter Fresh kit) www.pixelcanvas.co.nz; (ribbon from CU Bows & Ribbons kit) www.simply-scraps. net *Software:* (scrapbooking) Creative Memories **Finished size: 6" x 4"**

Deer Friend
Designer: Sherry Wright

SUPPLIES: *Cardstock:* (light blue) Prism *Patterned paper:* (Fawnd of You, Woo + Woo, All My Heart from My Dearest collection; Piccadilly from Pocket Full of Rosies collection; Gumdrop Garden from Sunshine Lollipop collection) Sassafras Lass *Chalk ink:* (Chestnut Roan, Tangerine) Clearsnap *Accents:* (chipboard letters) CherryArte; (orange rhinestones) Queen & Co. *Rub-on:* (sentiment) Paper Salon *Fibers:* (cream crocheted trim) Offray **Finished size: 5¼" x 6¼"**

A Cupcake Kind of Day!
Designer: Jen del Muro

SUPPLIES: *Cardstock:* (white) Papertrey Ink; (Pumpkin Pie) Stampin' Up!; (Aqua) Prism *Patterned paper:* (Funky Flowers, Pretty Petals from Day Dream collection) My Mind's Eye *Clear stamps:* (sentiment, cupcake from It's a Cupcake Kind of Day set) My Favorite Things *Pigment ink:* (Graphite Black) Tsukineko *Color media:* (assorted markers) Copic Marker; (colored pencils) Sanford *Accents:* (pink button, clear rhinestone) *Fibers:* (aqua ribbon) Ribbons and Bows Oh My! *Tool:* (scalloped border punch) Stampin' Up! **Finished size: 4¼" x 5½"**

Page 67
Hello Friend
Designer: Julia Stainton

SUPPLIES: *Cardstock:* (white) Prism *Patterned paper:* (Chrysanthemum from Freshcut collection) Autumn Leaves *Rubber stamp:* (sentiment from Friend Centers set) Cornish Heritage Farms *Dye ink:* (Tuxedo Black) Tsukineko *Accents:* (pink rhinestones) Doodlebug Design *Fibers:* (black ribbon) May Arts *Adhesive:* (foam tape) **Finished size: 5" square**

Good Luck
Designer: Mary MacAskill

SUPPLIES: All supplies from American Crafts unless otherwise noted. *Patterned paper:* (Bumper Cars, Funnel Cake, House of Mirrors from Celebration II collection) *Accents:* (staples) no source *Rub-ons:* (Rue alphabet, crown) *Stickers:* (Runway alphabet) *Fibers:* (pink star ribbon) *Adhesive:* (foam tape) no source **Finished size: 5" square**

Dream Big
Designer: Kristen Swain

SUPPLIES: *Cardstock:* (olive green, white) The Paper Company *Patterned paper:* (red jacquard, green dots from Alix collection) Anna Griffin *Specialty paper:* (Twirl die cut from Bloom collection) KI Memories *Accents:* (chipboard butterflies) Dollar Tree Stores; (acetate journaling box) Hambly Screen Prints; (green, red buttons) Darice *Rub-on:* (sentiment) Plaid *Fibers:* (white string) Darice **Finished size: 5½" x 5¼"**

Page 68
#1 Coach
Designer: Shanna Vineyard

SUPPLIES: *Cardstock:* (kraft, white) *Patterned paper:* (Little Star from So Handsome collection) My Mind's Eye *Accent:* (acetate star) My Mind's Eye *Rub-on:* (symbol) BoBunny Press *Stickers:* (Holly Doodle alphabet) Pink Paislee; (vinyl number) *Adhesive:* (foam tape) **Finished size: 5" x 6"**

Hit the Road, Jack!
Designer: Kimberly Crawford

SUPPLIES: *Cardstock:* (Vintage Cream, Kraft) Papertrey Ink *Patterned paper:* (Mr. Campy Flannel, Happy Campers from Mr. Campy collection) Cosmo Cricket *Clear stamps:* (sentiment, trailer, sun, cloud, tree, road signs from Road Trip set) Inkadinkado *Specialty ink:* (Burnt Umber, Sunflower, Water Lily Green, Jardin Moss hybrid) Stewart Superior Corp. *Color medium:* (assorted markers) Copic Marker *Fibers:* (brown string) Martha Stewart Crafts *Adhesive:* (foam tape) *Tool:* (corner rounder punch) **Finished size: 5½" x 4¼"**

Dotty Welcome
Designer: Julia Stainton

SUPPLIES: *Cardstock:* (Spring Willow Dark, Kraft) Prism *Patterned paper:* (Peppermint Sticks from Good Cheer collection) October Afternoon; (Euphoria from Frenzy collection) We R Memory Keepers *Rubber stamps:* (sheep from Sweet Spring set, sentiment from Baby Love set) Cornish Heritage Farms *Dye ink:* (Tuxedo Black) Tsukineko *Pigment ink:* (Frost White) Clearsnap *Accents:* (safety pin) Creative Impressions; (cream felt button) Making Memories *Fibers:* (blue pom-pom trim) Fancy Pants Designs; (green polka dot ribbon) Creative Impressions *Template:* (Swiss Dots embossing) Provo Craft *Tool:* (embossing machine) ProvoCraft **Finished size: 5¼" square**

Page 69
Catch U Later
Designer: Betsy Veldman

SUPPLIES: *Cardstock:* (kraft) Papertrey Ink *Patterned paper:* (Vivid, Chillin' from About a Boy collection) Fancy Pants Designs; (Secret Garden from Pocket Full of Rosies collection) Sassafras Lass; (Lipstick from Girls Only collection) My Mind's Eye *Paint:* (white) Plaid *Accents:* (yellow button) BasicGrey; (yellow felt fish) American Crafts *Stickers:* (sun) Sassafras Lass; (Cream Soda alphabet) American Crafts *Fibers:* (white string) *Dies:* (wave, catch, Sans Serif alphabet) Provo Craft *Tool:* (die cut machine) Provo Craft **Finished size: 5½" x 4¼"**

On the Road Again
Designer: Kimberly Crawford

SUPPLIES: *Cardstock:* (Dark Chocolate, white) Papertrey Ink; (Ocean) Bazzill Basics Paper *Patterned paper:* (Radical from Offbeat collection) BasicGrey *Clear stamps:* (sentiment, van from Road Trip set) Inkadinkado *Dye ink:* (Tuxedo Black) Tsukineko *Color medium:* (assorted markers) Copic Marker *Fibers:* (olive ribbon) May Arts; (white twine) Wrights *Adhesive:* (foam tape) **Finished size: 4¼" x 5½"**

Happy Day
Designer: Maren Benedict

SUPPLIES: *Cardstock:* (Pure Poppy, Vintage Cream) Papertrey Ink *Patterned paper:* (Beach Towel from Snorkel collection) Cosmo Cricket *Paint:* (Red Wagon) Making Memories *Accents:* (Tank Mix chipboard alphabet) Cosmo Cricket *Rub-ons:* (Snorkel alphabet) Cosmo Cricket *Fibers:* (red ribbon) Michaels *Adhesive:* (foam tape) *Tool:* (1" circle punch) Stampin' Up! **Finished size: 5½" square**

And They Lived
Designer: Maren Benedict

SUPPLIES: *Cardstock:* (Basic Gray) Stampin' Up! *Patterned paper:* (Something Borrowed from Everafter collection) Cosmo Cricket *Accents:* (beaded hat pin) Stampin' Up!; (white pearls) Martha Stewart Crafts; (sentiment label) Cosmo Cricket *Rub-on:* (floral spray) Cosmo Cricket *Fibers:* (silver ribbon) Martha Stewart Crafts **Finished size: 5½" x 4¼"**

July

Page 76
Happy Fourth
Designer: Wendy Sue Anderson

SUPPLIES: *Cardstock:* (gray) Bazzill Basics Paper *Clear stamp:* (branch from Birds & Branches set) Hero Arts *Chalk ink:* (Chestnut Roan) Clearsnap *Accents:* (red, blue chipboard birds, red chipboard stars) Creating Keepsakes; (flag clip, white scalloped border) Doodlebug Design *Stickers:* (Shin-Dig alphabet) Doodlebug Design *Fibers:* (red gingham ribbon) O'Scrap! *Adhesive:* (foam tape) **Finished size: 8½" x 4¼"**

Page 77
Canada, Eh?
Designer: Cathy Schellenberg

SUPPLIES: *Cardstock:* (red) Bazzill Basics Paper; (black) Stampin' Up! *Patterned paper:* (Fennel from Dill Blossom collection) SEI; (Ruby Ave. from Loveland collection, White Blue Grid Background) Scenic Route *Color medium:* (black pen) American Crafts *Rub-ons:* (Stony Island alphabet, Canada) Luxe Designs; (scalloped trim) **Finished size: 5½" x 4¼"**

Go Green
Designer: Teri Anderson

SUPPLIES: *Cardstock:* (white) *Patterned paper:* (Toadstools, Bear, Owl from Green collection) Die Cuts With a View *Accents:* (silver staples) Swingline *Font:* (CK Gutenberg) Creating Keepsakes *Tool:* (corner rounder punch) Creative Memories **Finished size: 4¼" square**

Da Rulz
Designer: Kim Kesti

SUPPLIES: *Cardstock:* (Raven, Lily White, Tropical, Marmalade, African Daisy, Pajama, Parakeet) Bazzill Basics Paper *Patterned paper:* (Passing Notes from Teen collection) American Crafts *Color medium:* (black pen) *Stickers:* (Tinsel alphabet) American Crafts *Font:* (your choice) *Adhesive:* (foam tape) **Finished size: 4¼" x 6¼"**

Page 78
Star-Spangled Day
Designer: Kimberly Crawford

SUPPLIES: *Cardstock:* (Vintage Cream) Papertrey Ink *Patterned paper:* (Scrap Strip, Grant Street from Liberty collection; Grey Cube on Worn Background) Scenic Route *Clear stamp:* (sentiment from Ready 4 Any Holiday set) Kitchen Sink Stamps *Specialty ink:* (L'Amour Red hybrid) Stewart Superior Corp. *Accents:* (red, white, & blue chipboard circles) Scenic Route *Sticker:* (blue star strip) Scenic Route *Adhesive:* (foam tape) *Die:* (label) Spellbinders *Tools:* (die cut/embossing machine) Spellbinders; (star punch) Fiskars **Finished size: 4¼" x 5½"**

Bright Birthday
Designer: Roree Rumph

SUPPLIES: *Cardstock:* (white) Bazzill Basics Paper; (Orange Glitter) Creative Café *Patterned paper:* (Candles & Cake, Celebrate from Candles & Cakes collection) Creative Imaginations; (Sublime from Kewl collection) Fancy Pants Designs *Accents:* (chipboard star) Li'l Davis Designs; (white glitter chipboard star) Making Memories; (teal button) BasicGrey; (red button) Creative Imaginations *Rub-on:* (celebration) Creative Imaginations *Stickers:* (candle, orange circle, red date circle) Creative Imaginations *Fibers:* (green ribbon) American Crafts *Adhesive:* (foam tape) **Finished size: 5½" square**

It's a Boy
Designer: Maren Benedict

SUPPLIES: *Cardstock:* (kraft, Vintage Cream) Papertrey Ink *Patterned paper:* (Handsome Henry from Lil' Man collection) Cosmo Cricket *Color medium:* (black marker) Copic Marker *Accent:* (chipboard arrow) Cosmo Cricket *Rub-ons:* (Lil' Man alphabet) Cosmo Cricket *Fibers:* (striped ribbon) Cosmo Cricket *Adhesive:* (foam tape) *Dies:* (circles) Spellbinders *Tool:* (die cut/embossing machine) Spellbinders **Finished size: 4½" x 4¼"**

Page 79
Sweet Baby Girl
Designer: Wendy Sue Anderson

SUPPLIES: *Cardstock:* (white, pink) American Crafts *Patterned paper:* (Little Bo-Peep from Baby collection) American Crafts *Stickers:* (Loopy Lou alphabet) Doodlebug Design; (pink tag, pink label, pink epoxy elephant, flowers) Making Memories *Fibers:* (brown ribbon) American Crafts; (pink trim) Making Memories; (white crochet thread) *Adhesive:* (foam tape) **Finished size: 4¾" square**

Vintage Friends
Designer: Maren Benedict

SUPPLIES: *Cardstock:* (Pumpkin Pie) Stampin' Up! *Patterned paper:* (Something Special from Everafter collection) Cosmo Cricket *Accents:* (best friends die cut) Cosmo Cricket; (orange buttons) BasicGrey *Fibers:* (orange gingham ribbon) Offray **Finished size: 4¼" x 5½"**

BFF
Designer: Danielle Flanders

SUPPLIES: *Cardstock:* (cream) Bazzill Basics Paper *Patterned paper:* (Bianca, Haley, Peyton from Fresh Twist collection) Melissa Frances *Transparency sheet:* Staples *Clear stamp:* (decorative bracket from Baroque set) Melissa Frances *Solvent ink:* (black) *Accents:* (ticket die cut) Melissa Frances; (pink rhinestone brad) Making Memories; (white button) Wrights *Rub-on:* (friend) Melissa Frances *Fibers:* (pink rickrack) Wrights; (cream ribbon) Offray; (twine) **Finished size: 5¾" x 4¾"**

Page 80
Thx
Designer: Alli Miles

SUPPLIES: *Cardstock:* (white) Papertrey Ink *Patterned paper:* (Pinstriped from Hog Heaven collection) Sassafras Lass *Accent:* (pink star stick pin) Fancy Pants Designs *Stickers:* (journal label) Sassafras Lass; (Playroom alphabet) American Crafts *Fibers:* (brown polka dot ribbon) Papertrey Ink **Finished size: 4¼" x 5½"**

Thanks for Delivering
Designer: Shanna Vineyard

SUPPLIES: *Cardstock:* (white) Bazzill Basics Paper *Paint:* (red) *Stickers:* (Tiny Alpha alphabet) Making Memories *Fibers:* (black floss) *Font:* (your choice) *Adhesive:* (foam tape) *Other:* (newspaper, cardboard) **Finished size: 5¼" x 3¾"**

Elephant Love You
Designer: Angie Hagist

SUPPLIES: *Cardstock:* (Cupcake, Aqua, Reed) Bazzill Basics Paper; (white) *Rubber stamp:* (elephant from Wild & Crazy Bunch set) Unity Stamp Co. *Dye ink:* (black) Close To My Heart *Color media:* (black pen) Sakura; (watercolor markers) *Accents:* (silver heart brads) Jo-Ann Stores *Rub-ons:* (flower, love you) October Afternoon *Adhesive:* (foam tape) **Finished size: 4¾" x 3½"**

Page 81
Silly Old Bear
Designer: Maren Benedict

SUPPLIES: *Cardstock:* (Wild Wasabi, Whisper White) Stampin' Up! *Patterned paper:* (Strip Tease, Lessons from Jacks World collection) Cosmo Cricket *Clear stamps:* (bear costume and doll from Isabelle Paper Dolls set) My Favorite Things *Dye ink:* (black) *Color medium:* (assorted markers) Copic Marker *Accents:* (white pearls) Martha Stewart Crafts *Fibers:* (white ribbon) Michaels *Adhesive:* (foam tape) **Finished size: 8" x 4¼"**

Have a Sweet Day
Designer: P. Kelly Smith

SUPPLIES: *Cardstock:* (Cricket) American Crafts *Patterned paper:* (Slurp from Backyard collection) American Crafts *Specialty paper:* (Petticoat die cut) SEI *Accents:* (blue rhinestones) Doodlebug Design *Stickers:* (Hopscotch alphabet) Doodlebug Design *Adhesive:* (foam tape) **Finished size: 7" x 5"**

Polka Dot Hello
Designer: Kimberly Crawford

SUPPLIES: *Cardstock:* (Summer Sunrise, kraft) Papertrey Ink *Patterned paper:* (text dots, green mini floral from Chloe's Closet collection) Making Memories *Accent:* (white grid paper flower) Making Memories *Rub-on:* (hello) American Crafts *Stickers:* (orange slice badge) American Crafts; (label) Martha Stewart Crafts *Adhesive:* (foam tape) *Tool:* (border punch) **Finished size: 5½" x 4¼"**

Page 82
Birdie Anniversary
Designer: Kim Moreno

SUPPLIES: *Cardstock:* (brown) Core'dinations; (white) *Patterned paper:* (Soiree, Wishes, Zoology from The Menagerie collection) Dream Street Papers *Chalk ink:* (Charcoal) Clearsnap *Color medium:* (black pen) American Crafts *Accents:* (red glitter glue) Ranger Industries; (blue rhinestones) Doodlebug Design *Rub-on:* (happy anniversary) American Crafts *Adhesive:* (foam tape) *Tools:* (border punch) Martha Stewart Crafts; (corner rounder punch) Creative Memories **Finished size: 5¼" x 3¾"**

Beach Run
Designer: Maren Benedict

SUPPLIES: *Cardstock:* (black) Stampin' Up!; (Summer Sunrise) Papertrey Ink *Patterned paper:* (Boardwalk, Elements from Snorkel collection) Cosmo Cricket *Stickers:* (clear epoxy dots) Cloud 9 Design *Fibers:* (yellow stitched ribbon) Papertrey Ink *Adhesive:* (foam tape) **Finished size: 5½" x 4¼"**

Crazy
Designer: Layle Koncar

SUPPLIES: *Cardstock:* (red, white) Bazzill Basics Paper *Patterned paper:* (Crush Notes, Heartland, Cupids from Crush collection) Teresa Collins Designs *Tool:* (dotted scalloped border punch) Fiskars **Finished size: 4¼" x 6½"**

Page 83
What's the Scoop?
Designer: Betsy Veldman

SUPPLIES: *Cardstock:* (Raspberry Fizz, Spring Moss, Aqua Mist, white, kraft) Papertrey Ink; (orange) Bazzill Basics Paper *Patterned paper:* (White Blue Grid Background) Scenic Route *Clear stamps:* (Simple Alphabet, ice cream cone, mini heart from Love Songs set; solid, outline polka dots from Polka Dot Basics set) Papertrey Ink *Dye ink:* (Pumpkin Pie, Green Galore) Stampin' Up! *Pigment ink:* (Fresh Snow) Papertrey Ink *Specialty ink:* (Raspberry Fizz, Spring Rain, Summer Sunrise, Lavender Moon hybrid) Papertrey Ink *Accent:* (orange button) BasicGrey *Fibers:* (lavender ribbon) Papertrey Ink; (white string) Provo Craft *Tool:* (die cut machine) Provo Craft **Finished size: 4¼" x 5½"**

Lollipop Love
Designer: Anabelle O'Malley

SUPPLIES: *Cardstock:* (white) *Patterned paper:* (Wake Up from Jacks World collection) Cosmo Cricket; (Cupid Straight Arrows from Quite Smitten collection) My Mind's Eye *Accents:* (pink rhinestones) Darice; (white enjoy tag) Making Memories *Sticker:* (pink rhinestone circle) Heidi Swapp *Fibers:* (pink ribbon) Three Bugs in a Rug *Dies:* (scalloped circle, circle) Spellbinders *Tools:* (decorative-edge scissors) Fiskars, Provo Craft *Other:* (lollipop) **Finished size: 4" x 6"**

Bright Friends
Designer: Rae Barthel

SUPPLIES: *Cardstock:* (white, white polka dots embossed) Bazzill Basics Paper *Patterned paper:* (Meadow from Beau Jardin collection) Tinkering Ink; (Preserves from Spring & Summer collection) American Crafts *Accents:* (green, red birds; red flowers) American Crafts *Rub-on:* (friends) Melissa Frances *Fibers:* (multi-colored ribbon) American Crafts; (black cord) *Adhesive:* (foam tape) *Template:* (frame die cuts) Cosmo Cricket **Finished size: 5½" square**

Page 84
Sweet on You
Designer: Beatriz Jennings

SUPPLIES: *Cardstock:* (blue) Bazzill Basics Paper *Patterned paper:* (pink floral, red hearts from Sweet Talk pad) K&Company *Vellum:* Hot Off The Press *Dye ink:* (Antique Linen) Ranger Industries *Paint:* (white) *Accents:* (white glitter) Martha Stewart Crafts;

(chipboard circle) Maya Road; (sweet on you die cut, red/pink fabric brad) K&Company; (cream flower) *Fibers:* (blue ribbon) *Tools:* (scalloped border punch) Martha Stewart Crafts; (decorative-edge scissors) Provo Craft **Finished size: 4¾" x 5"**

Pink & Black Birthday
Designer: Rae Barthel

SUPPLIES: *Cardstock:* (white) Hobby Lobby; (black scalloped) Bazzill Basics Paper *Patterned paper:* (black polka dot, pink medallions, black and pink dots from Sabrina collection) Making Memories *Chalk ink:* (charcoal) Clearsnap *Accents:* (small white pearls) Target; (pink flowers) Petaloo; (large white pearls) Hobby Lobby *Rub-on:* (birthday sentiment) Melissa Frances *Sticker:* (pink border) Making Memories *Fibers:* (pink ribbon) Hobby Lobby *Adhesive:* (foam tape) **Finished size: 5" square**

Miss You Travel
Designer: Angie Hagist

SUPPLIES: *Cardstock:* (white) American Crafts *Patterned paper:* (Young Street from Surprise collection) Scenic Route *Accent:* (suitcase with airplane) American Crafts *Stickers:* (Aqua Metro mini alphabet) Making Memories *Fibers:* (red ribbon) *Tool:* (corner rounder punch) Fiskars **Finished size: 4" x 7"**

Page 85
Friends Forever Flowers
Designer: Alli Miles

SUPPLIES: *Cardstock:* (white) Papertrey Ink *Clear stamps:* (flower stem from Wise Owl set, sentiment from Spiral Bouquet set) Papertrey Ink *Dye ink:* (Pear Tart) Tsukineko *Accents:* (yellow, teal buttons) My Mind's Eye; (red button) Making Memories *Dies:* (small, large rectangles) Spellbinders *Tool:* (die cut/embossing machine) Spellbinders **Finished size: 5½" x 4¼"**

Enjoy the Journey
Designer: Wendy Price

SUPPLIES: *Cardstock:* (light gray, dark gray) Bazzill Basics Paper; (white) *Rubber stamp:* (car from Things That Go set) Lizzie Anne Designs *Solvent ink:* (black) Tsukineko *Paint:* (watercolors) Winsor & Newton *Rub-on:* (sentiment) Making Memories *Fibers:* (black stitched ribbon) Michaels *Adhesive:* (foam tape) *Die:* (cityscape) Provo Craft *Tool:* (die cut machine) Provo Craft **Finished size: 4" square**

Medallion Thanks
Designer: Betsy Veldman

SUPPLIES: *Cardstock:* (Pure Poppy, Vintage Cream) Papertrey Ink *Patterned paper:* (Canopy from Brunch collection) Crate Paper *Clear stamps:* (circles, medallion, sentiment from Simply Stationery set) Papertrey Ink *Specialty ink:* (Pure Poppy, Ripe Avocado, Lemon Tart, Spring Rain, True Black hybrid) Papertrey Ink *Accents:* (green, blue, yellow buttons) BasicGrey; (journaling card) Collage Press *Sticker:* (flower) BasicGrey *Fibers:* (light blue ribbon) Papertrey Ink *Adhesive:* (foam tape) **Finished size: 3¼" x 6"**

Page 86
Polka Dot Floral Hello
Designer: Dawn McVey

SUPPLIES: All supplies from Papertrey Ink unless otherwise noted. *Cardstock:* (kraft, Dark Chocolate) *Vellum; Patterned paper:* (red polka dots from 2008 Bitty Dot Basics collection) *Clear stamps:* (flower, hello from Friends 'Til the End stamp set) *Specialty ink:* (Dark Chocolate hybrid) *Watermark ink:* Tsukineko *Embossing powder:* (white) *Accents:* (cream buttons) *Fibers:* (linen thread) Stampin' Up! *Adhesive:* (foam tape) no source **Finished size: 5" square**

Thanks
Designer: Heidi Van Laar

SUPPLIES: *Cardstock:* (white) Georgia-Pacific *Patterned paper:* (Checking Out, Lots of Dots, Fresh as a Daisy from Bloom & Grow collection) My Mind's Eye *Accents:* (orange flower, leaves die cuts) My Mind's Eye; (polka dot flower) Prima *Stickers:* (Chit Chat alphabet) American Crafts *Fibers:* (orange/white striped ribbon) American Crafts *Adhesive:* (foam tape) *Tools:* (border punch; medium, large corner rounder punches) EK Success **Finished size: 7" x 5"**

Imagine
Designer: Maren Benedict

SUPPLIES: *Cardstock:* (Ocean Tides) Papertrey Ink *Patterned paper:* (Handsome Henry from Lil' Man collection) Cosmo Cricket *Accents:* (chipboard baseball player, chipboard imagine) Cosmo Cricket *Fibers:* (cream stitched ribbon) Papertrey Ink *Adhesive:* (foam tape) *Die:* (scalloped square) Spellbinders *Tool:* (die cut/embossing machine) Provo Craft **Finished size: 4½" square**

Page 87
Safe Travels
Designer: Becky Olsen

SUPPLIES: *Cardstock:* (orange) Bazzill Basics Paper *Patterned paper:* (We'll Always Have Paris from Bibliography kit) Studio Calico; (Cutie Pie from Sweet Cakes collection) Pink Paislee; (Make a Wish from Sugar & Spice collection) My Mind's Eye *Accent:* (black button) Autumn Leaves *Stickers:* (Shin-Dig alphabet) Doodlebug Design *Fibers:* (blue trim) American Crafts; (black floss) DMC *Tool:* (scalloped border punch) Fiskars **Finished size: 8½" x 3¾"**

August
Page 88
Greetings from Camp
Designer: Wendy Sue Anderson

SUPPLIES: *Cardstock:* (white, red) *Patterned paper:* (Stripe from Passport collection) Making Memories; (Happy Campers from Mr. Campy collection) Cosmo Cricket *Chalk ink:* (Chestnut Roan) Clearsnap *Accents:* (journaling tags) Cosmo Cricket; (silver adventure clip, star brad) Making Memories *Rub-on:* (compass) Colorbok *Stickers:* (destination) Making Memories; (Just My Type alphabet) Doodlebug Design *Fibers:* (hemp cord) *Adhesive:* (foam tape) **Finished size: 4½" x 6"**

Arrrgh Birthday
Designer: Teri Anderson

SUPPLIES: *Cardstock:* (pink, white) WorldWin *Patterned paper:* (Chic from Moda Bella collection) American Crafts; (Lunch Hour from Office Lingo collection) Pink Paislee *Rubber stamps:* (arrrgh, skull from Ahoy Matey-Pirates set) Cornish Heritage Farms *Clear stamp:* (another birthday? from Mainly Men set) A Muse Artstamps *Dye ink:* (black) Marvy Uchida *Solvent ink:* (Jet Black) Tsukineko *Accents:* (vellum tag) Making Memories; (silver staples) Swingline *Sticker:* (conversation bubble) Colorbok **Finished size: 3½" x 5½"**

Page 95
What's Up?
Designer: Laura Williams

SUPPLIES: *Cardstock:* (Kiwi, Holiday Red, Ocean, Breeze, Sunny Yellow, black) Close To My Heart *Transparency sheet; Rubber stamps:* (Cityscape from DoodleFactory Urban set; hello there, what's up? from Comic Book Sentiments set) Starving Artistamps *Dye ink:* (Kiwi) Close To My Heart *Solvent ink:* (Jet Black) Tsukineko *Color medium:* (red, green, blue markers) *Accents:* (silver staples) **Finished size: 6" square**

Break a Leg
Designer: Susan R. Opel

SUPPLIES: *Cardstock:* (pink) Die Cuts With a View *Patterned paper:* (Pep Rally from Teen collection) American Crafts *Specialty paper:* (matte photo paper) *Accent:* (white glitter chipboard frame) American Crafts *Fibers:* (aqua trim) My Mind's Eye *Fonts:* (Bernard MT Condensed, Baskerville Old Face) www.fonts.com *Software:* (photo editing) *Adhesive:* (foam tape) **Finished size: 6" x 4"**

You Made My Day Butterfly
Designer: Lea Lawson

SUPPLIES: *Cardstock:* (black) Bazzill Basics Paper *Patterned paper:* (Cucumber Sandwiches, High Tea, English Garden from Spring & Summer collection) American Crafts *Chalk ink:* (Warm Red) Clearsnap *Accents:* (green, blue rhinestones) Doodlebug Design; (chipboard square) Rusty Pickle *Rub-ons:* (thank you, sentiment) Making Memories *Fibers:* (rainbow striped ribbon) Masterpiece Studios *Tool:* (corner rounder punch) EK Success **Finished size: 4¼" x 5½"**

Page 96
Candles
Designer: Mary MacAskill

SUPPLIES: *Cardstock:* (white, kraft) Bazzill Basics Paper *Patterned paper:* (House of Mirrors from Celebration II collection) American Crafts *Accents:* (pink brads) Jo-Ann Stores; (iridescent glitter glue) Ranger Industries *Rub-ons:* (sentiment, candles) *Fibers:* (pink dotted ribbon) American Crafts *Tool:* (decorative-edge scissors) **Finished size: 5½" x 4¼"**

Summertime
Designer: Betsy Veldman

SUPPLIES: *Cardstock:* (Ocean Tides, Pure Poppy, Aqua Mist, white) Papertrey Ink *Patterned paper:* (jelly balls from Hello Sunshine pad) Cosmo Cricket; (Straw from Urban Prairie collection) BasicGrey *Clear stamps:* (ice cream cone, tiny heart from Love Songs set) Papertrey Ink *Specialty ink:* (Summer Sunrise, Ripe Avocado, Berry Sorbet, Ocean Tides, Pure Poppy,

Lemon Tart hybrid) Papertrey Ink *Accents:* (journaling tag) Papertrey Ink; (red chipboard circle) Scenic Route *Fibers:* (pink stitched ribbon) Papertrey Ink *Adhesive:* (foam tape) *Dies:* (label, scalloped circle) Provo Craft *Tools:* (die cut machine, decorative-edge scissors) Provo Craft **Finished size: 4¼" x 5½"**

Birthday Buttons
Designer: Alisa Bangerter

SUPPLIES: *Cardstock:* (gray, hot pink, pink, white) *Clear stamp:* (happy birthday from Post Card Sentiments set) My Sentiments Exactly! *Dye ink:* (Weathered Wood) Ranger Industries *Accents:* (assorted buttons) Making Memories, Jesse James & Co. *Fibers:* (white organza ribbon) Offray; (white floss) **Finished size: 5½" square**

Page 97
Hi There Cherries
Designer: Maren Benedict

SUPPLIES: *Cardstock:* (Chocolate, Real Red, white) Stampin' Up! *Patterned paper:* (Berries from Hello Sunshine pad) Cosmo Cricket *Vellum; Rubber stamps:* (cherries, hi there from Mix Up of Cuteness set) Unity Stamp Co. *Color medium:* (assorted markers) Copic Marker *Accent:* (red rhinestone) My Mind's Eye *Fibers:* (red gingham ribbon) Offray *Adhesive:* (foam tape) *Dies:* (scalloped rectangles) Spellbinders *Tool:* (die cut machine) Spellbinders **Finished size: 4¼" square**

Kiss & Make Up
Designer: Kim Kesti

SUPPLIES: *Cardstock:* (Natural, Raven, Berry) Bazzill Basics Paper *Patterned paper:* (Norms News from Hometown collection) October Afternoon; (Zebra from Hot Mama collection) Glitz Design *Color medium:* (hot pink marker) *Rub-on:* (flowers with rhinestones) BasicGrey *Sticker:* (pink kiss badge) American Crafts *Font:* (Corbel) www.fonts.com *Adhesive:* (foam tape) *Tools:* (2" circle punch, 2½" scalloped circle punch, decorative-edge scissors) **Finished size: 3" x 4"**

Almost Human
Designer: Alicia Thelin

SUPPLIES: All supplies from Stampin' Up! unless otherwise noted. *Cardstock:* (Real Red, Not Quite Navy, So Saffron, Whisper White, kraft) *Clear stamp:* (rabbit with sentiment from Humorous Birthday set) Inkadinkado *Dye ink:* (Not Quite Navy) *Fibers:* (white polka dot ribbon) Michaels *Adhesive:* (foam tape) *Tool:* (spiral binding punch) **Finished size: 4¼" x 5½"**

Page 98
Special Delivery
Designer: Debbie Olson

SUPPLIES: *Cardstock:* (Poison Ivory) Arjo Wiggins *Patterned paper:* (Mischievous Max, Jumping Jack from Lil' Man collection) Cosmo Cricket *Rubber stamp:* (sentiment oval from Baby Stamp Ensemble set) JustRite *Clear stamp:* (special delivery from Favor It Baby set) Papertrey Ink *Dye ink:* (Antique Linen) Ranger Industries *Pigment ink:* (Turquoise Gem) Tsukineko *Accents:* (white buttons) Buttons Galore & More *Fibers:* (striped ribbon) Cosmo Cricket; (white twine) Coats & Clark *Adhesive:* (foam tape) *Dies:* (oval frame, tag, bracket label) Spellbinders *Tools:* (lattice punch) Martha Stewart; (die cut/embossing machine) Spellbinders; (corner rounder punch) Marvy Uchida *Other:* (chipboard, photo) **Finished size: 5½" x 4¼"**

Gingham Get Well
Designer: Rae Barthel

SUPPLIES: *Cardstock:* (white) Bazzill Basics Paper *Patterned paper:* (red branch, green grid from Friendly Forest collection) Colorbok *Chalk ink:* (Charcoal) Clearsnap *Accents:* (green rhinestones) Darice *Stickers:* (Whistle Stop alphabet) American Crafts *Fibers:* (yellow gingham ribbon) Michaels **Finished size: 7" x 4"**

Believe in Yourself
Designer: Julie Campbell

SUPPLIES: *Cardstock:* (Island Mist Dark, Birchtone Dark) Prism; (Serape from Flower Power collection) Core'dinations *Patterned paper:* (Jack's Beanstalk from Woodland Whimsy collection) Sassafras Lass *Rubber stamp:* (tree from Tiny Trinity set) Unity Stamp Co. *Watermark ink:* Tsukineko *Embossing powder:* (white) Stampendous! *Accent:* (yellow heart stick pin) Fancy Pants Designs *Rub-on:* (believe in yourself) Melissa Frances *Fibers:* (white lace ribbon) The Paper Studio; (hemp twine) *Adhesive:* (foam tape) *Die:* (oval) Spellbinders *Tool:* (die cut/embossing machine) Spellbinders *Other:* (cardboard) **Finished size: 4¼" x 5½"**

Page 99
Baby Butterflies
Designer: Maren Benedict

SUPPLIES: *Cardstock:* (Sweet Blush) Papertrey Ink *Patterned paper:* (Wednesday from Girl Friday collection) Cosmo Cricket *Accents:* (yellow chipboard butterflies, baby tag) Cosmo Cricket; (pink rhinestones) My Mind's Eye *Fibers:* (pink scalloped trim, yellow twill ribbon) Cosmo Cricket *Tool:* (corner rounder punch) Creative Memories **Finished size: 5½" x 4¼"**

September

Page 100
Thank You Very Much
Designer: Wendy Sue Anderson

SUPPLIES: *Cardstock:* (white) *Patterned paper:* (Twees, Together, Nesting from So Tweet collection) Pebbles Inc. *Accents:* (assorted buttons) Making Memories *Rub-on:* (thank you very much) American Crafts *Sticker:* (bubble tree) Pebbles Inc. *Adhesive:* (foam tape) *Template:* (Tiny Bubbles embossing) Provo Craft *Tool:* (embossing machine) Provo Craft **Finished size: 5" square**

Page 101
Back to School Apple
Designer: Charity Hassel

SUPPLIES: *Patterned paper:* (A is for Apple, Sweet Pea Blossoms from Autumn Afternoon collection) Scribble Scrabble; (Lessons from Jacks World collection) Cosmo Cricket *Accents:* (die cut trim, flocked chipboard apple) Scribble Scrabble; (green button) Autumn Leaves *Rub-ons:* (school sentiment) American Crafts; (Simply Sweet alphabet) Doodlebug Design *Fibers:* (red ribbon, green floss) **Finished size: 4½" x 6"**

School Days
Designer: Danielle Flanders

SUPPLIES: *Cardstock:* (red) *Patterned paper:* (Margaret, Alice) Melissa Frances *Paint:* (white) Delta *Accents:* (glitter chipboard alphabet negative) Melissa Frances; (yellow button, red heart button) *Rub-on:* (school days) Melissa Frances *Stickers:* (blue floral border, polka dot date square) Melissa Frances *Fibers:* (twine, red polka dot ribbon) **Finished size: 4¾" x 6½"**

Touch Lives Forever
Designer: Kimberly Crawford

SUPPLIES: *Cardstock:* (True Black, white) Papertrey Ink; (yellow) Die Cuts With a View *Patterned paper:* (Glitter Apples from Grade School collection) Die Cuts With a View *Clear stamp:* (teacher sentiment from Teacher's Apple set) Papertrey Ink *Specialty ink:* (New Canvas hybrid) Stewart Superior Corp. *Accents:* (red buttons) BasicGrey *Fibers:* (red ribbon) Papertrey Ink *Adhesive:* (foam tape) *Dies:* (square labels) Spellbinders *Tool:* (die cut machine) Spellbinders **Finished size: 4¼" x 5½"**

Page 102
Much Appreciated
Designer: Ashley C. Newell

SUPPLIES: *Cardstock:* (Aqua Mist, white) Papertrey Ink; (Chocolate Chip) Stampin' Up!; (red) *Clear stamps:* (much appreciated, flower solid, flower outline, dot from Garden of Life set) Papertrey Ink *Dye ink:* (Cranberry) Close To My Heart; (Chocolate Chip) Stampin' Up! *Specialty ink:* (Aqua Mist hybrid) Papertrey Ink *Accent:* (red brad) Close To My Heart *Fibers:* (red ribbon) Papertrey Ink *Adhesive:* (foam tape) *Die:* (circle) Spellbinders *Tool:* (die cut/embossing machine) Provo Craft **Finished size: 3¾" diameter**

Hi Flower
Designer: Teri Anderson

SUPPLIES: *Cardstock:* (white) Die Cuts With a View; (textured white) WorldWin *Patterned paper:* (Animal Friends from Jacks World collection) Cosmo Cricket *Accents:* (flower die cut) Crate Paper; (orange tag) Creative Café *Dies:* (Rockstar alphabet) QuicKutz *Tools:* (die cut machine) QuicKutz; (corner rounder punch) Creative Memories **Finished size: 3½" x 5½"**

So Stylish
Designer: Kristen Swain

SUPPLIES: *Cardstock:* (kraft, white, Espresso) The Paper Company *Patterned paper:* (Orange Dot from Bailey collection, Black Check from Elsie's Kitchen collection, Rose Etching from Maime collection) Anna Griffin *Accents:* (flower die cuts) Anna Griffin; (orange brads) Making Memories; (white pearls) Michaels *Rub-ons:* (so stylish circle) Anna Griffin *Fibers:* (twine) *Adhesive:* (foam tape) 3M *Tool:* (decorative-edge scissors) Provo Craft **Finished size: 5" x 5¼"**

Page 103
Heartfelt Flag
Designer: Charlene Austin

SUPPLIES: *Cardstock:* (kraft, white) Papertrey Ink; (blue, red) Stampin' Up! *Dye ink:* (Walnut Stain) Ranger Industries *Rub-ons:* (happy, Ned Jr. alphabet) American Crafts *Die:* (heart) Spellbinders *Tools:* (die cut/embossing machine) Spellbinders; (star punch) Marvy Uchida **Finished size: 5" square**

Read, Read, Read
Designer: Kim Moreno

SUPPLIES: *Cardstock:* (dark gray) Core'dinations *Patterned paper:* (Zoology, Wishes from Menagerie collection) Dream Street Papers *Accent:* (orange button) Sassafras Lass *Stickers:* (Lollipop Shoppe alphabet) BasicGrey; (Holly Doodle alphabet) Pink Paislee; (red alphabet) *Fibers:* (white string) Coats & Clark *Tools:* (doily border punch) Martha Stewart; (dotted scallops border punch) Fiskars; (corner rounder punch) Creative Memories; (⅛" circle punch) **Finished size: 4¾" x 4½"**

Happy Grandparents Day
Designer: Wendy Sue Anderson

SUPPLIES: *Cardstock:* (brown, white, green, light blue) *Patterned paper:* (Ella Animals from Animal Crackers collection) Making Memories *Color medium:* (black pen) American Crafts *Accents:* (blue, green buttons) Autumn Leaves *Fibers:* (hemp twine, black/tan gingham ribbon) *Tool:* (scalloped border punch) Fiskars **Finished size: 4" x 8½"**

Page 104
Miss You Butterflies
Designer: Rae Barthel

SUPPLIES: *Cardstock:* (white) Hobby Lobby *Patterned paper:* (Winsome, Citrus, Clementine, Smoke from Ambrosia collection) BasicGrey *Accents:* (chipboard heart buttons, corner button) Colorbok *Stickers:* (scalloped border, Ambrosia alphabet) BasicGrey *Fibers:* (gray printed ribbon) American Crafts; (orange raffia) Hobby Lobby *Adhesive:* (foam tape) **Finished size: 6" square**

America the Beautiful
Designer: Julie Campbell

SUPPLIES: *Cardstock:* (kraft) *Patterned paper:* (Orchard from Lemon Grass collection) Crate Paper; (Title Strips from Splendid collection) Fancy Pants Designs *Rubber stamp:* (sentiment from America the Beautiful set) Cornish Heritage Farms *Specialty ink:* (Pure Poppy hybrid) Papertrey Ink *Color medium:* (Stardust gel pen) Sakura *Accents:* (blue, red rhinestones) K&Company; (large brass eyelets) Stampin' Up! *Adhesive:* (foam tape) *Dies:* (circles, star) Spellbinders *Tool:* (die cut machine) Provo Craft *Other:* (denim fabric) **Finished size: 5" square**

Dots & Flowers Thank You
Designer: Heidi Van Laar

SUPPLIES: *Cardstock:* (white) Georgia-Pacific *Patterned paper:* (Full Moon Dot from Lotus Faded China collection) K&Company; (yellow swirls from Modern Milan stack) Me & My Big Ideas *Accents:* (cardstock flower die cut) K&Company; (dark gray, light gray, yellow flowers) Prima; (large gray brad) Eyelet Outlet *Stickers:* (yellow paper border) K&Company; (Cinnamon Stick alphabet) Cloud 9 Design *Fibers:* (yellow ribbon, white floss) *Adhesive:* (foam tape) **Finished size: 7" x 5"**

Page 105
Classy
Designer: Susan R. Opel

SUPPLIES: *Cardstock:* (red, silver) WorldWin; (white, black) Bazzill Basics Paper *Accents:* (red rhinestones) The Paper Studio *Stickers:* (JFK alphabet) American Crafts **Finished size: 7" x 5"**

Thanks Apples
Designer: Dawn McVey

SUPPLIES: *Cardstock:* (kraft, Dark Chocolate, Vintage Cream) Papertrey Ink *Clear stamps:* (apple outline, apple patterns, thank you from Teacher's Apple set) Papertrey Ink *Specialty ink:* (Pure Poppy, Dark Chocolate hybrid) Papertrey Ink *Accents:* (red rhinestones) Hero Arts *Fibers:* (red stitched ribbon) Papertrey Ink *Adhesive:* (foam tape) *Tools:* (rounded rectangle punch, scalloped edge punch) Stampin' Up! **Finished size: 5½" x 4¼"**

You Are a Peach
Designer: Dawn McVey

SUPPLIES: *Cardstock:* (Dark Chocolate, Ripe Avocado, Raspberry Fizz, Summer Sunrise, white) Papertrey Ink *Clear stamps:* (Fresh Alphabet; grid, flower from Guide Lines set) Papertrey Ink *Watermark ink:* Tsukineko *Specialty ink:* (Summer Sunrise hybrid) Papertrey Ink *Embossing powder:* (white) Papertrey Ink *Color medium:* (Chocolate Chip marker) Stampin' Up! *Accent:* (pink rhinestone) Hero Arts *Fibers:* (yellow ribbon) Papertrey Ink *Adhesive:* (foam tape) *Tools:* (scalloped oval punch) Marvy Uchida; (butterfly punch) Martha Stewart Crafts; (corner rounder punch, slit punch) Stampin' Up! **Finished size: 4¼" x 5½"**

Page 106
Happy Anniversary
Designer: Ashley C. Newell

SUPPLIES: *Cardstock:* (black) American Crafts; (So Saffron) Stampin' Up!; (Pure Poppy, Spring Moss) Papertrey Ink *Clear stamps:* (happy, anniversary, small heart, swirled heart from Heart Prints set) Papertrey Ink *Dye ink:* (Basic Black) Stampin' Up! *Watermark ink:* Tsukineko *Embossing powder:* (clear) *Accents:* (green button) SEI; (yellow felt flower) American Crafts *Sticker:* (rhinestone frame) Heidi Swapp *Fibers:* (green floss) Bazzill Basics Paper; (white ribbon) *Adhesive:* (foam tape) *Template:* (Swiss Dots embossing) Provo Craft *Die:* (scalloped square) Spellbinders *Tool:* (die cut/embossing machine) Spellbinders **Finished size: 4¼" x 5¾"**

Birthday Rainbow
Designer: Heidi Van Laar

SUPPLIES: *Cardstock:* (Hazard, Teal) Bazzill Basics Paper; (white) *Patterned paper:* (Fruit Slice Land from Sunshine Lollipop collection, Hooty from Pocket Full of Rosies collection) Sassafras Lass *Clear stamp:* (happy birthday from Collaged Expressions set) Inkadinkado *Chalk ink:* (Azurite) Clearsnap *Accent:* (clear button) Autumn Leaves *Fibers:* (pink polka dot ribbon) Michaels; (dark pink, light pink, white, orange floss) DMC *Adhesive:* (foam tape) *Tools:* (corner rounder punch, ¾" circle punch) EK Success **Finished size: 4½" x 7"**

Shabby Birthday
Designer: Beatriz Jennings

SUPPLIES: *Cardstock:* (pink) Bazzill Basics Paper *Patterned paper:* (Star Bright Dotty Dude, Day Dream Betty Confetti from Just Dreamy collection) My Mind's Eye *Dye ink:* (Old Paper) Ranger Industries *Accents:* (blue glitter brad) Making Memories; (blue, pink buttons; white flower) *Rub-on:* (happy birthday) Melissa Frances *Sticker:* (chipboard circle) Sandylion *Fibers:* (red rickrack, white ribbon, pink floss) **Finished size: 3¾" x 6"**

Page 107
Yo Matey
Designer: Kim Hughes

SUPPLIES: *Cardstock:* (Snow) Bazzill Basics Paper *Patterned paper:* (Honey from Granola collection) BasicGrey *Rubber stamps:* (parrot, skull, diamond, arrgh, yo matey from Ahoy Matey–Pirates set) Cornish Heritage Farms *Dye ink:* (Nightfall, Palm Grove) Storage Units, Ink *Color medium:* (black marker) Sakura *Accent:* (white button) Autumn Leaves *Fibers:* (twine) Creative Impressions; (netting trim) Beaux Regards *Adhesive:* (foam tape) Therm O Web *Tool:* (1³⁄₈" circle punch) Marvy Uchida **Finished size: 4½" x 5"**

5th Birthday
Designer: Shanna Vineyard

SUPPLIES: All supplies from BoBunny Press unless otherwise noted. *Cardstock:* (white) Bazzill Basics Paper *Patterned paper:* (Wasabi Dot from Double Dot collection; Poems, Stripe from It's My Party collection) *Color medium:* (black marker) no source *Accent:* (white chipboard number) *Rub-on:* (happy happy birthday) *Fibers:* (black polka dot ribbon) *Adhesive:* (foam tape) no source *Template:* (circle) no source **Finished size: 6½" x 5"**

Choo Choo
Designer: Maren Benedict

SUPPLIES: *Cardstock:* (white, Pure Poppy) Papertrey Ink *Patterned paper:* (Playtime from Jacks World collection) Cosmo Cricket *Rubber stamps:* (choo choo, train from Things That Go set) Lizzie Anne Designs *Dye ink:* (Tuxedo Black) Tsukineko *Color medium:* (assorted markers) *Accent:* (white chipboard tag) American Crafts *Fibers:* (red ribbon) Papertrey Ink *Adhesive:* (foam tape) *Tool:* (1¼" circle punch) Stampin' Up! **Finished size: 5" square**

Page 108
Autumn
Designer: Beatriz Jennings

SUPPLIES: *Patterned paper:* (Falling from Grateful collection) KI Memories; (Tree House from Spring Fling collection) Pink Paislee *Specialty paper:* (Flower Child Socialite die cut from Pop Culture collection) KI Memories *Dye ink:* (Old Paper) Ranger Industries *Accents:* (green printed flower) Prima; (orange glitter button) *Rub-on:* (autumn) Reminisce *Fibers:* (eyelet ribbon) Making Memories; (hemp twine) *Tool:* (corner rounder punch) **Finished size: 4" x 6"**

Hi Fall
Designer: Laura Williams

SUPPLIES: *Cardstock:* (Sunflower, Cranberry) Close To My Heart; (orange) Bazzill Basics Paper *Patterned paper:* (Pots A Plenty from Story of a Seed collection) Dream Street Papers *Rubber stamps:* (trees from Tiny Giggle Grove set) Unity Stamp Co. *Dye ink:* (Chocolate) Close To My Heart *Stickers:* (Chaos & Confusion alphabet) Three Bugs in a Rug *Adhesive:* (foam tape) *Tools:* (¹⁄₈" circle punch, ¹⁄₁₆" circle punch) **Finished size: 9¼" x 4"**

Bling Flowers With Gratitude
Designer: Gretchen Clark

SUPPLIES: All supplies from Stampin' Up! unless otherwise noted. *Cardstock:* (Whisper White, Groovy Guava, Chocolate Chip) *Clear stamps:* (flower solids, flower outlines, stem, sentiment from Spiral Bouquet

set) Papertrey Ink *Dye ink:* (Chocolate Chip, Blush Blossom, Groovy Guava, Mellow Moss) *Accent:* (iridescent glitter glue) Ranger Industries *Fibers:* (brown ribbon) *Adhesive:* (foam tape) **Finished size: 5½" x 4¼"**

Page 109
Oh Deer
Designer: Melissa Phillips

SUPPLIES: *Cardstock:* (Spring Moss, white) Papertrey Ink *Patterned paper:* (Adirondack, Beach Grass from Poppy collection) SEI; (Navy Tiny Dot from Trendy collection) Jenni Bowlin Studio *Clear stamps:* (deer, grass, sentiment from Forest Friends set) Papertrey Ink *Specialty ink:* (Pure Poppy, Spring Moss hybrid) Papertrey Ink *Paint:* (off-white) Delta *Accents:* (chipboard bookplate) Maya Road; (white glitter, red rhinestone) Doodlebug Design; (cream button) Papertrey Ink; (red glitter glue) Ranger Industries *Sticker:* (aqua paper ribbon) K&Company *Fibers:* (aqua ribbon) Papertrey Ink; (twine) *Template:* (Forest Branches embossing) Provo Craft *Tools:* (butterfly punch) Martha Stewart Crafts; (embossing machine, decorative-edge scissors) Provo Craft; (corner rounder punch) **Finished size: 5¼" x 4"**

Love You Forever
Designer: Dawn McVey

SUPPLIES: *Cardstock:* (Vintage Cream, Pure Poppy) Papertrey Ink *Clear stamps:* (grid, medallions from Guide Lines set, love you forever from Heart Prints set) Papertrey Ink *Dye ink:* (Tea Dye) Ranger Industries *Pigment ink:* (Vintage Cream) Papertrey Ink *Specialty ink:* (Pure Poppy hybrid) Papertrey Ink *Fibers:* (red ribbon) Papertrey Ink *Adhesive:* (foam tape) *Die:* (bird) Stampin' Up! *Tool:* (die cut machine) *Other:* (cork) **Finished size: 4¼" x 5½"**

Blooming Flower
Designer: Anabelle O'Malley

SUPPLIES: *Cardstock:* (white) Bazzill Basics Paper *Accents:* (fabric flower) Prima; (clear rhinestones) Heidi Swapp; (tag) Avery; *Rub-ons:* (flower, thank you) Making Memories *Fibers:* (red striped ribbon) MJ Trimming; (white/red ribbon) Caramelos *Tools:* (corner rounder punch) EK Success; (dotted scalloped border punch) Fiskars *Other:* (chipboard die cut packaging) Prima **Finished size: 4" x 6½"**

Page 110
With Sympathy Branches
Designer: Dawn McVey

SUPPLIES: *Cardstock:* (Gold Shimmer, Spring Moss, Ripe Avocado, Dark Chocolate, Vintage Cream) Papertrey Ink *Clear stamps:* (branch, leaves from Out on a Limb Revised set; sentiment from Paper Tray set) Papertrey Ink *Pigment ink:* (Gold) Tsukineko *Specialty ink:* (Dark Chocolate, Spring Moss, Ripe Avocado hybrid) Papertrey Ink *Accents:* (clear rhinestones) Mark Richards *Fibers:* (green ribbon) Papertrey Ink *Adhesive:* (foam tape) *Tool:* (slit punch) Stampin' Up! **Finished size: 4¼" x 5½"**

Leafy Birthday
Designer: Betsy Veldman

SUPPLIES: *Cardstock:* (green) Bazzill Basics Paper; (red) Prism *Patterned paper:* (Family Tree, Lineage from Family Tree collection) Bella Blvd *Accent:* (green button) BasicGrey *Rub-on:* (happy birthday) Crate Paper *Sticker:* (scalloped circle) Bella Blvd *Fibers:* (yellow polka dot ribbon) Papertrey Ink; (pink floss) DMC *Adhesive:* (foam tape) *Other:* (brown felt) **Finished size: 4¼" x 5½"**

Wishing You Well
Designer: Ashley C. Newell

SUPPLIES: *Cardstock:* (Vintage Cream, Ocean Tides) Papertrey Ink *Rubber stamp:* (grass from Inspired by Nature set) Stampin' Up! *Clear stamps:* (bird from Anniversary Birds set, wishing you well from Wonderful Wishes set) Verve Stamps *Chalk ink:* (Chestnut Roan) Clearsnap *Accents:* (green pearls) Queen & Co. *Fibers:* (brown ribbon) Michaels *Adhesive:* (foam tape) *Dies:* (scalloped oval, oval) Spellbinders *Tool:* (die cut/embossing machine) Provo Craft **Finished size: 4 ¼" x 5½"**

October
Page 111
Eek
Designer: Wendy Sue Anderson

SUPPLIES: *Cardstock:* (white) *Patterned paper:* (Glitter Crow from Spellbound collection) Making Memories; (Skullies from Hocus Pocus collection) Doodlebug Design *Dye ink:* (black) Stewart Superior Corp. *Accent:* (orange button) *Stickers:* (glitter foam stars, witch, eek) Making Memories *Fibers:* (orange striped ribbon) *Template:* (Swiss Dots embossing) Provo Craft *Tools:* (embossing machine) Provo Craft; (scalloped border punch) Fiskars **Finished size: 5½" x 4¼"**

Page 112
Birthday Countdown
Designer: Mary MacAskill

SUPPLIES: *Cardstock:* (kraft) Bazzill Basics Paper *Accents:* (green chipboard label, green plastic label) American Crafts; (clear rhinestones) Hero Arts *Rub-ons:* (sentiment, numbers) American Crafts **Finished size: 4½" x 3½"**

Butterfly Thanks
Designer: Mary MacAskill

SUPPLIES: *Cardstock:* (white, kraft, burgundy) Bazzill Basics Paper *Patterned paper:* (Blush Dot from Double Dot collection) BoBunny Press; (flowers ledger from Noteworthy collection notebook) Making Memories *Rubber stamp:* (Heart Winged Butterfly) Hero Arts *Clear stamps:* (sentiment from Frames and Messages set) Hero Arts; (flourish from It's All About... Hearts set) Banana Frog *Pigment ink:* (Pinecone) Tsukineko *Watermark ink:* Tsukineko *Color medium:* (colored pencils) Crayola *Accents:* (pewter eyelet) We R Memory Keepers; (brown buttons) *Fibers:* (pink ribbon) American Crafts; (hemp twine) *Adhesive:* (foam tape) *Tools:* (corner rounder punch) Marvy Uchida; (¹⁄₈" circle punch) **Finished size: 4¼" x 5½"**

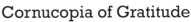

World Card Making Day
Designer: Kim Kesti

SUPPLIES: *Cardstock:* (white, Mexican Poppy, Festive, Bazzill Green, Dragonfly, Nutmeg, Blue Oasis) Bazzill Basics Paper *Specialty paper:* (photo paper) *Accent:* (silver staple) *Digital element:* (logo) www.PaperCraftsMag.com *Fibers:* (blue ribbon) Making Memories *Software:* (photo editing) *Adhesive:* (foam tape) *Tool:* (2" scalloped square punch) Marvy Uchida **Finished size: 4" x 6"**

Page 113
Earthy Thank You
Designer: Kimberly Crawford

SUPPLIES: *Cardstock:* (kraft, Ocean Tides, Ripe Avocado) Papertrey Ink *Rubber stamp:* (Four Leaf Grid) Hero Arts *Clear stamps:* (tiny circle, vines, woodgrain, flowers from Hello Circles set, sentiment from Thank You Messages set) Hero Arts *Watermark ink:* Tsukineko *Specialty ink:* (Dark Chocolate, Ripe Avocado hybrid) Papertrey Ink *Accents:* (brown buttons) BasicGrey; (wood buttons) *Fibers:* (white twine) **Finished size: 5½" x 4¼"**

Reasons to Smile
Designer: Alicia Thelin

SUPPLIES: All supplies from Stampin' Up! unless otherwise noted. *Cardstock:* (white, Kiwi Kiss, Bermuda Bay) *Rubber stamp:* (butterfly, sentiment from Reasons to Smile set) *Dye ink:* (Kiwi Kiss) *Pigment ink:* (Whisper White) *Embossing powder:* (white) *Accent:* (teal button) no source *Fibers:* (teal polka dot ribbon) *Adhesive:* (foam tape) *Tools:* (corner rounder punch, 1¾" circle punch) **Finished size: 5½" x 4¼"**

Sustaining Hope
Designer: Debbie Olson

SUPPLIES: *Cardstock:* (Gold Shimmer, Vintage Cream) Papertrey Ink *Clear stamps:* (sentiment, vines from With Sympathy set) Papertrey Ink *Watermark ink:* Tsukineko *Embossing powder:* (Gold) Papertrey Ink *Paint:* (gold paint pen) *Accents:* (gold stick pin, white bead) Blue Moon Beads *Fibers:* (gold ribbon) Papertrey Ink *Adhesive:* (foam tape) *Tools:* (⅛" circle punch, scoring tool) **Finished size: 4¼" x 5½"**

Page 114
What's Buggin' You?
Designer: Susan R. Opel

SUPPLIES: *Cardstock:* (black) American Crafts; (green) Bazzill Basics Paper; (yellow) Prism *Embossing powder:* (clear) Clearsnap *Color medium:* (embossing marker) EK Success *Accents:* (yellow rhinestones) Hobby Lobby; (chipboard glitter bug) Me & My Big Ideas *Fibers:* (black gingham ribbon) Michaels *Fonts:* (Antigoni) www.searchfreefonts.com; (Century Gothic) Microsoft **Finished size: 6½" x 5"**

Sparkle Thank You
Designer: Rae Barthel

SUPPLIES: *Cardstock:* (white, white Swiss dots embossed) Bazzill Basics Paper; (black) Hobby Lobby *Patterned paper:* (polka dots from Black & White pad) Me & My Big Ideas *Accents:* (black circles border) Making Memories; (large clear rhinestones) Darice; (small clear rhinestones) Hobby Lobby *Rub-on:* (thank you circle) Scenic Route *Adhesive:* (foam tape) *Tools:* (assorted circle punches) EK Success **Finished size: 4¼" x 5½"**

Shine!
Designer: Roree Rumph

SUPPLIES: *Cardstock:* (white, yellow) *Patterned paper:* (Bernice, Phyllis, Stella from the Retro Metro collection) Tinkering Ink *Accents:* (chipboard star) Li'l Davis Designs; (large green brad) Heidi Swapp; (purple, blue, orange brads) Making Memories *Rub-ons:* (Simply Sweet alphabet) Doodlebug Design *Fibers:* (black ribbon) Pebbles Inc.; (blue floss) DMC *Adhesive:* (foam tape) *Tool:* (corner rounder punch) EK Success **Finished size: 4" x 6"**

Page 115
Love Me
Designer: Maren Benedict

SUPPLIES: *Cardstock:* (white) Papertrey Ink *Patterned paper:* (Jack from Night Light collection) October Afternoon *Rubber stamp:* (sentiment from Love Etc. set) Unity Stamp Co. *Dye ink:* (black) Tsukineko *Color medium:* (red marker) Copic Marker *Accents:* (clear rhinestone heart) Me & My Big Ideas; (iridescent glitter glue) Ranger Industries *Fibers:* (red ribbon) Michaels *Tool:* (corner rounder punch) Creative Memories **Finished size: 3¾" x 4¼"**

Retro Thank You
Designer: Rae Barthel

SUPPLIES: *Cardstock:* (brown) Hobby Lobby; (white) Bazzill Basics Paper *Patterned paper:* (Radical from Offbeat collection) BasicGrey *Clear stamp:* (thank you) Studio G *Chalk ink:* (Chestnut Roan) Clearsnap *Accents:* (green rhinestones) Hobby Lobby *Tools:* (oval punch) Marvy Uchida; (corner rounder punch) EK Success **Finished size: 4¼" x 5½"**

Owl Thank You
Designer: Daniela Dobson

SUPPLIES: *Cardstock:* (black) Frances Meyer; (white) OfficeMax *Patterned paper:* (Unpredictable from Offbeat collection) BasicGrey *Rubber stamp:* (branch from AI: Branches set) Hero Arts *Clear stamps:* (leafy branch, thank you from Owl set) Sandylion *Pigment ink:* (Olive) Clearsnap *Solvent ink:* (Jet Black) Tsukineko *Chalk ink:* (Creamy Brown) Clearsnap *Color medium:* (yellow pencil) Prismacolor *Accents:* (black, yellow, red buttons) BasicGrey; (journaling card) BoBunny Press *Rub-on:* (owl) Maya Road *Fibers:* (yellow floss) DMC *Adhesive:* (foam tape) **Finished size: 6" x 4"**

Page 116
Birthday Star
Designer: Mary MacAskill

SUPPLIES: *Cardstock:* (white, kraft, orange) Bazzill Basics Paper *Patterned paper:* ('Allo from Everyday collection) American Crafts *Vellum:* The Paper Company *Clear stamps:* (stars from Super Stars set, flourish from It's All About…Circles set) Banana Frog *Solvent ink:* (Cotton White) Tsukineko *Watermark ink:* Tsukineko *Embossing powder:* (clear) Stampendous! *Accents:* (chipboard glitter star) Making Memories; (orange buttons) The Paper Studio *Rub-on:* (sentiment) American Crafts *Fibers:* (purple star ribbon) American Crafts; (orange floss) *Tools:* (circle cutter) Creative Memories; (border punch) Fiskars; (corner rounder punch) Marvy Uchida **Finished size: 5½" x 4¼"**

Cornucopia of Gratitude
Designer: Alice Golden

SUPPLIES: *Cardstock:* (natural) Bazzill Basics Paper; (Razzleberry Medium) Prism *Patterned paper:* (gold frames from Cornucopia pad) Me & My Big Ideas *Clear stamp:* (sentiment from First Fruits set) Papertrey Ink *Pigment ink:* (Raspberry) Tsukineko; (Gold) Tsukineko *Color medium:* (sand, sepia markers) Copic Marker *Sticker:* (cornucopia) Me & My Big Ideas *Fibers:* (plum ribbon) American Crafts; (brown ribbon) Strano Designs *Adhesive:* (foam tape) Therm O Web *Die:* (label) Spellbinders *Tool:* (die cut/embossing machine) Spellbinders **Finished size: 4¾" x 7½"**

Pineapple Thanks
Designer: Julie Masse

SUPPLIES: *Cardstock:* (Very Vanilla, Kiwi Kiss) Stampin' Up! *Patterned paper:* (Poppy Garden from Daydream collection) October Afternoon *Clear stamps:* (pineapple from 3 Step Aloha! set, ½ Pint Playful Alphabet Buddy set) Kitchen Sink Stamps *Dye ink:* (Cantaloupe, Potter's Clay, Pear Tart) Tsukineko; (Kiwi Kiss) Stampin' Up! *Fibers:* (green/white ribbon) Stampin' Up! *Adhesive:* (foam tape) *Dies:* (square, scalloped square) Spellbinders *Tools:* (slot punch) Stampin' Up!; (die cut machine) Spellbinders **Finished size: 4¼" square**

Page 117
Delicate Thank You
Designer: Sherry Wright

SUPPLIES: *Cardstock:* (pink, white) Bazzill Basics Paper *Patterned paper:* (Full Moon Dot, Lacework from Lotus Tea Box collection) K&Company; (blue distressed) *Chalk ink:* (blue) Clearsnap *Accents:* (pink rhinestones) Queen & Co.; (butterfly die cut) K&Company *Rub-ons:* (swirl) Autumn Leaves; (sentiment, frame) **Finished size: 5¼" square**

Strength
Designer: Melissa Phillips

SUPPLIES: *Cardstock:* (white, green) Bazzill Basics Paper *Patterned paper:* (Strong, Cheerful) Melissa Frances *Dye ink:* (Old Paper) Ranger Industries *Paint:* (off-white) Delta *Accents:* (pink crocheted flowers) Offray; (pink button) Creative Café; (white glitter) Doodlebug Design; (chipboard wings) Maya Road *Stickers:* (strength, sentiment) Melissa Frances *Fibers:* (pink rickrack) Offray; (pink ribbon, white string) *Tools:* (scalloped border punch) Martha Stewart Crafts; (corner rounder punch) **Finished size: 6½" x 3¾"**

Chocolate Cupcake Day
Designer: Wendy Sue Anderson

SUPPLIES: *Cardstock:* (white) *Patterned paper:* (Puppy Play from Park Buddies collection) SEI; (Faye Needleworth from Crafts Fair collection, Passing Notes from Teen collection) American Crafts *Clear stamps:* (cupcake liner, frosting from Cupcake Sprinkles set) Close To My Heart *Watermark ink:* Tsukineko *Chalk ink:* (Chestnut Roan) Clearsnap *Embossing powder:* (white) Ranger Industries *Accents:* (flower sequins) Doodlebug Design; (pink chipboard heart) Heidi Swapp; (metal tag rim) Making Memories; (pink seed beads) *Fibers:* (yellow polka dot ribbon) BoBunny Press; (brown ribbon) American Crafts *Font:* (SS Mono) Simple Scrapbooks *Software:* (word processing) Microsoft *Adhesive:* (foam tape) *Tools:* (scalloped border punch) Fiskars; (tag maker) Making Memories **Finished size: 4" x 5½"**

Page 118
Chocolate Cake Birthday
Designer: Tanis Giesbrecht

SUPPLIES: *Cardstock:* (French Roast) Core'dinations; (white) Bazzill Basics Paper *Patterned paper:* (Birthday Boy Dots, Plaid from Wild Asparagus collection) My Mind's Eye *Rubber stamps:* (happy birthday banner, cake from Whimsical Birthday set) Unity Stamp Co. *Dye ink:* (Tuxedo Black) Tsukineko *Color medium:* (teal, brown markers) BIC *Fibers:* (brown ribbon) **Finished size: 5½" x 4¼"**

Leaf Gratitude
Designer: Ashley C. Newell

SUPPLIES: *Cardstock:* (Kiwi Kiss, Bravo Burgundy) Stampin' Up!; (Dark Chocolate, Ripe Avocado) Papertrey Ink *Patterned paper:* (polka dot from Dark Chocolate Remix collection) Papertrey Ink *Clear stamp:* (sentiment from First Fruits set) Papertrey Ink *Dye ink:* (Chocolate Chip) Stampin' Up! *Accent:* (felt leaf) World Market *Fibers:* (green ribbon) Papertrey Ink *Adhesive:* (foam tape) Stampin' Up! **Finished size: 4¼" x 5½"**

Striped Thank You
Designer: Roree Rumph

SUPPLIES: *Cardstock:* (white) *Patterned paper:* (Rain Showers, Skipping Stones from Spring Fling collection) Pink Paislee *Accents:* (floral journaling tag) Pink Paislee; (green, blue flowers) Prima; (brown buttons) American Crafts *Stickers:* (Holly Doodle alphabet) Pink Paislee; (red labels) Jenni Bowlin Studio *Fibers:* (teal floss) DMC **Finished size: 4¼" x 5½"**

Page 119
Breast Wishes
Designer: Ashley Harris

SUPPLIES: *Cardstock:* (white) Bazzill Basics Paper *Patterned paper:* (Born and Bread from Mimi's Bakery collection) Treehouse Memories *Accent:* (red rhinestone) Creative Imaginations *Fibers:* (white eyelet trim, red polka dot ribbon) *Font:* (your choice) **Finished size: 4" square**

Congratulations Bouquet
Designer: Maren Benedict

SUPPLIES: *Cardstock:* (cream, peach, orange) Papertrey Ink *Rubber stamps:* (flower, congratulations from In the Nursery set) Lizzie Anne Design *Dye ink:* (Tuxedo Black) Tsukineko *Color medium:* (orange marker) Copic Marker *Accents:* (yellow brads) Queen & Co. *Fibers:* (orange gingham ribbon) Offray *Adhesive:* (foam tape) **Finished size: 4¼" x 5½"**

Hot Dawg
Designer: Becky Olsen

SUPPLIES: *Cardstock:* (white) Bazzill Basics Paper *Patterned paper:* (Henry from Night Light collection) October Afternoon; (Fifth Street from Appleton collection) Scenic Route *Rubber stamp:* (dog from Little Gal set) Cornish Heritage Farms *Watermark ink:* (clear) Tsukineko *Embossing powder:* (red) Ranger Industries *Stickers:* (Newsroom-Hometown alphabet) October Afternoon *Fibers:* (white pompom trim) May Arts **Finished size: 5½" x 4¼"**

Page 120
Thanks Coach
Designer: Lisa Dorsey

SUPPLIES: *Cardstock:* (white, yellow, black) *Patterned paper:* (Black & White Chic Stripe Reverse from Collection 3) KI Memories; (Yasoda Street from Metropolis collection) Scenic Route *Color medium:* (black marker) EK Success *Paint:* (Licorice) Plaid *Accent:* (chipboard circle) Magistical Memories *Digital element:* (soccer ball image) *Fibers:* (black striped ribbon) Making Memories *Font:* (your choice) *Software:* (word processing) Microsoft *Adhesive:* (foam tape) **Finished size: 7" x 4¾"**

Haunt Couture
Designer: Betsy Veldman

SUPPLIES: *Cardstock:* (Vintage Cream) Papertrey Ink; (black) Bazzill Basics Paper *Patterned paper:* (Halloween Words from Spellbound collection) Flair Designs *Rubber stamps:* (Witch Shoes, Haunt Couture) Just Johanna Rubber Stamps *Dye ink:* (black) Tsukineko *Specialty ink:* (New Canvas hybrid) Stewart Superior Corp. *Color medium:* (colored pencils) *Accents:* (journaling tag) Making Memories; (orange button) BasicGrey; (green brads) Die Cuts With a View *Fibers:* (white/yellow damask ribbon) Michaels; (green raffia) *Tool:* (corner rounder punch) Stampin' Up! **Finished size: 4¼" x 5½"**

Boo!
Designer: Angie Hagist

SUPPLIES: *Cardstock:* (black) American Crafts *Accents:* (eye die cuts) October Afternoon *Rub-ons:* (eyes) October Afternoon *Stickers:* (Newsroom-Hometown alphabet) October Afternoon *Adhesive:* (foam tape) **Finished size: 4¼" x 5½"**

Page 121
Beware
Designer: Stefanie Hamilton

SUPPLIES: *Cardstock:* (white) Creative Memories *Digital elements:* (yellow, green paper; beware, frame from Thrilling October kit; candelabra from Single Spooky Candelabra Brush kit) www.twopeasinabucket.com; (torn edge from Chunky Torn Paper Edges kit) www.designerdigitals.com *Software:* (photo editing) Creative Memories **Finished size: 4" x 6"**

Bejeweled Halloween
Designer: Kim Moreno

SUPPLIES: *Cardstock:* (purple, black) Core'dinations; (orange scalloped) Bazzill Basics Paper *Patterned paper:* (Polka Dot Stripe from Spellbound collection) Making Memories; (Halloween Circle Tags from Spooktacular collection) Teresa Collins Designs; (black polka dot) *Color medium:* (black pen) American Crafts *Accents:* (orange, purple rhinestones) Kaisercraft *Adhesive:* (foam tape) Therm O Web **Finished size: 4½" x 5"**

Trick or Treat
Designer: Sherry Wright

SUPPLIES: *Cardstock:* (black) Prism *Patterned paper:* (Hollow Moon, Full Moon, Night Owl from Vintage Moon collection) Pink Paislee *Chalk ink:* (Aquamarine, black) Clearsnap *Accents:* (chipboard circle) Pink Paislee; (chipboard sentiment) Making Memories; (black glitter glue) Ranger Industries *Sticker:* (owl circle) Pink Paislee *Fibers:* (black rickrack) Offray **Finished size: 5" square**

Page 122
Pumpkin Patch
Designer: Beatriz Jennings

SUPPLIES: *Cardstock:* (brown) DMD, Inc. *Patterned paper:* (Wesley) Melissa Frances; (cream floral from McKenna pad) K&Company *Dye ink:* (Old Paper) Ranger Industries *Accents:* (white, brass buttons) *Sticker:* (pumpkin patch) Melissa Frances *Fibers:* (cream crocheted trim) Making Memories; (brown polka dot ribbon, twine) **Finished size: 5" x 4¼"**

November
Page 123
Fall Blessings
Designer: Wendy Sue Anderson

SUPPLIES: *Cardstock:* (orange) *Patterned paper:* (Cozy Home, Picking Pumpkins from Weathervane collection) October Afternoon *Accents:* (leaves, apple tags) Three Bugs in a Rug *Stickers:* (Jewelry Box alphabet) American Crafts; (blessings tab) October Afternoon *Fibers:* (cream yarn) **Finished size: 4¾" x 6"**

Page 124
Birthday Wish Ticket
Designer: Sherry Wright

SUPPLIES: *Cardstock:* (green, cream) Bazzill Basics Paper *Patterned paper:* (Sonoma Verano Ave.) Scenic Route; (gray weave) *Chalk ink:* (Chestnut Roan) Clearsnap *Accents:* (wish ticket) Kenner Road; (red rhinestone) Queen & Co. *Rub-on:* (birthday) Scenic Route *Fibers:* (yellow ribbon) Kenner Road *Tools:* (covered button maker) Maxant Button & Supply; (decorative-edge scissors) *Other:* (red/green fabric, vintage book page) Kenner Road; (floral fabric strip) Vera Bradley; (button shell) Maxant Button & Supply **Finished size: 5" x 5½"**

Offbeat Birthday
Designer: Courtney Kelley

SUPPLIES: *Cardstock:* (kraft) Bazzill Basics Paper *Patterned paper:* (Light Hearted from Offbeat collection) BasicGrey; (Jack's Beanstalk from Woodland Whimsy collection) Sassafras Lass *Accents:* (red, orange, blue brads) Queen & Co. *Stickers:* (flower, Offbeat alphabet) BasicGrey *Fibers:* (black floss) Weeks Dye Works **Finished size: 5½" x 4¼"**

Newsprint Thank You
Designer: Dawn McVey

SUPPLIES: *Cardstock:* (Vintage Cream, Pure Poppy) Papertrey Ink *Clear stamps:* (sentiment, finial from Simply Stationery set; grid, medallions from Guide Lines set) Papertrey Ink *Dye ink:* (Tea Dye) Ranger Industries *Pigment ink:* (white) *Specialty ink:* (Dark Chocolate, Pure Poppy hybrid) Papertrey Ink *Accents:* (yellow buttons) Rusty Pickle; (brown flowers) Bazzill Basics Paper *Fibers:* (brown ribbon) Papertrey Ink; (hemp twine) Stampin' Up! *Die:* (flower) Ellison *Tools:* (die cut machine) Ellison; (scallop punch) Stampin' Up! *Other:* (vintage book page) **Finished size: 5½" x 4¼"**

Page 125
Always
Designer: Maren Benedict

SUPPLIES: *Cardstock:* (Pure Poppy) Papertrey Ink *Patterned paper:* (Something Special, Elements from Everafter collection) Cosmo Cricket *Accents:* (chipboard flourishes) Cosmo Cricket; (pearl brad) Creative Imaginations *Fibers:* (white ribbon) May Arts *Adhesive:* (foam tape) *Tool:* (flower punch) Stampin' Up! **Finished size: 4¼" x 5½"**

Autumn Glow Birthday
Designer: Rae Barthel

SUPPLIES: *Cardstock:* (black) Bazzill Basics Paper *Patterned paper:* (Mandarin, Citrus, Clementine from Ambrosia collection) BasicGrey *Accent:* (black lace paper border) Creative Imaginations *Rub-on:* (happy birthday) Breezy Design **Finished size: 4" x 6"**

Simply Red
Designer: Maren Benedict

SUPPLIES: *Cardstock:* (white) Papertrey Ink *Patterned paper:* (Wink from Chemistry collection) Cosmo Cricket *Accents:* (white brad) Heidi Swapp; (red felt flowers) Chatterbox *Fibers:* (red stitched ribbon) Papertrey Ink; (white lace trim) *Tool:* (corner rounder punch) **Finished size: 5½" x 4¼"**

Page 126
Layered Hello
Designer: Kimberly Moreno

SUPPLIES: *Cardstock:* (white) Core'dinations *Patterned paper:* (Lyrics, Lighthearted, Frolic, Lullaby from Heartsong collection) Dream Street Papers *Rubber stamp:* (hello from Scripty Words set) Cornish Heritage Farms *Chalk ink:* (black, blue, orange, pink) Clearsnap *Accents:* (orange button) Sassafras Lass; (pink epoxy dots) Cloud 9 Design *Fibers:* (orange gingham ribbon) Michaels; (white ribbon) *Adhesive:* (foam tape) Therm O Web *Tools:* (eyelet, scalloped border punches) Martha Stewart Crafts; (dotted scallop border punch) Fiskars **Finished size: 3¼" x 5¾"**

Blessing
Designer: Alice Golden

SUPPLIES: *Cardstock:* (Iced Pink, Intense Kiwi) Prism *Patterned paper:* (Posh from Sultry collection) BasicGrey *Clear stamp:* (sentiment from Loving Words set) Technique Tuesday *Dye ink:* (Chocolate) Close To My Heart *Specialty ink:* (Raspberry Fizz hybrid) Papertrey Ink *Accents:* (green flower) Petaloo; (pink buttons) Autumn Leaves *Fibers:* (orange, green floss) Karen Foster Design; (pink ribbon) May Arts

Adhesive: (foam tape) Therm O Web *Die:* (scalloped rectangle) Spellbinders *Tool:* (die cut/embossing machine) Spellbinders **Finished size: 6" square**

For You
Designer: Danielle Flanders

SUPPLIES: *Cardstock:* (Bluebird Gossip die cut from Pop Culture collection) KI Memories *Patterned paper:* (Lovey Dovey, Cutie Pie, Sweet Nothings from Sweet Cakes collection) Pink Paislee *Accent:* (clear heart rhinestone) The Beadery *Rub-on:* (sentiment) Melissa Frances *Stickers:* (Fashion Script alphabet) Pink Paislee; (make a wish, red polka dot frame) Making Memories *Fibers:* (blue gingham ribbon) Making Memories *Adhesive:* (foam tape) *Other:* (chipboard) **Finished size: 4¾" x 5¼"**

Page 127
Welcome to the Neighborhood
Designer: Nicole Maki

SUPPLIES: *Cardstock:* (Simon) Bazzill Basics Paper *Patterned paper:* (Cozy Home, New Pencils, Sweater Weather from Weathervane collection) October Afternoon *Chalk ink:* (Chestnut Roan) Clearsnap *Accent:* (yellow button) Autumn Leaves *Fibers:* (blue gingham ribbon) Offray *Tools:* (scalloped circle punch) Marvy Uchida; (circle cutter, corner rounder punch) Creative Memories; (decorative-edge scissors) **Finished size: 5½" x 4¼"**

Freedom
Designer: Alli Miles

SUPPLIES: *Cardstock:* (white) Papertrey Ink; (brown) Prism *Patterned paper:* (Daniel) Melissa Frances; (Grant Street, Franklin Street from Liberty collection) Scenic Route *Rubber stamps:* (Freedom, Proud Eagle) Cornish Heritage Farms *Dye ink:* (Espresso) Ranger Industries *Pigment ink:* (Snow Cap) Ranger Industries *Color medium:* (assorted markers) Copic Marker *Accent:* (blue button) Making Memories *Fibers:* (red stitched ribbon) Papertrey Ink; (hemp twine) *Adhesive:* (foam tape) **Finished size: 4¼" x 5½"**

Simply Marvelous
Designer: Maren Benedict

SUPPLIES: *Cardstock:* (Pure Poppy, Ocean Tides, Vintage Cream) Papertrey Ink *Patterned paper:* (Mischievous Max, Jumping Jack from Lil' Man collection) Cosmo Cricket *Accents:* (pewter brad, epoxy brad top) Stampin' Up!; (blue, cream brads) BasicGrey; (chipboard clouds, plane) Cosmo Cricket *Rub-on:* (sentiment) Cosmo Cricket *Fibers:* (teal ribbon) Papertrey Ink *Adhesive:* (foam tape) *Tool:* (¾" circle punch) Stampin' Up! **Finished size: 4¼" x 5½"**

Page 128
Adore U
Designer: Sherry Wright

SUPPLIES: *Cardstock:* (red) *Patterned paper:* (Elizabeth Berry from 5th Avenue collection; Red Dot Floral from Love Story collection) Making Memories *Rubber stamps:* (circle border from 10 Designer Centers & Borders set; Times New Roman alphabet) JustRite *Dye ink:* (black) *Accent:* (adore bingo card) Jenni Bowlin Studio *Fibers:* (white ribbon) Offray *Adhesive:* (foam tape) *Tool:* (decorative-edge scissors) **Finished size: 5" x 6"**

Flourish of Thanks
Designer: Charity Hassel

SUPPLIES: *Cardstock:* (Oasis, Petra, Caspia from Oasis collection) SEI; (white) *Patterned paper:* (Begram from Oasis collection) SEI *Clear stamps:* (flower, flourishes from Floral Flourishes set) Sweet 'n Sassy Stamps *Dye ink:* (brown) Clearsnap *Accent:* (brown button) Harmonie *Rub-on:* (thanks) American Crafts *Stickers:* (flourishes; large, small medallions; border) SEI **Finished size: 5" x 7"**

Botanical Birthday Wishes
Designer: Alli Miles

SUPPLIES: *Cardstock:* (cream) *Patterned paper:* (Quinn, Isabel from Honey Pie collection) Cosmo Cricket *Rubber stamps:* (floral stems, dragonfly from Nature's Silhouette set; sentiment from Silhouette Blooms II set) Cornish Heritage Farms *Dye ink:* (Espresso, Willow, Mountain Rose, Vintage Photo) Ranger Industries *Accents:* (brown buttons) My Mind's Eye *Fibers:* (twine) *Tool:* (corner rounder punch) *Other:* (acrylic sheet) Cornish Heritage Farms **Finished size: 5" square**

Page 129
You are So Thoughtful
Designer: Mary MacAskill

SUPPLIES: *Cardstock:* (white, yellow) Bazzill Basics Paper *Patterned paper:* (Happy Dots, Happy Flourish from Happy Day collection) Chatterbox; (green polka dot) Ann Griffin *Clear stamp:* (sentiment from Thoughtful Messages set) Hero Arts *Watermark ink:* Tsukineko *Embossing powder:* (white) Stampendous! *Accents:* (chipboard frame) Heidi Swapp; (chipboard butterflies) Chatterbox; (red buttons) Autumn Leaves; (clear red button) The Paper Studio *Fibers:* (yellow checked ribbon) American Crafts; (red floss) *Template:* (Swiss Dots embossing) Provo Craft *Tools:* (embossing machine) Provo Craft; (decorative-edge scissors) CRI **Finished size: 4¼" x 5½"**

Blue & Green Thinking of You
Designer: Alice Golden

SUPPLIES: *Cardstock:* (natural) Bazzill Basics Paper *Patterned paper:* (blue/green from Cornucopia pad) Me & My Big Ideas *Clear stamp:* (sentiment from Thinking of You set) Technique Tuesday *Pigment ink:* (Bamboo, Lagoon Blue) Tsukineko *Accents:* (pearl; blue, yellow rhinestone brads) Karen Foster Design *Fibers:* (turquoise printed ribbon) May Arts *Adhesive:* (foam tape) Therm O Web **Finished size: 8½" x 3¾"**

Elegant Best Friends
Designer: Maren Benedict

SUPPLIES: *Cardstock:* (Vintage Cream, kraft) Papertrey Ink *Patterned paper:* (Something Borrowed from Everafter collection) Cosmo Cricket *Accents:* (best friends chipboard label) Cosmo Cricket; (large clear rhinestone) Me & My Big Ideas; (clear rhinestones) Kaisercraft *Fibers:* (blue printed ribbon) Cosmo Cricket; (cream ribbon) Michaels *Adhesive:* (foam tape) **Finished size: 4¼" x 5½"**

Page 130

Thinking of You
Designer: Ashley C. Newell

SUPPLIES: *Cardstock:* (Pure Poppy, white) Papertrey Ink; (So Saffron) Stampin' Up!; (black) American Crafts *Patterned paper:* (Avenue from Metropolitan collection) American Crafts *Clear stamp:* (circles heart from Heart Prints set) Papertrey Ink *Pigment ink:* (Basic Black, Whisper White) Stampin' Up! *Accents:* (green pearls) Queen & Co.; (chipboard bird, branch) Maya Road *Rub-on:* (sentiment) Stampin' Up! *Dies:* (circles) Spellbinders *Tool:* (die cut machine) Spellbinders **Finished size: 4¼" x 5½"**

Red & Black
Designer: Maren Benedict

SUPPLIES: *Cardstock:* (black) Stampin' Up!; (Pure Poppy, white) Papertrey Ink *Rubber stamps:* (flower, leaf flourish from Damask set) Lizzie Anne Designs *Dye ink:* (black) Tsukineko *Fibers:* (red ribbon) Michaels *Adhesive:* (foam tape) **Finished size: 4¼" x 5½"**

Vintage Make a Wish
Designer: Melanie Douthit

SUPPLIES: *Cardstock:* (brown, green, ivory) Bazzill Basics Paper *Patterned paper:* (Olive Ave, Madera Street from Sonoma collection) Scenic Route *Chalk ink:* (Chestnut Roan) Clearsnap *Accents:* (platinum glitter glue) Ranger Industries; (cream button) *Rub-on:* (sentiment) Imaginisce *Fibers:* (cream ribbon) Offray; (brown rickrack) Wrights; (jute twine) *Adhesive:* (foam tape) *Dies:* (circles, scalloped circle) Provo Craft *Tool:* (die cut machine) Provo Craft **Finished size: 5½" x 4"**

Page 131

Thanks Leaves
Designer: Teri Anderson

SUPPLIES: *Cardstock:* (white) *Patterned paper:* (Worn Blue Grid Background) Scenic Route; (Tarragon, Carraway from Dill Blossom collection) SEI *Rub-on:* (thanks) American Crafts *Tools:* (circle punch) We R Memory Keepers; (corner rounder punch) Creative Memories **Finished size: 4¼" x 5½"**

Grateful Wreath
Designer: Ashley C. Newell

SUPPLIES: *Cardstock:* (Chocolate Chip) Stampin' Up!; (Canary) Close To My Heart; (orange, olive) Bazzill Basics Paper; (burgundy) Die Cuts With a View *Rubber stamp:* (Rose Hip Wreath) PSX *Clear stamp:* (grateful from Say It in Style set) Close To My Heart *Dye ink:* (Chocolate Chip) Stampin' Up! *Watermark ink:* Tsukineko *Accents:* (copper, cinnamon glitter glue) Ranger Industries *Fibers:* (orange ribbon) Michaels *Adhesive:* (foam tape) **Finished size: 4¼" x 5½"**

November
Designer: Betsy Veldman

SUPPLIES: *Cardstock:* (brown) Bazzill Basics Paper; (Vintage Cream) Papertrey Ink *Patterned paper:* (Voigt Street, Alder Ave from Sumner collection) Scenic Route *Clear stamps:* (circle tag from Boxes, Bags & Tags set; sentiment from Year-Round Puns set) Papertrey Ink *Dye ink:* (Tempting Turquoise) Stampin' Up! *Specialty ink:* (Pure Poppy, Summer Sunrise hybrid) Papertrey Ink *Color medium:* (colored pencils) *Accents:* (calendar card) Jenni Bowlin Studio; (brown button) BasicGrey; (brown brads) Die Cuts With a View; (silver bookplate) Making Memories *Fibers:* (brown ribbon) Papertrey Ink; (jute twine) *Adhesive:* (foam tape) **Finished size: 4¼" x 5½"**

Page 132

So Thankful
Designer: Kristen Swain

SUPPLIES: *Cardstock:* (black) Making Memories *Patterned paper:* (Swirl from Splendor collection) BoBunny Press; (green distressed) *Transparency sheet:* (Journaling Bits) Hambly Screen Prints *Color medium:* (yellow marker) Sanford *Accents:* (brown, gold felt leaves) Me & My Big Ideas; (black button) Darice *Stickers:* (Life's Journey alphabet) K&Company *Fibers:* (cream/black checked ribbon) Offray; (twine) Darice *Other:* (green felt) **Finished size: 7" x 4¼"**

Grateful Silhouette
Designer: Ashley C. Newell

SUPPLIES: *Cardstock:* (Lemon Tart, Vintage Cream, Ripe Avocado, Dark Chocolate) Papertrey Ink *Clear stamps:* (grateful, leaf from First Fruits set) Papertrey Ink *Dye ink:* (olive) Close To My Heart *Fibers:* (brown ribbon) Papertrey Ink *Adhesive:* (foam tape) **Finished size: 4¼" x 5½"**

Thank You So Much
Designer: Charlene Austin

SUPPLIES: *Cardstock:* (Vintage Cream, Spring Rain, Ripe Avocado) Papertrey Ink *Patterned paper:* (Flower & Vine from Brown Transferware collection) Jenni Bowlin Studio *Rub-on:* (sentiment) Stampin' Up! *Fibers:* (brown trim) Making Memories *Adhesive:* (foam tape) *Tool:* (corner rounder punch) Stampin' Up! **Finished size: 4¼" x 5½"**

Page 133

Princess for a Day
Designer: Dawne Ivey

SUPPLIES: *Cardstock:* (black) Bazzill Basics Paper *Patterned paper:* (Black/Pink Stripes from Bella Girl collection) Teresa Collins Designs *Accents:* (acrylic circle frame) Heidi Swapp; (chipboard crowns) Maya Road; (gold, red glitter) Martha Stewart Crafts; (clear, red, green rhinestones) Offray *Rub-on:* (princess) BoBunny Press *Stickers:* (Tiny alphabet) Making Memories *Tools:* (dotted scalloped border punch) Fiskars; (ticket corner punch) **Finished size: 4¼" x 4"**

Red Medallion Thanks
Designer: Melissa Phillips

SUPPLIES: *Cardstock:* (white) *Patterned paper:* (gray medallions from Lotus Tea Box pad) K&Company *Clear stamps:* (finial, thank you, medallion from Simply Stationery set) Papertrey Ink *Specialty ink:* (Pure Poppy, Spring Moss, True Black hybrid) Papertrey Ink *Embossing powder:* (clear) *Accents:* (green buttons) *Fibers:* (red stitched ribbon) Papertrey Ink *Tools:* (corner rounder, scalloped circle punches) **Finished size: 3" x 5½"**

Warm Wishes
Designer: Mary MacAskill

SUPPLIES: *Cardstock:* (kraft, white) *Patterned paper:* (Lizzie Polka Dot Paisley from Funky Vintage collection) Making Memories *Transparency sheet:* *Rubber stamps:* (tree from Creative Trees set, Old Letter Writing) Hero Arts *Solvent ink:* (black) *Watermark ink:* Tsukineko *Color medium:* (pearlescent white chalk) Pebbles Inc. *Paint:* (Cranberry) Making Memories *Accents:* (clear buttons) Wal-Mart; (iridescent glitter glue) Ranger Industries *Rub-on:* (warm wishes) American Crafts *Sticker:* (acrylic scroll) American Crafts *Fibers:* (white embroidered ribbon) Offray; (white crochet, scalloped trim) Rusty Pickle; (white floss) *Adhesive:* (foam tape) **Finished size: 5½" x 4¼"**

December

Page 134

Joy Defined
Designer: Wendy Sue Anderson

SUPPLIES: *Cardstock:* (white) *Patterned paper:* (Peppermint Sticks from Good Cheer collection) October Afternoon; (Number from FaLaLa collection) Making Memories *Accent:* (green button) Autumn Leaves *Sticker:* (snowflake) K&Company; (joy circle) October Afternoon *Fibers:* (olive snowflake ribbon) SEI; (burgundy striped ribbon, white yarn) *Template:* (Swiss Dots embossing) Provo Craft *Tools:* (scalloped border punch) Fiskars; (embossing machine) Provo Craft; (snowflake punch) EK Success **Finished size: 4½" x 5½"**

Page 135

Classic Congrats
Designer: Rae Barthel

SUPPLIES: *Cardstock:* (Salt embossed) Bazzill Basics Paper *Patterned paper:* (houndstooth from Black & White pad) Me & My Big Ideas *Accents:* (black lace paper border) Creative Imaginations; (clear rhinestones) EK Success *Rub-on:* (congrats) Breezy Design *Fibers:* (black ribbon) Hobby Lobby *Tool:* (corner rounder punch) **Finished size: 3½" x 6"**

Celtic Friend
Designer: Melanie Douthit

SUPPLIES: *Cardstock:* (brown) Bazzill Basics Paper; (cream) Stampin' Up! *Patterned paper:* (Novelty from Mairzy Doats collection; Zinnia from Mod Posy collection) Dream Street Papers *Rubber stamp:* (friend from A Little Somethin' set) Stampin' Up! *Dye ink:* (Chocolate Chip) Stampin' Up! *Accent:* (brown button) *Fibers:* (ivory ribbon) Stampin' Up!; (hemp twine) *Adhesive:* (foam tape) *Tools:* (oval, scalloped oval punches) Marvy Uchida; (doily border punch) Martha Stewart Crafts; (corner rounder punch) **Finished size: 5½" x 4¼"**

Wings to the Heart
Designer: Alli Miles

SUPPLIES: *Cardstock:* (white, kraft) Papertrey Ink *Patterned paper:* (Houndstooth from Paperie Poolside collection) Making Memories; (red polka dot) My Mind's Eye *Clear stamp:* (sentiment from Heart Prints Sentiments set) Papertrey Ink *Dye ink:* (Chocolate Chip) Stampin' Up! *Pigment ink:* (Vintage Cream) Papertrey Ink *Accents:* (clear rhinestone wings) Prima; (acrylic plaid ribbon) Chatterbox *Sticker:* (red stitched felt heart) Chatterbox *Adhesive:* (foam tape) *Dies:* (label, circle) Spellbinders *Tool:* (die cut/embossing machine) Spellbinders **Finished size: 4¼" x 5½"**

Page 136
Cold Outside
Designer: Julie Masse

SUPPLIES: *Cardstock:* (Dark Chocolate, Vintage Cream, kraft) Papertrey Ink *Patterned paper:* (Tinsel from Good Cheer collection) October Afternoon *Rubber stamp:* (deer from Enjoy Your Story… Laugh set) Unity Stamp Co. *Dye ink:* (Rich Cocoa) Tsukineko *Color medium:* (brown, dark brown pencils) Prismacolor *Accent:* (red rhinestone) *Rub-ons:* (snowflakes, sentiment) October Afternoon *Fibers:* (blue lace trim) Pink Paislee *Adhesive:* (foam tape) Stampin' Up! *Die:* (rectangle) Spellbinders *Tools:* (die cut/embossing machine) Spellbinders; (corner rounder punch) **Finished size: 5" square**

Vintage Christmas
Designer: Beatriz Jennings

SUPPLIES: *Cardstock:* (red) Bazzill Basics Paper *Patterned paper:* (Bunny Hill from Dasher collection, Vintage Ornament/Pine from Fruitcake collection) BasicGrey *Dye ink:* (Old Paper) Ranger Industries *Accents:* (cardstock sentiment label) My Mind's Eye; (red button) *Fibers:* (red trim) Making Memories; (cream ribbon, string) **Finished size: 5½" x 3½"**

Believe in Joy
Designer: Carla Peicheff

SUPPLIES: *Cardstock:* (pink) Bazzill Basics Paper *Specialty paper:* (Flurry Pure die cut from Festive collection) KI Memories *Pigment ink:* (white) Stampin' Up! *Accents:* (chipboard snowflake) Scenic Route; (white glitter) Stampin' Up!; (sheer believe journaling tag) Maya Road; (red, clear rhinestones) K&Company; (pink button) *Stickers:* (Playroom alphabet) American Crafts *Fibers:* (pink striped ribbon) American Crafts; (twine) **Finished size: 5" square**

Page 137
Gift at Christmas
Designer: Beatriz Jennings

SUPPLIES: *Cardstock:* (tan) DMD, Inc. *Patterned paper:* (Holly) Melissa Frances *Dye ink:* (Old Paper) Ranger Industries *Accents:* (chipboard snowflake) Melissa Frances; (white, brown buttons) *Sticker:* (sentiment label) Melissa Frances *Fibers:* (white ribbon, lace trim, string) **Finished size: 5" square**

Merry Christmas Leaves
Designer: Rebecca Oehlers

SUPPLIES: All supplies from Papertrey Ink unless otherwise noted. *Cardstock:* (Dark Chocolate, white) *Patterned paper:* (green circles from Holiday Vintage Prints collection) *Clear stamps:* (leafy branch from Beautiful Blooms set, sentiment from Silent Night set) *Watermark ink:* Tsukineko *Specialty ink:* (Ripe Avocado hybrid) *Embossing powder:* (white) *Color medium:* (red marker) Copic Marker *Accents:* (white pearls) no source *Fibers:* (red, green ribbon) *Adhesive:* (foam tape) no source **Finished size: 5" x 5½"**

Three Trees Christmas
Designer: Maren Benedict

SUPPLIES: *Cardstock:* (Ripe Avocado, Vintage Cream) Papertrey Ink *Patterned paper:* (Yuletide from Oh Joy collection) Cosmo Cricket *Rubber stamps:* (trees, sentiment from Holiday Cheer set) Lizzie Anne Designs *Dye ink:* (Old Olive) Stampin' Up!; (Antique Linen) Ranger Industries *Watermark ink:* Tsukineko *Embossing powder:* (white) Stampendous! *Accents:* (red rhinestones) Me & My Big Ideas *Fibers:* (cream ribbon) Papertrey Ink *Adhesive:* (foam tape) *Dies:* (oval, scalloped oval) Spellbinders *Tool:* (die cut/embossing machine) Spellbinders **Finished size: 4¼" x 5½"**

Page 138
Happy Hanukkah
Designer: Betsy Veldman

SUPPLIES: *Cardstock:* (Night Sky Shimmer, kraft) Papertrey Ink *Patterned paper:* (Forest Glade from Once Upon a Time collection) Die Cuts With a View *Clear stamps:* (sentiment, star, menorah from Mazel Tov set) Papertrey Ink *Watermark ink:* Tsukineko *Specialty ink:* (Dark Chocolate hybrid) Papertrey Ink *Embossing powder:* (gold) Stewart Superior Corp. *Accents:* (blue rhinestones) Doodlebug Design; (gold, blue pearl stick pins) *Rub-on:* (scrollwork) BasicGrey *Fibers:* (blue printed ribbon) KI Memories *Adhesive:* (foam tape) *Tool:* (decorative-edge scissors) Provo Craft **Finished size: 4¼" x 5½"**

Menorah Card
Designer: Nichole Heady

SUPPLIES: *Cardstock:* (Enchanted Evening, Ocean Tides, Vintage Cream) Papertrey Ink *Clear stamps:* (menorah, medallion, sentiment from Mazel Tov set) Papertrey Ink *Watermark ink:* Tsukineko *Specialty ink:* (Vintage Cream, Enchanted Evening hybrid) Papertrey Ink *Color medium:* (silver paint pen) Marvy Uchida *Accent:* (silver glitter) Ranger Industries *Tools:* (corner rounder punch) Fiskars; **Finished size: 5½" x 4"**

Festival of Lights
Designer: Stefanie Hamilton

SUPPLIES: All supplies from Creative Memories unless otherwise noted. *Cardstock:* (white) *Digital elements:* (blue patterned paper, sentiment from Jewel Hanukkah Additions kit, wire from Hardware kit) *Software:* (scrapbooking) *Other:* (digital photo) **Finished size: 6" x 4"**

Page 139
'Tis the Season
Designer: Beatriz Jennings

SUPPLIES: *Cardstock:* (red) DMD, Inc. *Patterned paper:* (Decoration, Wonderland) Melissa Frances; (red filigree from McKenna pad) K&Company *Dye ink:* (Old Paper) Ranger Industries *Accents:* (white glitter chipboard star, keyhole) Melissa Frances; (red rhinestone) *Rub-on:* (sentiment) Melissa Frances *Fibers:* (green ribbon, cream trim) **Finished size: 4½" x 5"**

Winter Wonderland
Designer: Maren Benedict

SUPPLIES: *Cardstock:* (Ruby Red) Stampin' Up!; (Dark Chocolate, Vintage Cream) Papertrey Ink *Patterned paper:* (Frosty from Oh Joy collection) Cosmo Cricket *Rubber stamp:* (trees from Christmas Elegance set) Unity Stamp Co. *Dye ink:* (Rich Cocoa) Tsukineko *Color medium:* (assorted markers) Copic Marker *Accents:* (brown buttons, copper brads) American Crafts; (sentiment card) Cosmo Cricket *Fibers:* (brown ribbon) May Arts; (white crochet thread) *Adhesive:* (foam tape) **Finished size: 4¼" x 5½"**

Christmas Reindeer
Designer: Ivanka Lentle

SUPPLIES: *Cardstock:* (black) The Paper Company; (gold) Prism *Patterned paper:* (Christmas Swirls Red from Christmas Basics collection) Reminisce; (cream reindeer) Anna Griffin *Chalk ink:* (black) *Accents:* (cream flower, red rhinestone flourish) Prima; (gold/pearl button) *Rub-on:* (sentiment) American Crafts *Sticker:* (reindeer) Anna Griffin *Fibers:* (gold ribbon) Michaels; (gold cord) *Adhesive:* (foam tape) *Template:* (D'Vine Swirl embossing) Provo Craft *Tool:* (embossing machine) Provo Craft **Finished size: 5" square**

Page 140
Rudolph the Reindeer
Designer: Laura Williams

SUPPLIES: *Cardstock:* (Kiwi, white) Close To My Heart; (black) Bazzill Basics Paper *Patterned paper:* (Memories Polka Dots from Confetti collection) My Mind's Eye; (Green Street from Providence collection) Scenic Route *Clear stamp:* (Rudolph from Christmas Melodies set) Close To My Heart *Dye ink:* (red) Close To My Heart *Accents:* (green rhinestones) K&Company *Fibers:* (red gingham ribbon) May Arts *Adhesive:* (foam tape) **Finished size: 5½" x 4¼"**

Houndstooth Trees
Designer: Kimberly Crawford

SUPPLIES: *Cardstock:* (Dark Chocolate, Spring Moss, white) Papertrey Ink *Vellum:* (Linen) Papertrey Ink *Rubber stamp:* (Fine Houndstooth Scrapblock) Cornish Heritage Farms *Clear stamps:* (tree from Made of Snow set; snowflakes, sentiment from Rustic Snowflakes set) Papertrey Ink *Dye ink:* (Tuxedo Black) Tsukineko *Watermark ink:* Tsukineko *Specialty ink:* (New Canvas hybrid) Stewart Superior Corp. *Accents:* (red rhinestones) Hero Arts; (iridescent glitter glue) Ranger Industries *Adhesive:* (foam tape) **Finished size: 4¼" x 5½"**

Home for the Holidays
Designer: Debbie Olson

SUPPLIES: *Cardstock:* (Vintage Cream, Pure Poppy, white) Papertrey Ink *Patterned paper:* (polka dot from Holiday Vintage Prints collection) Papertrey Ink *Clear stamps:* (house from Boards & Beams set; window, door, fence, garland, lamppost, snow, sentiment from Home for the Holidays set) Papertrey Ink *Dye ink:* (black) Tsukineko; (Antique Linen) Ranger Industries *Watermark ink:* Tsukineko *Embossing powder:* (white) Papertrey Ink *Color media:* (red, clear gel pens) Sakura; (assorted markers) Copic Marker *Accents:* (copper eyelet) We R Memory Keepers; (white liquid appliqué) Marvy Uchida *Fibers:* (red ribbon) Papertrey Ink *Adhesive:* (foam tape) *Tools:* (airbrush system) Copic Marker; (corner rounder punch) Marvy Uchida; (1/8" circle punch) **Finished size: 4¼" x 5½"**

Page 141
Merry Wishes
Designer: Gretchen Clark

SUPPLIES: All supplies from Stampin' Up!. *Cardstock:* (Very Vanilla, Real Red, kraft) *Patterned paper:* (red stripes from Dashing collection) *Rubber stamps:* (sentiment from Lots of Thoughts set, deer from Merry & Bright set) *Dye ink:* (Chocolate Chip) *Accent:* (red rhinestone brad) *Fibers:* (brown ribbon) *Adhesive:* (foam tape) *Tools:* (scalloped circle, 1⅜" circle punches) **Finished size: 4¼" x 5½"**

Snowflake Joy
Designer: Heidi Van Laar

SUPPLIES: *Cardstock:* (tan, red) Core'dinations *Patterned paper:* (Chiffon Dot, Coffee Dot from Double Dot collection) BoBunny Press *Rubber stamp:* (Tiny Snowflake) Plaid *Solvent ink:* (Timber Brown) Tsukineko *Accents:* (acrylic snowflakes) Heidi Swapp; (clear button) Autumn Leaves; (acrylic alphabet) Jo-Ann Stores *Fibers:* (twine) *Adhesive:* (foam tape) *Tools:* (¾" circle punch) Marvy Uchida; (scoring tool) *Other:* (acrylic card) SheetLoad ShortCuts **Finished size: 4¼" x 5½"**

Soft Snow
Designer: Maren Benedict

SUPPLIES: *Cardstock:* (Vintage Cream, Ocean Tides) Papertrey Ink *Patterned paper:* (Frosty, Wrapping Paper from Oh Joy collection) Cosmo Cricket *Accent:* (sentiment card) Cosmo Cricket *Fibers:* (red/white twine) Martha Stewart Crafts *Adhesive:* (foam tape) **Finished size: 4¼" x 5½"**

Page 142
'Tis the Season to be Jolly
Designer: Maren Benedict

SUPPLIES: *Cardstock:* (Vintage Cream) Papertrey Ink *Patterned paper:* (Yuletide from Oh Joy collection) Cosmo Cricket *Rub-ons:* (pinwheel border, sentiment) Cosmo Cricket *Fibers:* (white ribbon) May Arts **Finished size: 4¼" x 5½"**

Happy Festivus
Designer: Laura O'Donnell

SUPPLIES: *Cardstock:* (brown, white) *Rubber stamps:* (Kelly's Gnome with Flag, Kelly's Patchwork Chubby Gnome) Just Johanna Rubber Stamps *Dye ink:* (Tuxedo Black) Tsukineko *Color medium:* (assorted markers) Copic Marker **Finished size: 5" x 4"**

Birthday Trees
Designer: Julie Masse

SUPPLIES: *Cardstock:* (Really Rust, Always Artichoke) Stampin' Up!; (Vintage Cream) Papertrey Ink *Patterned paper:* (Birch, Ebb, Equinox from Mellow collection) BasicGrey *Rubber stamps:* (Itsy Bitsy Giggles) Unity Stamp Co.; (Stripes) Stampin' Up! *Clear stamp:* (sentiment from It's a Celebration set) Papertrey Ink *Dye ink:* (Rich Cocoa) Tsukineko; (Really Rust) Stampin' Up! *Accents:* (copper brads) Stampin' Up! *Fibers:* (linen thread) Stampin' Up! *Dies:* (rectangle, scalloped rectangle) Spellbinders *Tool:* (die cut/embossing machine) Spellbinders **Finished size: 5½" x 3¾"**

Page 143
Christmas Tickets
Designer: Mary Jo Johnston

SUPPLIES: *Cardstock:* (green, white) Bazzill Basics Paper *Patterned paper:* (Tinsel from Figgy Pudding collection) BasicGrey *Dye ink:* (Vintage Photo) Ranger Industries *Accents:* (holly leaves/berry brad) Making Memories *Digital elements:* (tickets from Tickets – Christmas kit) www.peppermintcreative.com *Software:* (photo editing) *Tool:* (decorative-edge scissors) EK Success **Finished size: 6½" x 4¼"**

Happy Kwanzaa
Designer: Layle Koncar

SUPPLIES: *Cardstock:* (kraft) Bazzill Basics Paper *Patterned paper:* (Parkman Road from Garland collection, Scrap Strip 2 from Sonoma collection) Scenic Route *Color medium:* (black pen) *Digital element:* (kinara clip art) Microsoft *Stickers:* (Omaha alphabet) Scenic Route *Software:* (word processing) Microsoft **Finished size: 7" x 5½"**

Simple Hi
Designer: Ashley C. Newell

SUPPLIES: *Cardstock:* (Sweet Blush) Papertrey Ink; (Ruby Red) Stampin' Up! *Rubber stamp:* (hi from Say It with Scallops set) Stampin' Up! *Watermark ink:* Tsukineko *Embossing powder:* (white) *Accents:* (pink rhinestones) Kaisercraft *Fibers:* (white ribbon) Jo-Ann Stores; (orange polka dot ribbon) Michaels *Adhesive:* (foam tape) **Finished size: 4¼" x 5½"**

Page 144
Beep! Beep!
Designer: Maren Benedict

SUPPLIES: *Cardstock:* (black, white) Stampin' Up! *Patterned paper:* (Hula Hoop, Clover, Hop Scotch from Hello Sunshine pad) Cosmo Cricket *Rubber stamps:* (car, sentiment, swirl from Things that Go set) Lizzie Anne Designs *Dye ink:* (Tuxedo Black) Tsukineko *Color medium:* (silver glitter pen) Copic Marker *Fibers:* (yellow ribbon) Michaels *Adhesive:* (foam tape) *Tools:* (assorted circle punches) Stampin' Up! **Finished size: 4¼" x 5½"**

New Year Clock
Designer: Heidi Van Laar

SUPPLIES: *Cardstock:* (white) Bazzill Basics Paper; (black) The Paper Company *Patterned paper:* (Skyline, Fountain from Metropolitan collection) American Crafts *Accents:* (acrylic clock face) Heidi Swapp; (black chipboard clock hands, black brad) Tim Holtz; (clear rhinestone flourishes) Me & My Big Ideas *Stickers:* (Metro Mini Shimmer alphabet) Making Memories *Adhesive:* (foam tape) *Die:* (circle) Spellbinders *Tools:* (die cut machine) Spellbinders; (corner rounder punch) EK Success **Finished size: 5½" square**

Party Like it's 1999
Designer: Charlene Austin

SUPPLIES: *Cardstock:* (kraft, white) Papertrey Ink *Clear stamps:* (Simple Alphabet) Papertrey Ink *Pigment ink:* (Fresh Snow) Papertrey Ink *Specialty ink:* (Burnt Umber hybrid) Stewart Superior Corp. *Accents:* (chipboard party) Maya Road; (aqua glitter, clear rhinestones) Martha Stewart Crafts *Rub-ons:* (stars) Stampin' Up! *Stickers:* (glitter numbers) Forever in Time **Finished size: 5" square**

Page 145
Bubbly New Year
Designer: Maren Benedict

SUPPLIES: *Cardstock:* (Pure Poppy, white) Papertrey Ink *Clear stamp:* (goblet with bubbles, sentiment from Happy Occasions set) My Favorite Things *Dye ink:* (Tuxedo Black) Tsukineko *Paint:* (Pearl) Ranger Industries *Accents:* (metal-rimmed tag, red flower stick pin) Making Memories *Fibers:* (red gingham ribbon) Offray *Tool:* (scallop punch) Stampin' Up! **Finished size: 4¼" x 5½"**

Patterns

Enlarge all patterns 145% except where otherwise noted.

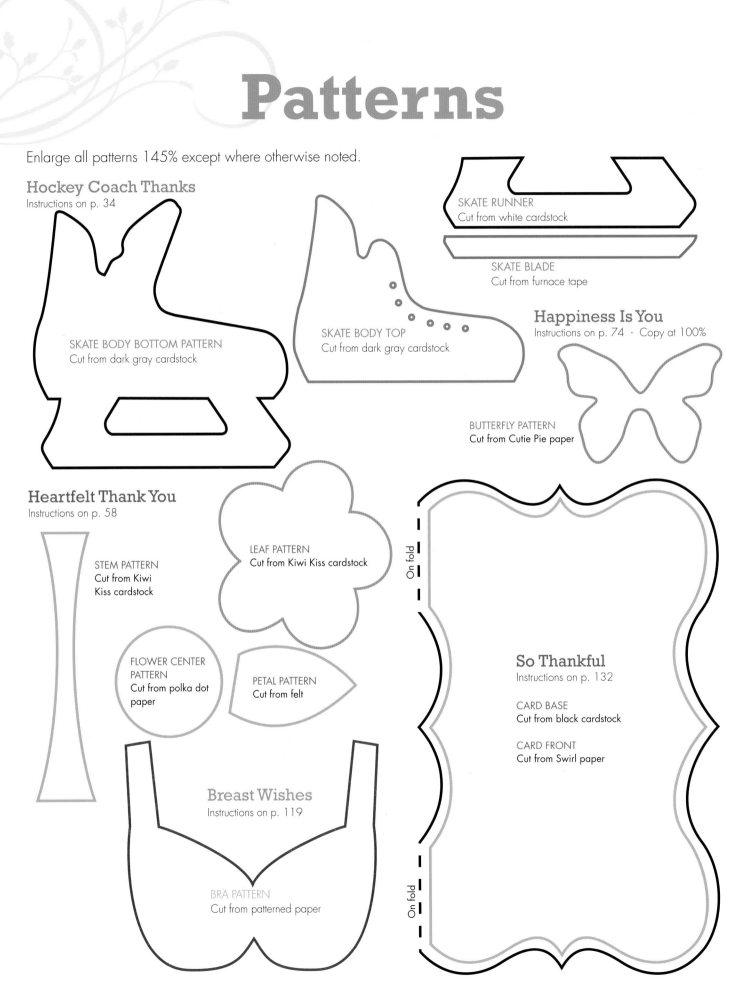

Hockey Coach Thanks
Instructions on p. 34

SKATE RUNNER
Cut from white cardstock

SKATE BLADE
Cut from furnace tape

SKATE BODY BOTTOM PATTERN
Cut from dark gray cardstock

SKATE BODY TOP
Cut from dark gray cardstock

Happiness Is You
Instructions on p. 74 · Copy at 100%

BUTTERFLY PATTERN
Cut from Cutie Pie paper

Heartfelt Thank You
Instructions on p. 58

STEM PATTERN
Cut from Kiwi
Kiss cardstock

LEAF PATTERN
Cut from Kiwi Kiss cardstock

FLOWER CENTER
PATTERN
Cut from polka dot
paper

PETAL PATTERN
Cut from felt

On fold

So Thankful
Instructions on p. 132

CARD BASE
Cut from black cardstock

CARD FRONT
Cut from Swirl paper

Breast Wishes
Instructions on p. 119

BRA PATTERN
Cut from patterned paper

On fold